T0311592

# The Professionalisation of Human Resource Management

Evolving economies, the emergence of new technologies and organisational forms are all features of late capitalism. Among this milieu, a marked feature has been the emergence and recognition in society of new occupations. The claim upon a body of knowledge and practice, and a societal domain in which to exercise expertise characterise these occupations. Status and recognition may ensue; in short, they claim 'professionalism'. 'Professionalism' is a word resonant with allusions to a particular time and place, loosely located in the United States and England in the twentieth century, although its roots are far earlier, and its present branches are far-reaching.

The text is an account of the human resource management occupation's search for status, legitimacy and "professionalism" and illustrates how key agents wove a purposeful plan in pursuit of goals through changing socio-economic and political contexts.

The text also discusses the changed meanings of and opportunities for professionalism for individual agents, as members of a social grouping that is the occupation.

This text is an analysis of the recent development of the human resource occupation, against the backdrop of changing meanings and models of professions and professionalism and the traditional signifier of professionalism in the UK, the Royal Charter. The original research from the UK outlines the efforts undertaken between 1968 and 2000 by the professional body, the present day Chartered Institute of Personnel and Development (CIPD, the Institute), to attain a Royal Charter.

This text addresses the following:

- The role of key agents and institutions on shaping social structures and practice regimes
- The changing construction and meanings of professionalism and professional occupations
- The role of the collective professional body in shaping occupational practices in human resource management and human resource development and their effect upon working lives
- The continuing significance of the Royal Charter as an ancient institution with deep societal effect

**Ruth Elizabeth Slater** is a chartered member of the Chartered Institute of Personnel and Development (CIPD) and holds a PhD from the Department of Organisation, Work and Technology, Lancaster University.

**Routledge Research in Employment Relations**
Series editors: Rick Delbridge and Edmund Heery
*Cardiff Business School, UK.*

Aspects of the employment relationship are central to numerous courses at both undergraduate and postgraduate level.

Drawing from insights from industrial relations, human resource management and industrial sociology, this series provides an alternative source of research-based materials and texts, reviewing key developments in employment research.

Books published in this series are works of high academic merit, drawn from a wide range of academic studies in the social sciences.

For more information about this series, please visit: https://www.routledge.com

# The Professionalisation of Human Resource Management

Personnel, Development and the Royal Charter

Ruth Elizabeth Slater

Routledge
Taylor & Francis Group

NEW YORK AND LONDON

First published 2020
by Routledge
605 Third Avenue, New York, NY 10017

and by Routledge
2 Park Square, Milton Park, Abingdon, Oxon, OX14 4RN

First issued in paperback 2021

*Routledge is an imprint of the Taylor & Francis Group, an informa business*

*Library of Congress Cataloging-in-Publication Data*
A catalog record for this book has been requested

ISBN 13: 978-1-03-208562-3 (pbk)
ISBN 13: 978-1-138-49249-3 (hbk)

Typeset in Sabon
by Apex CoVantage, LLC

# Contents

# Preface

This book concerns the present-day Chartered Institute of Personnel and Development (CIPD, the Institute), the professional body for HR practitioners in the UK, but with members living and working abroad. The Institute's public face on the internet declares that its purpose and mission is:

> Championing better work and working lives—because we believe work can and should be a force for good that benefits everyone.[1]

The webpage, which is all too transient as is the nature of digital media, continues to explain the mission. The CIPD's vision is:

> We want to create a world of work that's more human. By changing hearts and minds about the purpose of work, the value of people and the role of people professionals, we'll help ensure that work creates value for everyone.
> We'll do this by:
>
> - influencing policy and practice to convince decision makers that when you put people first in decisions about work, everyone stands to gain
> - establishing an internationally recognised gold standard for HR and people development, to ensure that the people profession is universally trusted and valued as principles-led, evidence-based and outcomes-driven community of experts who can make work generate value for everyone.

The CIPD did not always articulate its mission and vision in this way; however, in the words captured on 15 January 2019, lies the essence of what this book is about: the nature and status of the practices which practitioners execute and the relationship between that recent statement and what went before. The statements from the present webpages reveal several other issues concerning the relationship between the Institute in its various incarnations, professionalism in the traditional model exemplified by occupations such as law and medicine, and the unique British institution of the Royal Charter. The nature and meaning of the Royal Charter will unfold in subsequent chapters; however, it is an award administered on behalf of the Sovereign by the Privy Council. It is granted to "eminent professional bodies or charities".[2] Practitioners and other interested parties consider the Institute, an organisation existing since 1913, as the professional body for practitioners working in the field of personnel management and human resource management.

In organisational studies, several writers have highlighted the significance and impact which organisations have in society. Organisations have had and continue to have beneficial effects in many ways by developing ideas and creating goods and services which satisfy consumer needs and desires. Organisations also improve and provide the means whereby many people can provide for themselves. In the stage of capitalism which prevailed over the twentieth century and into the twenty-first, this idea appears self-evident and much lauded, but it is over-simplistic and does not recognise the potentially damaging effects of both production and consumption.

Organisations are not, therefore, neutral; they have effects and the actions of their leaders have consequences because the organisation connects to wider society, both shaping and being shaped by it. This is what makes the study of the Institute an important undertaking. This is because it is a professional body with a Royal Charter (and therefore some societal pre-eminence) whose practitioners execute practices which influence the lives of individuals both at work and personally. I should declare my interest in the organisation and the train of events which is at the core of this text.

In 2000, the Institute received a Royal Charter,[3] and three years later, the Institute's members who were appropriately qualified became entitled to call themselves chartered members of the Institute. This prompted some scholars[4] to write about the CIPD's "professional project", claiming it had been "rather successful". So, what was a "professional project", and what did this mean?

At the end of 2008, listeners to the BBC Radio 4 Today programme may have been surprised to hear a new Director of Public Policy and the Chief Economist for the Chartered Institute of Personnel and Development (CIPD) speaking on economic matters and introducing the Institute's new Public Policy Department. The CIPD Director of Public Policy and Chief Economist said:

> The workplace affects the lives of every employee, the success of every business and the performance of the entire economy. The CIPD's new Public Policy Department will devote itself to creating better work. We'll represent the views of our members—the real

workplace experts—in the corridors of power. And we'll work with Government, politicians, officials and opinion formers to ensure the economic and social benefit of good management is maximised.[5]

As a member of the CIPD and a former HR practitioner, this was evidence of a phenomenon about which I had become aware: the Institute's increasing presence on the national stage and the part it appeared to be playing in the socio-political arena. It is a matter of fact, known only to a few followers of private online discussion boards, that this event created considerable debate around the question "Does the CIPD really need a Chief Economist?" and "Is HR really a profession?"

This event increased my curiosity about the "professional project" and the questions I had burgeoned—what does a "professional project" mean, what is the Institute's claim to professionalism, and what is the societal need for such a thing? The Chief Economist evidently thought that the Institute and the area of social life, in which the Institute operated, existed for social benefit.

So I set off on a journey to explore the relationship between the Institute and the Royal Charter, and the antecedents and the consequences of this event. It is impossible to investigate this without examining the context and the other institutional actors which had been in play. It soon became clear that a "professional project"[6] was linked to characteristics found in the public understanding of the traditional professions.

This text is the outcome of that journey and is a study of a single occupation and its attempted professionalisation through a state institution, the Royal Charter. The text will explore what the Institute has done and what it has achieved, the actions of several actors in the Institute and the consequences of actions. In doing this, there will be explanations and interpretations of what the Institute's place in society is, and the question "for whose benefit does it exist?" Organisational actions do not take place within a vacuum but within an institutional environment, which exerted an influence upon actors to the extent that some actions will be deliberate and purposive, and some actions will be accidental or will occur through opportunism and capitalising upon the prevailing context. But more of that later.

The text also concerns the desires and stratagems of key elite actors to acquire a Royal Charter on behalf of an entire occupation of practitioners within the field of workforce management, workforce development and employer-employee relations; these are the present-day practitioners of human resource management (HRM). By working towards that event, the practitioners and their leaders aimed to achieve a longed-for legitimacy because, in a British context, a Royal Charter promotes legitimacy which society confers. It is a step in the professionalisation of an occupation in the British context.

This book is important because highlighting the case of the Institute and its pursuit of a Royal Charter, a symbolic award, historically located in Britain, reveals several important ideas. This is an example of the development of one occupational group as seen through the goals and objectives of the elites of the occupation, and it may be possible to draw inferences which apply to the development of other occupational groups. The practices which the occupational group espouse may be shifting sand dunes at the mercy of the prevailing interests and agency of the occupational elites. By piecing together and interrogating traces of action, activities and pronouncements which those involved have long forgotten about, it is possible to see the manoeuvring and devices to secure desires and objectives. So, this story also shows how the elite in society, as shown by the dealings of the Privy Council, who administer and award the Royal Charter, seek to hold back the tides of change because to change would diminish their status and the status of elite institutions. In short, such a trawl through the traces left of this lengthy event exposes how things come to be the way they are and exposes the lodestone of professionalism as a shifting, historical construct.

This book reflects a triangular relationship between three institutions —the institution of the traditional professional model, the Royal Charter and the Chartered Institute of Personnel and Development.

## Sources

It is incumbent upon me, as the storyteller, to tell the reader about how this material was assembled, what sources feature and through what lenses I viewed and interpreted the material. I shall deal with the sources first.

This book is the outcome of research into the present-day Chartered Institute of Personnel and Development and the Royal Charter. I began to gather sources for this project in October 2008. The sources relate in the main to the activity in the period between 1968 and 2003. This period holds some of the most significant activities of the Institute towards a "professional project".[7] The sources comprise a tranche of documents from the Privy Council outlining the dealings between the Privy Council and the Institute and a jigsaw in whose box contained pronouncements and commentary which were in the public domain. I searched, rendered readable, interpreted and matched with other contemporaneous material. There was also a series of interviews, some of which were more significant than others. This is the story of how this book came to be and what I found out, interpreted and concluded.

### Documentary Sources

The Institute inhabits a textual world in that it produces many documents for consumption by a range of audiences and through a range of media. This is discourse which has agency in the social world through the ways it is created, organised and disseminated.[8] Discourse, defined in this way, therefore, has a role in constructing reality.[9] There are other factors that contribute to the connected nature of the texts, such as medium, authorship and audience. Sources are found in physical artefacts and texts but increasingly appear in transient text containing data which are bounded in context, have the properties of intentionality and so construct action and convey meaning. These discursive phenomena have intertextuality as past, present and future, and examples in this study include the Institute's conference material, commentary and research, articles and pronouncements in the Institute's own journals and comment from interested participants.

Entities such as organisations incur "organizational events [that] . . . unfold over time and leave a substantial archival residue".[10] Some are official and need to be kept, but most are considered detritus and are frequently discarded. The official archive for the Institute is held at the Modern Records Office at Warwick University in the UK, and at the time of the research, the holdings ceased in 1985. These holdings cover the events which Margaret Niven wrote about in the first official biography of the Institute.[11] There was no curated archive relevant to the Institute for the period that focused upon the Royal Charter, or other key events in this period, in the expected places. I discovered that there is a repository of documents for the period after 1985 but that it was in storage outside Heathrow Airport, London.[12]

Wishing to examine the Institute's "professional project", I wanted to research naturally occurring 'documents' that represented elements of such a process. I, therefore, created and curated an archive relevant to the research. When the Privy Council documents became available, I incorporated them into the archive of my own creation and treated them in the same ways as other secondary documentary sources I had discovered, with the research focus and purpose in mind. It is important to acknowledge that the Privy Council appeared not to regard the documents with the significance that I have accorded them. Furthermore, the papers only represent what the Privy Council Office kept, in the order in which they kept them. Appendix I gives a summary of these documents.

The archive created for this project includes interview material, some of which presents oral histories of life and work in the late twentieth century and early twenty-first centuries. This material enhances and contextualises the documentary sources as a way "to preserve and access our past and generate future knowledge".[13]

Contained within the Privy Council Papers and the other documentary sources are several topics that matter to the Institute's "professional project". These topics concern the combination of the occupational domains of personnel management and training in 1994, the acquisition of the Royal Charter, the occasions on which the Institute reworked its professional standards and qualifications, and the effort the Institute expended pursuing a goal of seeking legitimacy among its consumers. These key events are in the public domain, known to members and accounted for in various media such as press releases from the Institute, the Institute's journals *Personnel Management* and *People Management*, which also form part of this archive. The Privy Council Papers also give some important detail about the Institute that most accounts found in many contemporary textbooks on human resource management[14] do not discuss.

I visited the Institute's library, where I have full access as a chartered member, in Wimbledon on four occasions between November 2008 and September 2010, where I was able to access documents giving the content of the Institute's Annual Conferences between 1971 and 2007. The data about qualification schemes came from the unlikely source of the Privy Council Papers, the Institute's practitioner journals, *Personnel Management* and *People Management*, and for the later period that this text covers, the Institute's website.

### Oral Sources

To complement the documentary sources, I was able to conduct twenty-four interviews to work alongside documentary sources because it would permit the key informants to re-create a social world through their own sense-making and articulation that was prompted by my opening questions on the themes I was interested in.

The choice of key informants was both purposive and "organic",[15] the interview growing and developing as the project progressed, sometimes based on opportunism on my part. However, I selected all the informants based on an association with the Institute and knowledge of the Institute's sphere of influence. These were Institute members, Institute insiders and academics. Several of the interviewees were or had been senior Institute employees, the "elites",[16] people who were uniquely placed to elaborate upon or clarify what other sources might suggest or what was already known.[17]

When interviewing key informants from the Institute, I was keen to hear about their roles in the Institute to gain a better understanding of certain events in the Institute's story. From practitioners, I was interested in their experiences as members of the Institute, how they perceived issues of professionalism and professionalisation, their views, if any, on the acquisition of the Royal Charter and observations on their relationship with the Institute. From the academics, I wanted to find out their experiences of working with and perceptions of the Institute and the extent to which the Institute's occupational strategies had affected their work. There were varying plans for the oral account depending upon the informant. There were themed opening questions relating to the focus of the research. Some questions for practitioners were biographical, allowing informants to give their accounts, filtered through their meaning-making processes, of working in personnel and human resource management; the purpose was to identify the kind of relationship the participant had with the Institute, their understanding of their role and their identity.

Where possible, interviews were recorded and transcribed. Some interviewees skilfully ensured that it would be pointless for me to even ask to record the interview by suggesting that we had our 'discussion' over a coffee in a noisy coffee shop, thus removing any possibility of capturing the interview electronically; sometimes, the din made even hearing and attending difficult. It is tempting to infer that this was a deliberate strategy on the participant's part, but I cannot be certain.

The interviews were conducted between February 2010 and September 2010.

For the purposes of this text in recognition of the different incarnations of this professional body, the text will refer to the CIPD as *the Institute* so that despite the reincarnations of the body and the changes of name which have occurred since the Institute's beginning in 1913, it is clear that I am discussing the same entity.

The sources for this text are rich and varied, but they represent a snapshot of the material which was, or could have been, available. This, therefore, is unlikely to be the last word on the subject. I hope not; I hope other material will become known and continue the exploration of societal practice, beliefs and values of societies, and help explain how things come to be the way they are. I have done my best to represent faithfully what was said to me, and what appeared in the documentary sources— where quotations appear ungrammatical, that is because they appeared that way in the text; where a source has used American English, I have reproduced that, although I prefer to write using British English—this explanation will, I hope, account for any perceived inconsistencies.

## Further Avenues of Inquiry

Gender is not a focus for this book; however, the gendered nature of the traditional professions and the personnel function is worthy of inquiry. Traditional professional work has tended to be masculine and patriarchal, and "semi-professions" have tended to employ women.[18] The reasons are historically and socially constructed by societal expectations of familial roles and lack of access to educational opportunities for women. This is out of step with contemporary notions, but it does place the issue of gender centre stage in discussions of the professions historically[19] and especially in the field of HR.

For anyone interested in the changing shape, packaging and execution of the practices for the management and development of people at work, watching, mapping and comparing developments in practice will continue to be important. Student and practitioner textbooks will always perform this role; however, to interrogate and interpret these developments in a historical and sociological vein, then, I argue, there will need to be someone to take hold of the Institute's footprint. The Institute has, however, turned to a presence which is increasingly mediated by the internet. It is fast, "abundant"[20] and transient. How actors choose to represent their ideas and the Institute, and observe, make sense of and communicate the social phenomena which are relevant to the Institute's sphere of operation will also influence how wide of an audience can see the Institute's future trajectory. This difficulty will present a challenge for source criticism—the why, who, what, where, when and why—because of its transient nature, the problem of "link rot"[21] and the difficulty of establishing intertextuality, authenticity of representativeness of the source—but then, I have found this to be a challenge in this present project. I have operated in a predominantly digitised archive which began at a canter and accelerated as a full gallop towards the finishing line of new archive material being born digital. This has presented a challenge now when examining pronouncements, policy documents, professional standards and qualification arrangements. But, preserving this information is important because it shows the signs of the times, the preoccupations of the practitioners and their elites. It is even more relevant and urgent: HR practitioners deal with the worker in the arena of employment relations and their statutory rights—even more reason that the public should know and be able to scrutinise the Institute's actions and those of actors in related fields.

## A Chapter by Chapter Focus of the Book

The book is divided into three parts. Part One examines the background and explains important matters about the key actors in the professionalisation of HR; it sets the scene.

Part Two considers the path the Institute trod in order to approach a kind of professionalism, and has three chapters which follow the chronology of the Privy Council Papers, supplemented with material from other contemporary and reflective sources. The chapter examines the period of 1968 to 2003 and shows how the Institute began to petition the Privy Council for a Royal Charter. Over the course of working with the documents and comparing them with other material, it becomes clear that the Privy Council Office maintained a firm association between the granting of a Royal Charter and the traditional professional model. There are allusions to status and legitimacy, and although it is not entirely clear what the motivations were for the Institute to seek a Royal Charter, the Institute would have understood the widely held associations between the Royal Charter and the traditional professional model, and professionalism.[22] With the Royal Charter won in 2000, Part Two concludes with a discussion of the meaning of the Royal Charter for the Institute and practitioner, set against continuing change within the meaning of

classical professionalism, and the socio-political and organisational practice context. It shows how although the acquisition was important in
many ways, the professionalisation of the HR function was incomplete
for many reasons. This discussion will also include the ways in which the
Institute seeks to steer a way through the change to maintain its position
as conferred by the Royal Charter.

Part Three develops the argument that the Royal Charter could not,
and did not, complete the professionalisation that some commentators
would have expected. There were several reasons for this, one of which
was the evolving nature of the traditional model. Pressures from government interventions and from societal expectations, perhaps beginning at a
glacial pace in the twentieth century, began to accelerate towards the end
of this period and into the twenty-first century. These pressures wrought
significant change to those traditional and elite professions which commentators, governments and the public had found so fascinating. Many
other occupations had emerged and evolved and sought to elevate the
status of the practitioners and the practices. Some of these occupations
have achieved social or occupational closure, as would have been seen in
Larson's "professional project".[23] This is achieved by supra-occupational
bodies retaining lists of qualified practitioners and the state requiring
regulation and reaccreditation. Many of the professional bodies for these
occupations have Royal Charters.

Whatever the Institute's motivation for seeking the Royal Charter, its
acquisition could never achieve professionalism in the traditional professional model. Therefore, on the one hand, the key actor responsible for
maintaining the momentum for the Royal Charter had been realistic in
his ambitions, and on the other, the classical model of professionalism
had been fragmenting over many years and was no longer the force it
was. In discussing the meaning of the Royal Charter for the Institute, this
chapter argues that a different kind of professionalism is emerging that
is far-reaching in most occupations and uses the HR practitioner as an
illustration of this.

## Acknowledgements

I have completed this book after several years of pondering the myster-
ies of the Chartered Institute of Personnel and Development (CIPD)—
without this institution and without the participation of key respondents
associated with the Institute, from member practitioners to senior officials past and present, this would not have been possible.

I am also indebted to members of the Privy Council Office who gener-
ously allowed me access to their records about the CIPD and the institution of the Royal Charter.

I most particularly want to thank my supervisors, Professor Bill
Cooke and Dr Karen Dale in the Department of Organisation, Work and

Technology, Lancaster University Management School where this book began as a doctoral study. I also wish to acknowledge the support and interest of many members of the Department of Organisation, Work and Technology, and fellow PhD candidates. I have had the most intellectually stimulating time ever within the embrace of this department. Finally, I would like to thank my present institution for believing that I could complete this.

So, how might you approach this text? I have tried to write this text in a logical and focused way. Readers who are interested in an account of social phenomena may appreciate the entire text a worthwhile read. Students of organisational theory may find in Part Two an interesting example of organisational logics and effort at play. Scholars and students of the professions and modern occupations may find a useful development of thinking about contemporary occupations in Chapter 5. My wish is that students of HR will read this, find it interesting and be willing and open to questioning the practices and how they have come to be the way they are.

Whatever your interest and motivation in selecting this book I hope you find something to stimulate your interest further.

## Notes

1. CIPD *Our Purpose and Vision*, www.cipd.co.uk/about/who-we-are/purpose, accessed 15 January 2019.
2. Chartered Bodies http://privycouncil.independent.gov.uk/royal-Charters/ Chartered-bodies/, accessed 30 November 2012; "A Royal Charter is an instrument of incorporation, granted by The Queen, which confers independent legal personality on an organisation and defines its objectives, constitution and powers to govern its own affairs. The terms of each Charter are therefore somewhat different, depending on the individual requirements of the type of organisation that is being incorporated", https://privycouncil. independent.gov.uk/royal-charters/chartered-bodies/, accessed 3 May 2019.
3. In Britain, the granting of a Royal Charter to an organisation like a professional body appears to be indicative to many commenters of that body as a profession like the traditional model that has so defined thinking about occupations. The Royal Charter, and the strategies pursued by the Institute to achieve it, is an essential component of the Institute's "professional project". This is because the Royal Charter is an institution as a signifier of preeminence and state recognition and therefore, in a British context, linked to a "professional project".
4. Gilmore S and Williams S (2003) *Constructing the HR Professional: A Critical Analysis of the Chartered Institute of Personnel and Development's "Professional Project"*; (2007) "Conceptualising the 'Personnel Professional': A critical analysis of the chartered institute of personnel and development's professional qualification scheme"; Gold J and Bratton J (2003) "The dynamics of professionalization: Whither the HRM profession?"
5. CIPD Press Release 2 December 2008.
6. Larson M S (1977) in *The Rise of Professionalism: A Sociological Analysis* coined the term "professional project" to denote the professionalising

strategies of occupations to achieve *professionalism*; other scholars also took up the notion in relation to other occupations. In relation to the occupation of human resource management, the idea of closure can be seen in the work of Gilmore and Williams 2003 ibid; Gold and Bratton 2003 ibid.

7. Larson 1977 ibid.
8. Discourse is ". . . an interrelated set of texts and the practices of their production, dissemination and reception", Hardy C and Phillips N (2002) "Discourse analysis: Investigating processes of social construction", page 3. See also Alvesson M and Kärreman D (2000) "Taking the linguistic turn in organisational research: Challenges, responses, consequences".
9. The nature of discourse constitutes a representation of reality as it "does not emanate from a freeplay of ideas in people's heads but from a social practice which is firmly rooted in an orientation to real material structures", Fairclough N (1992) *Discourse and Social Change*, page 66.
10. Gephart R P (1993) "The textual approach: Risk and blame in disaster sensemaking".
11. Niven M M (1967) *Personnel Management 1913–1963: The Growth of Personnel Management and the Development of the Institute*. In his interview in February 2010 the former Director-General admitted that he had not appreciated the historical value of the Institute's documents. Margaret Niven (1967) had already observed that many of the documents dated between 1913 and 1967 she needed for her book had already been destroyed.
12. I attempted to obtain access to these documents in return for cataloguing any documents for future keeping at the Modern Records Office; however, the request went unanswered and I did not over-press my inquiry for fear of alerting attention to my inquiry in a way that might jeopardise the interviews I had set up with some of the key informants at the Institute.
13. Lucas B E and Strain M M (2010) "Keeping the conversation going: The archive thrives on interviews and oral history", page 273. Very often a researcher enters an archive in hope, not knowing whether the information which she requires exists, and stumbles across those documents. Alternatively, a researcher may enter an archive without knowing for certain that documents relating to a topic are there, and so there is also the possibility of discovering something previously unacknowledged, which is what happened in this case.
14. University Forum for Human Resource Development *About*.
15. Mason J (2002) *Qualitative Researching*, page 127.
16. Lilleker D G (2003) "Interviewing the political elite: Navigating a potential minefield", "all elected representatives, executive officers of organisations and senior state employees" with "close proximity to power or policy making".
17. However, interviews are, as Langley says, "artificial interactions that can be influenced by lapses of memory, impression management, the moods of the participants and the quality of the rapport between interviewer and interviewee" Langley A (2009) "Studying processes in and around organizations".
18. Etzioni A (1969) *The Semi-Professions and Their Organization: Teachers, Nurses, Social Workers*, page xi.
19. The continuing legacy of this is illustrated in work by Crompton R (1987) "Gender, status and professionalism"; Phillips M (2005) "A gentlemanly body: The (excessive) case of the institute for the motor industry"; Roberts J and Coutts J A (1992) "Feminization and professionalization: A review of an emerging literature on the development of accounting in the United Kingdom"; Andrews T M and Waerness K (2011) "Deprofessionalization

of a female occupation: Challenges for the sociology of professions" and Noordegraaf M (2011) "Remaking professionals? How associations and professional education connect professionalism and organizations".
20. Fickers A (2012) "Towards a new digital historicism? Doing history in the age of abundance".
21. Ogden J, Halford S and Carr L (2017) "Observing web archives: The case for an ethnographic study of web archiving", June.
22. Throughout the Institute's story, there have been a few significant voices against the professionalisation of the occupation of personnel management, see for example Seears N (1979) "Can personnel managers deliver?"; a senior practitioner at the time immediately preceding the new institute joining the occupational practices of training with personnel management, in Personnel Management (1993) "The case for combination".
23. Larson 1977 ibid.

# Bibliography

Alvesson M and Johansson A W (2002) "Professionalism and politics in management consultancy work", in T Clark and R Fincham (eds) *Critical Consulting: New Perspectives on the Management Advice Industry*, Oxford: Blackwell.

Alvesson M and Kärreman D (2000) "Taking the linguistic turn in organisational research: Challenges, responses, consequences", *Journal of Applied Behavioural Science* 36: 136–158.

Burrage M (1990) "Introduction: The professions in sociology and history", in M Burrage and R Torstendahl (eds) *Professions in Theory and History: Rethinking the Study of the Professions*, London: Sage Publications.

Crompton R (1987) "Gender, status and professionalism", *Sociology* 21(3): 413–428.

Etzioni A (ed) (1969) *The Semi-Professions and Their Organization: Teachers, Nurses, Social Workers*, New York: Free Press.

Fairclough N (1992) *Discourse and Social Change*. Cambridge, MA: Polity Press.

Fickers A (2012) "Towards a new digital historicism? Doing history in the age of abundance", *VIEW Journal of European Television History and Culture* 1(1): 19–26.

Gephart R P (1993) "The textual approach: Risk and blame in disaster sensemaking", *Academy of Management Journal* 36(6): 1465–1514.

Hardy C and Phillips N (2002) "Discourse analysis: Investigating processes of social construction", *Qualitative Research Methods Series* 50.

Langley A (2009) "Studying processes in and around organizations", in D Buchanan and A Bryman (eds) *The Sage Handbook of Organizational Research*, London: Sage Publications, Chapter 24, pages 409–429.

Larson M S (1977) *The Rise of Professionalism: A Sociological Analysis*, London and Berkeley: University of California Press.

Lilleker D G (2003) "Interviewing the political elite: Navigating a potential minefield", *Politics* 23(3): 207–214.

Lucas B E and Strain M M (2010) "Keeping the conversation going: The archive thrives on interviews and oral history", in A E Ramsey, W E Sharer, B L'Eplattenier and L S Mastrangelo (eds) *Working in the Archives: Practical Research Methods for Rhetoric and Composition*, Carbondale, IL: Southern Illinois University, pages 259–277.

Mason J (2002) *Qualitative Researching*, 2nd edition, London and Thousand Oaks, CA: Sage Publications.

Niven M M (1967) *Personnel Management 1913–1963: The Growth of Personnel Management and the Development of the Institute*, London: Institute of Personnel Management.

Noordegraaf M (2011) "Remaking professionals? How associations and professional education connect professionalism and organizations", *Current Sociology* 59(4): 465–488.

Ogden J, Halford S and Carr L (2017) "Observing web archives: The case for an ethnographic study of web archiving", in *Proceedings of the 2017 ACM on Web Science Conference*, ACM, pages 299–308, June.

Phillips M (2005) "A gentlemanly body: The (excessive) case of the institute for the motor industry", in C Gustafsson, A Rehn and D Skold (eds) *Excess and Organization: Proceedings of SCOS XXIII: Stockholm 2005*, Stockholm, Sweden: Royal Institute of Technology.

Roberts J and Coutts J A (1992) "Feminization and professionalization: A review of an emerging literature on the development of accounting in the United Kingdom", *Accounting, Organizations and Society* 17(3–4): 379–395.

University Forum for Human Resource Development *About*, www.ufhrd.co.uk/wordpress/?page_id=5, accessed 25 November 2010.

Part 1

# The Century of Occupational Development and Change

# 1 Professionalism, the Institute and the Royal Charter

This book is about the perceived professionalisation of the field of human resource management (HR) as told through the relationship between the Chartered Institute of Personnel and Development (CIPD, the Institute), the professional body for Human Resource Management practitioners in the UK and the Royal Charter. The Institute is an association of practitioners within the field of workforce management, workforce development and employer-employee relations. Based in Britain, with members and reach across the globe, this organisation has had an evolving development because of a confluence of historical context, the socio-economic and political context, and the desires of key elites. Its origins stem from the industrial welfare workers movement of the late nineteenth and early twentieth centuries.[1]

## Introducing the Players

There are several important actors and institutions in the story of the professionalisation of HR. These are the Institute itself, the Institute's membership and their practices and the ancient British institution of the Royal Charter.

The story to unfold here takes place in a context with many actors, both organisational and human, involved in the professionalisation of HRM. There are, however, two main actors involved in the professionalisation of HRM—the Institute itself in a variety of incarnations and the Privy Council who administer Royal Charters on behalf of the Sovereign. The context is complex and multi-layered. This is the field of action, the stage upon which the action takes place, and includes organisational actors with an interest in the work of the Institute, such as the Institute's members, and actors with interests in the regulation and conduct of the employment relationship, as well as the state actor, the Privy Council. It is the traditional professional model which links the two and completes the triangle. There is also a minor player—the Institution of Training Officers Limited (ITOL, which later became the Institute of Training and Development, ITD)—whose fortunes nest within the Institute's story, but whose significance in the professionalisation of HRM is important because of the Institute's actions in relation to the requirements of the Privy Council.[2]

## The Lure of the Traditional Professional Model

I cannot address the professionalisation of the modern occupation of human resource management without discussing the model of professionalism or occupational organisation which characterises the traditional profession against which HRM has been judged. The professionalisation of HR needs an understanding of why and how such occupations form, and the recognition that the formation is both historically, institutionally and geographically grounded.[3] The traditional professions belong to an important institution, that of the traditional professional model, which is embedded in a society, and is, within the context of this book, in the Anglophone world. The traditional professional model is also a historical construct and as societies develop, technologies of work and practice evolve, and so we would expect it to evolve as occupations change and new occupations arise. Indeed, this has happened because elements of this construct have persisted well beyond their original meaning.

Since Adam Smith's treatise, *On the Wealth of Nations*,[4] there has been a continuing fascination with professionalism in the Anglophone tradition. Adam Smith recognised "lawyers and physicians" as "liberal professions" and artists and sculptors as "ingenious professions". He compared the "liberal" and "ingenious" professions with experienced tradespeople and made much of their superior knowledge, training and reward. This tradition came to be associated with other established occupations found in the Anglican Church, the military, medicine and the law. These are indeed old occupations and since the grouping named first, other occupations have become associated with the traditional professional model by modelling themselves on the characteristics of the older traditional professions. The occupations of architecture, accountancy and engineering are examples of professions in this model.

So, the traditional professions are a constellation of occupations that, according to a body of literature,[5] have common characteristics and exist to achieve certain purposes.[6] This model of a profession has become solidly ingrained in the collective consciousness of the Anglophone societies to the extent that if anyone claims to be a professional, to belong to a profession or to have professionalism, there are unspoken and agreed on assumptions about that person. Therefore, although we know what is meant, and what type of occupations are professions, these are occupations which are in flux and have always been changing, but their potency lasts. The professions have cast "a long shadow" over society.[7]

The traditional professional model is a principal element of the professionalisation stories because this model, and its assumed characteristics, has prompted discussion about other occupations' professionalisations or "professional projects" including that of HR.[8]

Why does the epithet "professional" have so much currency and appeal to individuals and representatives of occupational groups? The appeal derives from the inference of separation and superiority. Superiority derives from the education and training, socialisation, perceived and received expertise, and consequent reward, from which status and standing in the social world derives.

The claims made for the beneficial characteristics of the traditional professional model are large. For example, one claim is that the stability and welfare of society rest upon "the effective organisation of professional work" promising "to deliver work of high standard" and "keep us healthy and safe every day[9]". Not only does the public consider the notion of a 'profession' and 'professional work' important, but it is a powerful notion for governments too. In the belief that the professions have high status and reward, governments look to develop policies that improve social mobility through access to the professions.[10]

## The Traditional Model of Professions

Some twentieth-century accounts of the professions give a sense of how to recognise the traditional model. These accounts have examined the traditional professions from the perspectives of how they go about their craft and how people gain access to the professional group, and these observations have dominated the literature of much of the twentieth century and public consciousness. This example from 1953[11] exemplifies this tendency to show defining characteristics:

> A profession is a vocation whose practice is founded upon an understanding of the theoretical structure of some department of learning or science, and upon the abilities accompanying such understanding. This understanding and these abilities are applied to the vital practical affairs of man (sic). The practices of the profession are modified by knowledge of a generalized nature and by the accumulated wisdom and experience of mankind, which serve to correct the errors of specialism. The profession, serving the vital needs of man, considers its first ethical imperative to be altruistic service to the client.

The quotation is representative of the thinking about the professions and their association with underpinning knowledge, the performance of competence, the garnering of experience, the properties of a public good, ethical behaviours and altruism. It is a view which persisted beyond the twentieth century as modern scholars attest, noticing the same or similar characteristics in contemporary occupations.

The making of the traditional model of professionalism includes localised but defined and codified knowledge which has come from some scientific discipline. The practitioners translate the knowledge to expertise and practice, which they execute with skill and competence. The underpinning knowledge is kept up to date and put into the service of others. The traditional professions have legal and ethical responsibility created through normative value systems, often codified as a code of professional conduct. The effect, therefore, is a societal good, an "anchor of order".[12] Through their association with other professionals and operating inside the boundaries of the professional body, professionals have control over their affairs and create a hierarchy of membership.

A profession has a monopoly for the expert services it provides; it is autonomous and self-governing. The training is specific, programmed and erudite. Consumers or clients of the service have trust in the perceived competence of the practitioner and the practices. As a result, consumers afforded the practitioner legitimacy—all told, a profession was "of special importance for society and the common weal".[13] Professionals have considerable societal status and reward to match, which is why governments are interested in the traditional model of the professions as an encouragement to social mobility. "Differential occupational prestige" between occupations claiming professionalism and the association with prestige, high reward[14] are two attributes which contribute to the notion of the professions being elitist.[15]

The approaches to understanding professions which appeared in most of the twentieth century[16] did not address the issues of occupational control, power and the charges of monopoly and elitism. This oversight was addressed after the 1970s[17] but by then the same scholars saw traditional professionalism in decline, and in respect of the traditional profession of medicine in Britain, they may have been right.[18] Although the power of the traditional professions may be declining, professional power is still a highly desirable resource. Such power derives from the "specialised occupational skills" that create relationships of "social and economic dependence". Dependency creates asymmetry, "social distance", which creates space for autonomy.[19] This analysis shows how professions derived their power and privilege from the trust and deference afforded to the professional by their "consuming public". These are the societal effects which made the traditional professional model attractive for new and emerging occupations to imitate.

The wealth of commentary applied to the professions or single occupations which aspire to traditional professionalism shows a scholarly interest in how people spend their time at work. There is interest in the knowledge and preparation needed to be competent and interest (both prurience and envy) in the pay and rewards. High reward shows an individual's worth, value or measure of esteem and status. The public trust their professionals, and many people look to join the ranks of professionals themselves. The work, the assumed collegiality, reward and esteem appear as objects of great meaning to society.

Professions are inscribed in social acceptance, and they have longevity; the practices purveyed are executed as a skill which is underpinned by a recognised body of knowledge from some branch of trusted science. Professionals exercise their skill and knowledge in places where others are not capable or qualified. As a result, recipients of a professional's expertise and service trust the professional. The professional, in return, may charge a fee for the service rendered. So, the societal benefits attributed to professional work are in exchange for esteem, privilege and trust, the consumer believing that only the professional can solve the client's problem. In that belief, the effect is good and necessary, and the consumer grants legitimacy.

## Accounts of Professions

In the context of this book, the traditional professional model is socially and historically located in the Anglophone world, and there is a wealth of literature concerning occupations in this model. Much of it, however, is accounts of single professions, or two professions, where writers see comparisons or similarities. These have, however, tended to be "complimentary"[20] and deferential, focusing upon the "elite of the profession" and the preoccupations of "their governing bodies", the professional body.

Accounts of the traditional professions have discussed traits, functions and characteristics which appear to have set the standard for all other aspiring occupations. These accounts[21] offer the public some key characteristics ranging from how the professionals go about their craft, how people gain access to the professional group and what the public might expect from an encounter with the professional. The accounts are freighted with desirable characteristics which have become institutionalised to the extent that everyone knows a profession when they encounter it. These accounts and observations have dominated the literature of much of the twentieth century and entered the public consciousness. Furthermore, the traditional professional model conveys notions of prestige, recognition and reward,[22] and therefore it became an aspirational model to which occupations in collective formation aspire. The professional model has become institutionalised, and the reasons relate to characteristics of self-regulation and self-generation observed in institutions.[23]

Although there appears to be agreement as to what constitutes a profession this is an *ideal type*, with some distinctive features which create that common, institutionalised understanding of an occupation with professionalism because it displays, to some degree, some of the institutionalised characteristics which are found in the ideal view of the typical traditional model.[24] The *ideal type* embodies the characteristics of the collective formation and "a system of rewards (monetary and honor-ary)".[25] These are emblematic of "work achievement" and are symbolic of collective identity being "ends in themselves, not means to some end of individual self-interest".[26]

Different types of occupations fall somewhere on the continuum which has the ideal at its centre point, depending upon the extent to which they exhibited the characteristics of the traditional professional model. So, there are occupations which are fully organised in the model of the tradi-tional profession, those which are semi-professions and those which are non-professions.[27] For example, the semi-professions had shorter train-ing, less status in society, less privilege, a less significant body of knowl-edge and less autonomy for the practitioner. Semi-professionals worked in organisations, an idea which contrasted with the work done by the traditional professional who was not subject to administrative or organi-sational control (a notion which turned out to be fanciful). The semi-pro-fessions seek full professional status through professionalisation because they wish to differentiate themselves from a blue-collar or an unskilled worker; this idea adds to the charge, directed at the traditional profes-sions, that they are elitist.[28] The continuum idea offers a broader scope for analysis that would, therefore, include occupations such as pharma-cists, nurses, teachers, architects and practitioners of alternative medi-cine. These occupations are perceived to have aspiration (and often fail) to "match up to many criteria of a classical profession".[29] I might argue that personnel management/human resource management falls into this category since the site of practice is in an organisational setting, but, as this book will show, there has been a concerted attempt to organise and regulate the personnel/human resource practitioner for over a hundred years.[30]

There are other views about the traditional profession which examine the purpose of the traditional professional model[31] and focus upon pro-cesses such as professionalisation and "professional projects" or effects such as power, exclusivity and occupational closure and monopoly.[32] These purposes and processes appear to distil to privilege, exclusivity, status and power—the "professions-as-conspiracy" view.[33]

The separate discussions and arguments are, however, artificial as there is interconnectedness between the different forms of analysis, as organi-sation, history and process, and societal effect overlap. More than that, however, this thinking has contributed to elongating the "long shadow"[34] cast by the traditional professional model, to the extent that it has become institutionalised as a societal benefit.[35] Professions create and maintain social institutions through theorising, working in domains such as poli-tics, the law and management, and stitching together the fabric of social life.[36] Thus, the aspects of professions—knowledge, the professional as an expert, the kind of work, the orientation to that work, permanence, stability and longevity are the characteristics by which professions may be identified and are relevant to the study of the HR occupation.[37] This is the essence of traditional *professionalism* and where we might see professionalisations and "professional projects"[38] among occupations aspiring for such status.

But what of the work, and the body of knowledge which is key to the traditional profession? Professions create practices, which accumulate over time, diffuse and which other groups adopt.[39] Furthermore, traditional professions wield influence through their legitimacy and their status and prestige. These are "symbolic elements, social activities and material resources".[40] The importance of this conception of the professional model lies in its capture of the social imagination not only for their benefits but also their pervasiveness, recognised by characteristics of permanence, stability, longevity and acceptance. Professions are important because of their:

> distinct and identifiable structures of knowledge, expertise, work, and labor markets, with distinct norms, practices, ideologies and organizational forms.[41]

These foci often omit issues about the effects of the profession on society, their clients, the voiceless, and the struggles that lay underneath the linear and trouble-free path towards professionalism. As an antidote to such flattering and uncritical accounts, there has been increasing recognition of the historical, socio-political factors contingent upon the emergence and progress of a profession. By examining contingent accounts or documents such as case reports, statutes and government reports, a less one-sided picture and more critical approach to studying the British legal profession emerges, rather than relying upon the sources from the profession itself.[42] In a similar way, the trace characteristics underpinning the traditional professional model are inscribed in statements on the Institute's website, and because of the association between the traditional profession model and the Royal Charter: it is a triangular relationship and the focus of this book.

To conclude, the characteristics which much of the literature about these occupations identified may be summarised in four parts: they have a collective organisation; they have a body of knowledge which underpins practice and which is curated and developed; they have values of altruism for social good; and the profession regulates itself through the license to practice, the register of members and codes of professional conduct.

Professionalisations are both the attainment of professionalism as an end-state[43] and "professional projects".[44] Although earlier studies of single professions tended to ignore context and the role of other agents, it is important to consider the effects of context and of several actors who were instrumental in the emergence and progress of a profession.[45] The features of the traditional professional model come about because of professionalisation. Professionalisation concerns the regulation of the production of producers (qualification into the profession and closure) and the regulation of the production by producers (the behaviour of qualified professionals and standards).[46]

More factors also include the potential for inter-professional rivalry and the outcomes of such jurisdictional conflict,[47] and the story of the professionalisation of HR through the Institute's dealings with the Privy Council bears this out. Professionalisation is:

> the aspiration that an occupational group cherishes to reach exclusive societal advantages and preference of interpretation within their special field of knowledge and praxis.[48]

In 1969, Hickson and Thomas argued that instead of asking what a profession is, a more profitable inquiry would be the extent to which occupations have *professionalised* along a pathway which was shown in the literature and in ordinary understanding.[49] Hickson and Thomas (1969) reviewed earlier literature to find a scale of professionalisation based upon the extent to which an occupation had acquired certain characteristics. This approach foregrounded the prominence of key attributes of the traditional professional model which determined how far an occupation had progressed along a continuum towards professionalism in the traditional model.

Key elements along a professionalisation pathway include matters of education, training, testing for competence, organisation and a code of conduct. These staging points, although not as linear and processual as they appear, nevertheless indicate collective organisation, the presence of a body of knowledge and a mimetic orientation towards the public good. This is relevant to the Institute's "professional project" as one of the triggers for the original study into the Institute and the Royal Charter was the observation that the Institute's "professional project" had been "rather successful".[50] So, what is a "professional project"?

THE "PROFESSIONAL PROJECT"

A "professional project" referred to occupational strategies to professionalise for the purposes of exclusivity and monopoly (and status and privilege). The "professional project" said Larson in 1977:

> organizes the production of producers and the transaction for services of a market.[51]

This is an interesting phenomenon as it shows that the traditional professional model is performative, enabling occupations to garner a range of resources, material and intangible. The material resources include high rewards, but intangible resources include power, prestige, social standing and legitimacy. Organisation, ideology and persistence together constitute "the remarkable uniformity and consistency in the goals of professions", and an occupation achieves this through the completion of a "professional project".[52]

Occupations engaging in a "professional project" enact strategies to achieve "professionalism" in the traditional model.[53] For example, as part of a "professional project", an occupation might engage in a strategy of "jurisdictional expansion" to strengthen boundaries, whose purpose was a closed labour market, with high and exclusive barriers to entry and have an accomplished "professional project".[54] The result is a high demand for services that only practitioners within that market can perform. This situation leads, therefore, to charges of exclusivity and high status, which is an attribute highly prized by society. These are attributes of a "professional project" because the project relies upon the efforts and aggrandisement strategies of the collective, the professional body.

The barriers to entry into the occupational territory are deliberately exclusionary, and this is relevant when considering how the Institute has tried to capture and keep a market for specialised labour. There are a number of ways to describe the closure of an occupation, whose ultimate state was "the license to practice". One way is the expression of two polar opposites—"exclusionary closure" and "demarcationary" closure.[55] Exclusionary closure refers to situations when occupations try to improve status, privilege and earnings and derive from "intra-occupational relationships". Strategies to secure closure may concern "jurisdictional conflict".[56] This is because the profession, to achieve its goals, needs to eliminate the potential threats to either its claims to be the voice of practitioners or to have sole authority over the domain and the associated knowledge and skill. An example of "jurisdictional conflict" is the intra-occupational rivalry shown between the professional bodies involved in accounting,[57] and this phenomenon is relevant to the Institute's "professional project".

In contrast, in attempting demarcationary closure, occupations try to gain control over domains of work where perceived boundaries are porous or overlapping, a situation which occurs in many management fields. This is an inter-occupational conflict which is "a fundamental fact of professional life" and applies in the case of personnel/human resource management practitioners.[58] These notions are important for the meaning of the Institute's "professional project" because the original observation of a "professional project"[59] appears to refer to both types of closure and is thus typical of the notions of jurisdictional conflict which characterise "professional projects".

The "professional project" suggests a linear process, but it is one situated in an institutional environment which at one time provides progress towards professionalism and at another time interferes with progress. To have reached "professionalism", the occupation needs to meet certain conditions of having legitimate power over the supply of services, control over who is admitted to membership and "a sustaining ideology" that has "the appearance of benefiting consumers through the monopoly position".[60] In this way, the occupation can protect the consumers of its services without interference from the state, through a sustaining ideology. These conditions are relevant when it comes to examining the professionalising tendencies of the Institute but also the seeds of its inchoate "professional project".

The aspects of the traditional professional model acquired a certain stickiness and featured in the literature either side of the year 1968, when the record shows that the Institute first enacted what Niven suggests the welfare workers had done in 1913 and 1917—professionalise through acquiring a Royal Charter, the badge of recognition of the day. Appendix II shows how the defining features of the traditional professional model can be distilled to collective organisation, knowledge and values.

OCCUPATIONS ORGANISING

Practitioners of a discipline, craft or trade who see themselves as superior in education and training, expertise and status have consistently found it more helpful to seek communion and common cause with others, whose interests most closely match those of their own. Coalescence concentrates resources to pursue helpful ends. Such common interest has moved practitioners, like particles in motion, to form new shapes and constellations which are products of their social and political time, and which are reflective of localised knowledge. Once grouped, practitioners erect new boundaries which serve to protect practitioners, guard and develop the knowledge upon which the practice derives and exclude the unqualified.

The presence of a professional association illustrates the weight given to the collective of practitioners, as an indicator of an occupation that is professionalising or has a "professional project" is important in the case of the Institute.[61]

A profession's altruism and contribution to society are two aspects in the traditional professional model which suggested effects such as the perpetuation of elitism, power and privilege; this is because of the trust conferred upon them by the profession's consumers. Therefore, professional work becomes a monopoly[62] and the profession will do everything it can to keep that monopoly. The profession and its agents, the professional body, carry out this through erecting exclusionary fences around a collective of practitioners.

A professional body is the overarching organising mechanism protecting and promoting a set of practices which have arisen in the occupational field. The practices begin at the job level and by social processes become occupations. The practices need protection, as do practitioners, and the act of coming together as a group enables the building of fences of exclusion. The professional occupational body is a stronghold, a castle's barbican, the first line of defence against persons who might weaken the practices. It is essential to guard against infiltration from the unsuitable, the charlatan, the unqualified. The barbican is the "qualifying association",[63] a purveyor of credentials and shaper of practitioner identity. The "qualifying association" curates and develops the shared body of knowledge and practice which bind practitioners together and support standards of practice.

Scholars have recognised the dominance of the model of traditional professionalism, with its assumed characteristics, linear processes of emergence and mimetic charm. There have been efforts to find traditional professionalism within a class structure, as a social stratum which afforded opportunities for advancement.[64] So, professionalism of this type applied to the traditional professions results in power, prestige, trust and legitimacy, and these are properties looked for in professionalising strategies of imitation.

## The Royal Charter

The Royal Charter is an ancient British institution which exudes power and elitism because only the Sovereign's Privy Council can make such an award. The Royal Charter conveys symbolic meaning about pre-eminence, quality and status. Its association with the traditional professions comes from the fact that many of the traditional professions representing occupations hold Royal Charters. These occupations are the traditional professions which have long held a fascination for the public, state actors and academics and social commentators alike.

The main reasons for this are that professionals occupy a significant place in society and social hierarchy. They have status and high reward and are associated with desirable social mobility; for example, it remains aspirational to enter the field of medicine or law. These occupations appear exclusionary in that they self-regulate having the autonomy to choose who will or who will not be admitted to the profession. Furthermore, the public attribute many benefits and privileges to being members of a profession and make consequent assumptions about the practitioner of the profession in terms of their status, trustworthiness and probity.

The institution of a Royal Charter in Britain dates from the thirteenth century and was the only way individuals could act as legal entities with rights and purposes. The most common early corporations were the universities of Cambridge (1231) and Oxford (1248), and associations and guilds such as the Grocers Company (1428), the Brewers Company (1437) and the Royal Botanic Society for London (1839). In

September 2012, the most recent Charter was granted to The Worshipful Company of Lightmongers, a body representing all parts of the lighting and electrical industry from contractors, manufacturers, designers, architects and engineers.[65] What unites these Chartered bodies is their purpose to advance knowledge and science and perform a social benefit. Queen Elizabeth's Privy Council Office administers Royal Charters[66] on behalf of the Sovereign. At the time I was undertaking research for this project, the Privy Council website said:

> New grants of Royal Charters are these days reserved for eminent professional bodies or charities which have a solid record of achievement and are financially sound. In the case of professional bodies, they should represent a field of activity which is unique and not covered by other professional bodies.[67]

This book is the story of how the Institute won a Royal Charter, against a backdrop of changing socio-political-economic conditions, against an evolving and eventually fragmenting professional model.

In the British context the acquisition of the Royal Charter is a signifier of pre-eminence and has been, and still is, an institution which carries symbolic meaning.

It has been the Royal Charter which has tended to link occupations with a "professional project",[68] or professionalisation in which the occupation evolved, and observers saw that the occupation was mimicking the traditional professions in both organisation, interests and goals. A goal of a "professional project" or professionalisation included closing off the occupation to persons who were not fit and proper and qualified practitioners. It was the strategy of excluding the non-qualified which created a labour market for professional labour.

### The Link With Professionalism and a Royal Charter

The main factor in the professionalisation of HR is the occupational strategies through the acts of the Institute to professionalise, and the assumption that a Royal Charter would contribute to the goal. The features of the traditional professions which have persisted in the literature[69] also are important to the Privy Council who award Royal Charters. The record appears to show that the features were both important and used as obstacles for the Institute to scale. The following extract from the Privy Council Office website from November 2012:

> At least 75% of the corporate members should be qualified to first degree level standard. Finally, both in the case of charities and professional bodies, incorporation by Charter should be in the public interest.

The Royal Charter is, therefore, a form of state recognition of a defined domain of occupational practice underpinned by some branch of knowledge (preferably with a scientifically testable and provable basis) and in which practitioners are qualified and competent. It is not surprising, therefore, to recognise that many associations of traditional professional occupations do have a charter—the Royal College of Surgeons (1800), the Law Society (1845), the Institute of Chartered Accountants in England and Wales (1880), and The Royal College of General Practitioners (1972) are all examples.

A further hallmark of a profession is state recognition and occupational closure—the license to practice. The license to practice is variously a barrier to entry, restrictor of quackery and a way for an occupation to control its own domain of work. It is however surprising to note that many modern occupational associations associated with knowledge and practice in the service and protection of the public do not have charters but have achieved recognition for the occupation and its practitioners through the license to practice, the register of practitioners. Examples of such occupational associations include the Institute of Teaching and Learning and the Healthcare Professions Council.

The characteristics of the traditional professional model were still visible at the time the Institute first made its representation to the Privy Council for a Royal Charter.[70]

Some Institute insiders had expressed doubts about the desirability of professionalisation[71] because of the association between the Royal Charter and professionalism which would mean closure and a license to practice. However, despite this, the Institute won a Royal Charter in 2000, to much publicity and celebration at the Institute and among members.

## The Institute's Origins

The Institute is *the* professional association for people working in the field of personnel/human resource management.[72] In 2013, the Institute celebrated its 100th year as an organising mechanism for practitioners of routines in workplaces for dealing with the problem of the worker, and everything which that entailed. An organisational centenary is an achievement; it is also an example of the passing of social time and is redolent with meanings constructed by organisational elites and members who forget how things have come to be as they are. One hundred years of existence suggests longevity and permanence and enables the Institute to boast of its dominance and competence over its field of practice. Such attributes turn out to be relevant to the Institute's professionalisation, its perceived "professional project".

The early forerunner of the modern-day HR practitioner was the welfare worker,[73] and that is where the Institute's story really begins. In her historiography[74] written in 1967, Niven wrote appreciatively of the Institute's progress from 1913, through various name changes, and, as the Institute published the book, introduced a willing audience to the foundation stories of the early "pioneers" in the field of welfare. The story is that the work in Britain began with the welfare tradition of the nineteenth and early twentieth centuries set up among many enterprises owned and managed by benevolent families, with the approval of the Factory Inspectorate.[75]

In 1913, a group of welfare workers and their employers met at the invitation of Seebohm Rowntree in York. Many of the thirty-four welfare supervisors who met in 1913 were employees in family-owned enterprises, often run following religious principles and beliefs. In this type of organisation practices for the dual purpose of worker betterment and organisational productivity came together as 'welfare'; occasionally a firm's 'social department' oversaw the welfare practices. According to Niven,[76] the Institute's biographer, the meeting in York was because of "the need of the early welfare workers for association with their fellows".[77] Whilst there is little doubt that this was the case, it is also important to recognise that employers and their welfare workers had a shared interest in the problem of the worker. The workers were the human factor in industry[78] and an integral part of the means by which organisations created wealth for the owners.

An occupation laying claim to a domain of work, welfare work, needed to organise, but the fragmented situation which existed in the early twentieth century did not bode well if the welfare workers were to arise as an organised profession.[79] This was important for the elites of the occupations, such as those meeting in York, if they were to unite and align members behind specific goals. Niven suggests that the founders of the Institute had the professionalism shown in the traditional professions within their sights.

Although collective organisation was an aim, there was little progress in 1913: the Great War intervened, and other national priorities took centre stage. However, in response to the threat of the continuing fragmentation of practice, the welfare workers regrouped in 1917 with the formation of the Central Association for Welfare Workers when:

> it was finally agreed that the association should be a 'professional' body of all engaged in welfare work in industrial and business enterprises.[80]

Niven's historiography of 1967 overlooked the fact that what passed for industrial welfare work at the time the welfare officers met to form their association for the second time in 1917 was already part of practices in welfare and was a strategy for organisational efficiency in many large organisations. Niven's foundational story promoted the idea of unanimity among employers; however, this was not always the case. Edward Cadbury, for example, was one dissenting voice. He did not see the need for a social department as he said in his introduction to his volume that "business efficiency and the welfare of employees are but different sides of the same problem".[81]

A professional occupation has distinctive practices; whilst it is true that some of the origins of welfare work appeared as an amalgam of activities labelled variously as "social" and "employment" work, these were practices which as "welfare work" went on in workplaces "unobserved" before they were "named".[82] "Indeed, it might almost be said that there is nothing new in Welfare Work, except the name," claimed one commentator, concluding that welfare work was concerned with:

> the voluntary efforts on the part of employers to improve, within the existing industrial system, the conditions of employment in their own factories.[83]

After the First World War, the requirement for welfare workers diminished, but the Institute remained though it did not yet have a monopoly over a domain of work. As the Institute refocused its endeavours to reflect its changing spheres of activity, away from welfare work, to include labour management, and personnel management activities, so the practices were broadly recognised in the changed names of the Institute: Central Association for Welfare Workers (Industrial) (1919), Welfare Workers Institute (1919) and in 1924, the Institute became the Institute of Industrial Welfare Workers Incorporated. In 1931, the body became the Institute of Labour Management.

Both World Wars had left residual effects upon the British economy—changing work practices, changing social mores, changing demographics, recessions and resultant (un)/employment, and industrial relations issues.[84] From the early 1920s, there were developments in other 'scientific' disciplines, particularly in industrial psychology. The Institute accumulated this body of knowledge because practitioners could see that the practices were relevant. Many practitioners wrote textbooks[85] because practitioners had adopted and adapted the practices to suit the work which organisations needed to manage the workforce.

The emerging discipline of industrial psychology contributed to the development of practices for the recruitment, choice and measurement of the employee. Labour economics as a discipline claimed in labour management were borrowed from the accounting and economics bodies of knowledge. These 'borrowed' bodies of knowledge from concrete disciplines of a scientific nature lent weight to the appearance of rigour in the practices and body of knowledge, and therefore acquired legitimacy.

## The Development of the Qualification and the Relationship With Universities

A body of knowledge was construed in the traditional professional model as belonging to a "theoretical structure of some department of learning or science"[86] and as such the idea was laden with symbolism. Two factors emerging in the 1980s contributed to the Institute's endeavours in this regard: the emergence of the human resource management discourses and the associated research, and the attention being paid in the UK to management education. The Institute has been associated with the development of management education in Britain.[87]

Human resource management discourses were increasingly being taken up in organisations and were also being noticed by the academic community.[88]

The developing practices and body of knowledge became associated with the attributes of the traditional model of professionalism giving opportunities for the Institute to develop qualifications which practitioners increasingly wanted and needed to gain employment in the field, and which employers expected so that they would not have to train the practitioner themselves.

The Institute revised the qualifications in 1979/80, and subsequently. Although there was a hiatus in the Institute's dealings with the Privy Council about the Royal Charter, there was continued work upon the qualifications. The Institute's qualification scheme became much more formalised, moving away from the experiential and practitioner-based learning. The aim of the new programme was to enhance the practitioner's "professional knowledge and competence".[89] The scheme reflected practice at the time and consisted of three stages: stage one provided a foundation in aspects of management and organisations; stage two provided study in the three major functional areas of personnel management-employee relations, employee development and employee resourcing; and stage three involved an organisationally based project and demonstration of practical experience.

By reworking the qualifications in 1980, the Institute attempted to exercise a gate-keeping role to membership of a "distinct profession".[90] The scheme of the 1980s represented the tussle between those who perceived the practices as essentially vocational which were at their best when executed in specific and localised contexts and those who appear to argue for standardisation and credentialing of practitioners. These positions also represented the debate about the extent to which the occupation should professionalise.[91]

In 1991, again in pursuit of the Royal Charter, the Institute submitted an account of a new qualification system, the Professional Management Foundation Programme (PMFP). However, the reason given for the revision of the 1980s scheme was:

> The IPM was conscious that its qualification process to date had produced good personnel specialists, *but not necessarily good managers.*

The IPM was convinced by the work of the CNAA[92] and the Management Charter Initiative (MCI) that what was required within its qualification was an initial management programme to develop the core competence required of all managers. It considered that its own specialist training in personnel management would follow very naturally from this core management programme.[93]

By the time the PMFP was in operation, discourses around human resource management were beginning to make their way into personnel management practice in organisations, and new business practices such as Business Process Reengineering and Total Quality Management were being 'sold' into organisations as solutions by a growing band of consultants to an eager managerial cadre. Furthermore, the Conservative government introduced the *Investors in People* standard which focused on "transforming business performance through people".[94]

The endeavours of employees in organisations became fundamental to human resource management as conceived in the form received from the American literature. Correct control of employees fell under the purview of the personnel department, and practitioner had to navigate this—a task made all the more difficult by pressure from senior organisational members who were not necessarily practitioners.[95] The Institute needed to demonstrate timeliness, but the PMFP was only just beginning to reflect some of these developing ideas which indicated a shift from the focus on the practitioner as a traditional professional to expert.[96]

The Institute was known as the Institute of Personnel Management (IPM) from 1946 until 1993 when the name changed to the Institute of Personnel and Development (IPD). This came about when the occupational field of training and development came within the hinterland of the Institute. This was a strategy of "occupational upgrading" or a "professional project",[97] and is an event with a unique place in the professionalisation of HR.[98]

It also settles an idea that the hitherto separate fields of training (or learning and development) and personnel management ought to combine.[99] The event was also an illustration of the pursuit of elite interests and goals which characterise both the development of this organisation, this occupation and these practices. The event is by no means as benign as it sounds and needs exploration further in this book.

As part of the Institute's context, some background information about the state and status of training is required. The field had developed separately, having become an object of interest for successive governments as a route to successful national outcomes such as greater productivity, employment and skills transfer. As a result, training had become subject not only to the vagaries of government "ideology" but also "jurisdictional conflict"[100] and battles for legitimacy among different agents.

Prior to 1994, Education and Training (ET) policy in Britain had either been voluntarist or from 1964 prescribed under the Industrial Training

Boards (ITBs). The result was a fragmentation of provision with the field divided between the ITBs (until their abolition in the 1980s), the Institution of Training Officers founded in 1964, the British Association for Commercial and Industrial Education (BACIE) formed in 1919 and the Institute (IPM). The discipline itself was often seen as within the field of personnel management but of lower status than personnel management, with "specialist training staff" who reported to personnel managers.[101]

As prospects for Britain's post-war economy appeared to decline over the 1960s and 1970s, so too did confidence in the training field. This appeared to be over the ineffectuality of the ITBs.[102] There had long been a feeling among some practitioners of personnel management and some training practitioners that there should be one overarching body for practitioners from the fields of training and personnel management. Indeed, many personnel management practitioners were also engaged in the practice of training activity.[103] Furthermore, many practitioners belonged to both the Institute of Personnel Management and the Institute of Training and Development, and this was the case at the time the two institutes came together in 1993.

Writing in the *Journal of Industrial and Commercial Training* in 1979,[104] and with some foresight recognising the oncoming significance of changing practices and the advancing discourses of human resource management which acknowledges interdependence of both domains of practice,[105] Patrick H Sharpe revealed that in 1963 the Institute and British Association for Commercial and Industrial Education (BACIE)[106] had entered discussions to set up a "professional trainers' organization". The attempt of 1963 failed.

Following the failure of the IPM/BACIE discussions in 1963, Sharpe became a founder member of the British Institution of Training Officers in 1964. The British Institution of Training Officers developed a global reach and attracted "700 members in 53 overseas" countries.[107] With its international orientation, the organisation changed its name to the Institution of Training Officers (ITOL).[108]

Discussions to combine the two fields of practice continued between 1972 and 1979, unsuccessfully and rancorously. In fact, Sharpe suggests that the talks to merge the two were fractious and debilitating, and once again they came to no satisfactory conclusion. However, the Institution of Training Officers changed its name to the Institute of Training and Development, in recognition of the growing field of learning and development which was more focused upon the active participation of employees as trainees and learners, in contrast to the 'sheep-dip' approach that had characterised workplace training.

Sharpe resigned along with "a breakaway group of personnel and training managers" and set up an organisation whose focus was to be:

> providing a service to the many personnel and/or training managers who need national representation and down-to-earth grassroots support in their day to day jobs.[109]

This detour into the realm of training and ITOL serves to illustrate the occupational rivalry which has characterised the processes of HR professionalisation. The Institute launched a predatory raid on the successor organisation, the Institute of Training and Development, in 1994; the field of training and development became subject to the vagaries of circumstances and the whim, pursuits and interests of powerful individuals.[110]

This event appears again in a later chapter; however, developments at the national level were important in the 1994 combination of the two institutes. Making the case for a combined field of practice, practitioners observed the national developments taking place in Vocational and Educational Training (VET), and the rise of the National Vocational Qualification (NVQ) being overseen by the Training and Development and Personnel Standards Lead Bodies (TDLB and PSLB) which practitioners saw as providing "a professional infrastructure which permeates rather than reinforces the boundaries between those concerned with people at work". The rise of the NVQ could have provided a challenge for the Institute to be able to claim primacy and dominance over the knowledge associated with a field of practice, which was essential if the Institute was to be awarded a Royal Charter.[111]

As a professional association, the Institute assumes the role of developing credentialing qualifications for practitioners in the field, which education providers make available to aspirant practitioners within their own academic offerings. There are courses leading to qualification run internally by CIPD or by higher education bodies whose corresponding qualifications the Institute has previously accredited and put through quality assurance processes.

It is also important to acknowledge that the Institute is an employer and has organised its affairs like a rational-legal bureaucracy. As such it is subject to the same financial, commercial and employment legislation, although its charitable status[112] gives some concessions for tax purposes in Britain.

As an employer, many of the Institute's operational functions do not necessarily employ practitioners in the field of personnel/human resource management, but other "organizational professionals"[113] such as workers in finance, media, public relations and marketing. Many employees make a career at the Institute and move on to other employment, as in the case of the Chief Economist and other senior staff such as the Chartered Secretaries whose role features in the professionalisation story.

Over the years, the Institute has actively developed research programmes, commissioning research by academics. In addition to performing the role of a membership association, the connections with academics have enabled the Institute to develop an extensive publishing enterprise, publishing *toolkits* for practitioners and textbooks for use by students and their universities on the qualification programmes. There were many opportunities for members to meet at the Annual Conference and Exhibition (ACE).[114] The Institute has always traded commercially but under the auspices of another wholly owned subsidiary, rather than through the professional association.[115]

It is an unfortunate fact that the status of the practitioner has always been a preoccupation for the Institute, and professionalisation and the attainment of the Royal Charter were strategies to address it. The practitioner's status is an outcome of the nature of the practices and the site of practice. The practitioner is an employee of an organisation which, because of its structural and operational choices, has a function responsible for policies which the Institute itself has described loosely as the "management and development of people within organisations".[116]

Nevertheless, Mr Dryburgh, a former Institute President, writing in the Institute's journal *Personnel Management* in 1972, captures the position of the practitioner well with the following quotation:

> Nearly always he (sic) is the "man in the middle". For management, who pay his salary, he must argue the company case; from the union viewpoint he is expected to negotiate acceptable terms and conditions for the staff. If the personnel man adopts a progressive policy, management says "slow down". If he goes at the pace of many employers associations he is accused by the unions of "lagging behind". Equally, what do the staff members think of their personnel man? Is he a friend or a foe? Frequently the personnel man has a bigger struggle with the attitudes of his own management to change than he does with the attitudes of those on the shop floor.[117]

This quotation is illustrative of the type of ambiguity found in the orientation of the practitioners—stuck between the management and the worker. Although the practitioner may have both knowledge and ability, they are often unable to exercise it without the agreement of the employer. Many commentators and authors have covered these aspects more extensively than I propose to do here.[118]

Margaret Niven in her history of the Institute from 1967 remarked that the welfare workers who first formed the Institute had appointed the practices as "part of management".[119] Identification with values and freedoms found in the traditional professional model "would prevent identification as general management" even though the pursuit of status was an attraction.[120] Being "part of management" is a constant thread in the story of the Institute and the practitioners and commentators spoke of the "struggle" for personnel/human resource management practitioners to become "full members of the management team".[121] The ability to contribute to the business's financial success was how organisations and other managers judged the practitioner's success.[122]

Textbooks began to acknowledge the need for qualification amongst practitioners; this is one such example from 1949:

> personnel work is a recognised profession for which university training is required.[123]

*The Development of Practices and Practitioners*

The Institute claims to be an occupational association representing the personnel/human resource management practitioner. It is therefore important to acknowledge the Institute's role and involvement within this field of practice. A practitioner textbook from 1949 credits four bodies as having contributed most to the development of personnel management: the Industrial Health Research Board in 1918, the National Institute of Industrial Psychology in 1921, the Industrial Welfare Association (formerly the Boys' Welfare Society formed by Robert Hyde) and the Institute (as the Institute of Personnel Management).[124]

The CIPD's claimed domain of the "management and development of people within organisations",[125] known more generally as the field of personnel management or human resource management, has evolved over the twentieth century, due to several factors. One of those factors is the developing higher education sector in Britain and the growth of professional associations[126] in Britain. However, of equal significance are the socio-economic context and the rise of jobs in organisations which need cognitive and behavioural labour rather than physical labour. These roles enable organisations to monitor and survey other workers to ensure they fulfil organisational tasks in prescribed ways to reduce aberrant behaviour and unexpected results. The practitioner of personnel or human resource management is one such role.

After the period of welfare management, personnel management settled into a recognisable set of practices as the textbooks and the Institute's qualification structures show.[127] Recruitment, information storage and processing, and the provision of employee services appear within a familiar core of personnel management activities. Industrial relations became a focus for some practitioners in the 1960s and 1970s, however the skilled practitioner, as negotiator and trouble-shooter, tended to undertake those activities.[128]

In the 1970s, empirical studies[129] into the function of personnel management from the perspective of those performing what was recognised as 'personnel management' found ambiguity and tension in the role. This research was set against a backdrop of industrial turmoil. The authority of personnel specialists was unclear, and management could ignore their advice. Their contribution was "unmeasurable"; additionally, the title 'manager' was problematic because it was difficult to discern what they were managing, but perhaps the biggest tension and ambiguity arose from the question "whose side are they on?" The practitioners were very much "in the middle" between employee representatives against management but knowing that their allegiance was to the management and the organisation (if they were to keep their jobs).

As for any notion of professionalisation, professionalism was an image, an icon of aspiration, and a discursive resource to rely on. One respondent in one study said:

It needs a professional approach but it doesn't need the IPM.[130]

Perhaps practitioner members of the Institute had become aware of professionalisation and perhaps some remembered or knew about the Institute's desire for a Royal Charter; they were not especially exercised about it.

The Conservative administration in 1979 signalled a shift in the socio-political environment; this had already begun but was coming to fruition as a neo-liberal project. The practices which characterised post-war personnel management and industrial relations as mechanisms for managing people at work also changed. This is not to say that practitioners did not need to undertake the traditional practices described in textbooks[131]; organisations and practitioners required elaborate ways of accomplishing old functions to appear relevant, modern and important. In the neo-liberal world, traditional modes of governing and employing appeared redundant, along with many jobs in many traditional industries; however, there was the promise of renewed purpose and status as indicated in this quotation:

> management development, career development, reward and contract structures, and organisational flexibility. [. . .] Forward-thinking organisations regard the management of human resources as a critical and integral part of the strategic planning process.[132]

In the same article, another senior practitioner acknowledged the changed practices:

> The people management job has changed considerably over the last decade. The key personnel tasks are seen to be much wider than recruitment and employee relations, and line managers have a high level of commitment to employee motivation and development.[133]

At that time, developments at the national level took place in Vocational and Educational Training (VET), including the rise of the National Vocational Qualification (NVQ). The Training and Development and Personnel Standards Lead Bodies (TDLB and PSLB) were overseeing the development of NVQs in both fields. Even practitioners saw this development as providing "a professional infrastructure which permeates rather than reinforces the boundaries between those concerned with people at work".[134]

Practitioners also saw the relationship between the practitioner and the line manager changing, and another senior practitioner writing in 1993 said:

> Managing and developing human resources on a day-to-day basis is now seen as part of a manager's role. Providing human resource strategies and technical support falls to the human resource function.[135]

Without explicit reference to the Royal Charter, other senior practitioners[136] were already linking both fields of practice under a joint institute to increased influence on a wider social stage and to increased standing for the practitioner.

The writer continued:

> A new institute that can capture and disseminate all that is best in managing people and organisations would be a great national asset.

Additional commentary showed that the contribution made by "the collective human resource management function" to the organisational strategy was essential in providing the infrastructure to cope with change, which was a preoccupation of the business and management communities at this time. Further discourses included the absorption of the notion of "customer care" and Total Quality Management (TQM).[137]

The socio-political climate under the Conservative government led by Margaret Thatcher was also a significant institutional factor with its focus upon performance and entrepreneurialism. Whilst the Institute appeared not to rush to overtly absorb the emerging discourses of human resource management (the Director-General, interview 20 February 2010), there was a sense of something happening to the employment relationship that required investigation. Wishing to forge closer relationships with universities, the Institute sponsored the peer-reviewed *Human Resource Management Journal* in 1990.[138] A significant amount of space in the practitioner journal was devoted to accounts of practices in exemplar organisations as well as shorter versions of academic research that had appeared in peer-reviewed academic journals.[139] In this way, the Institute appeared to be aiming to engage with a number of constituents, including universities, organisations and members.

The connection with universities was not only important for research relevant to the occupation's activities but also to meet the needs of the "professional project".[140] As one former Institute Examiner in June 2010 said in an interview, a university education even for vocational occupations was becoming essential for "the sort of people who are going to smooth their way into management and therefore into more influential positions".

There appears to have been a struggle for control of the curriculum between the Institute and the university sector.[141] Despite these territorial disputes, a symbiotic relationship arose between the universities and the Institute in which the universities began to accept that the Institute's support as the professional body was important. The relationship appeared to flourish between 1990 and the revised Professional Standards of 2010.[142]

Throughout this period there is a strong sign of the future trajectory of human resource management, which laid the ground for receptiveness of the ideas around a strategic role for the function, and the strategic business partner.[143]

The practices and routines in present-day human resource management are organising mechanisms to achieve standardisation of worker output and behaviour within contemporary management practice which attempts to create conditions under which employees work compliantly, without overt coercion, but with maximum commitment. The practices became normalised, taken for granted and institutionalised to the extent that the risks of not organising and managing the worker in these ways are too great. Practitioners look for customary practice, with underpinning knowledge of some scientific aspect and look to become qualified and exclusive.

The focus for the management of the human factor of production transferred to the individual who because of the prevailing economic conditions and neo-liberal ideology must invest in themselves. This is indicative of the transference of ideas about individual self-sufficiency, individualism as a necessary condition for survival in competitive and sometimes hostile environments which characterised late capitalism.

Through its association with the British universities, the Institute developed its role as a professional body in relation to the practices of personnel/human resource management and the credentialing of practitioners. These are essential elements of the Institute's "professional project" and its thirty-year longing for a Royal Charter.

## Setting the Stage for Part Two

The Institute did win a Royal Charter in 2000 after over thirty years of endeavour during which time key actors changed, as did their interests and their ability to act. In a similar fashion, practitioners followed more powerful actors in the field and rebranded themselves and the practices. The words of the Institute's Director-General just after the award of the Royal Charter in 2000 explained the significance of the Royal Charter to members reading the journal *People Management*:

> First, it recognises the professionalism, body of knowledge and practical competence of our members. By becoming chartered we have joined the premier league[144] of professional bodies. Second, it makes us even more of a "must belong" body for anyone who is professionally involved in people management and development. Third, our charter means that we are recognised as a "must consult" body by policy-makers in government and elsewhere on the whole range of people issues and work.[145]

He later rowed back on that view or at least lessened its import by saying in an interview in 2010 that the Royal Charter:

> It (the Royal Charter) was a big deal, very important psychologically—in reality, it wasn't worth much . . . you couldn't go to

your boss and say, "give me another £2000" . . . but it removed a negative.[146]

The "negative" of which the Director-General spoke concerned the continuing feeling that the function was weak and without organisational purpose.[147] It also shows that a key driver of the eventually successful application for a Royal Charter concerned the search to prove the legitimacy and status of the occupation. This contrasts with the idea of the occupation becoming closed or achieving "social closure"[148] which was the presumed goal of professionalisation, and which was a fact in the case of many traditional professions whose regulatory bodies had Royal Charters. There are many examples of the word "status" and associated notions in many of the Director-General's own words captured in interviews with *Personnel Management* and *People Management*.[149]

The stage is now set to raise the curtain on the drama that is the Institute's "professional project", its search for legitimacy, and a Royal Charter, the hallmark of legitimacy, exclusivity and the professionalisation of HR.

## Notes

1. See Drake McFeely M (1988) *Lady Inspectors: The Campaign for a Better Workplace 1893–1921*; Niven M (1967) *Personnel Management 1913–1963: The Growth of Personnel Management and the Development of the Institute.*
2. Other actors are also complicit in this story, but these are the main ones.
3. Walker S P (1995) "The genesis of a professional organization in Scotland: A contextual analysis", page 286, Willmott H (1986) "Organising the profession: A theoretical and historical examination of the development of the major accountancy bodies in the UK"; Sciulli D (2010) *Structural and Institutional Invariance in Professions and Professionalism.*
4. Smith A (n.d.) *An Inquiry into the Nature and Causes of the Wealth of Nations.*
5. Carr-Saunders A M and Wilson P A (1933) *The Professions*; Parsons T (1939) "The professions and social structure"; Greenwood E (1957) "Attributes of a profession"; Cogan M L (1953) "Towards a definition of profession".
6. Sciulli 2010 ibid.
7. Hodgson D (2008) "The new professionals: Professionalisation and the struggle for occupational control in the field of project management", page 232.
8. Gold J and Bratton J (2003) "The dynamics of professionalization: Whither the HRM profession?"; Gilmore S and Williams S (2003) *Constructing the HR Professional: A Critical Analysis of the Chartered Institute of Personnel and Development's "Professional Project"*; (2007) "Conceptualising the 'Personnel Professional': A critical analysis of the chartered institute of personnel and development's professional qualification scheme".
9. Adler P S, Kwon S-K and Heckscher C (2008) "Professional work: The emergence of collaborative community", page 359; Craig J (2006) *Production Values, Futures for Professionalism*, page 13.
10. As this research began, as part of a social mobility project, the (then) Labour government stated its intention to open the professions to young people from

backgrounds less advantaged than those traditionally associated with the traditional professions—see Cabinet Office (2009b) *Panel on Fair Access to the Professions Announced—New Opportunities White Paper*.

11. Cogan 1953 ibid.
12. Adler et al 2008 ibid; Dent M and Whitehead S (2002) *Managing Professional Identities: Knowledge, Performativity and the "New Professional"*.
13. Burrage M (1990) "Introduction: The professions in sociology and history".
14. Barber B (1963) "Some problems in the sociology of the professions", pages 671–672.
15. Johnson T J (1972) *Professions and Power*; Larson M S (1977) *The Rise of Professionalism: A Sociological Analysis*; Evetts J (2003) "The sociological analysis of professionalism: Occupational change in the modern world".
16. Carr-Saunders and Wilson 1933 ibid; Parsons 1939 ibid.
17. Johnson 1972 ibid; Larson 1977 ibid; Abbott A (1988) *The System of Professions*.
18. Johnson 1972 ibid; Larson 1977 ibid; Lewis R and Maude A (1953) *The English Middle Class*.
19. Johnson 1972 ibid, page 421ff.
20. Burrage 1990 ibid, page 6.
21. For example, Carr-Saunders and Wilson 1933 ibid; Parsons 1939 ibid.
22. Greenwood 1957 ibid; Barber 1963.
23. Leicht K T (2005) "Professions", page 604; Phillips N, Lawrence T B and Hardy C (2004) "Discourse and institutions", page 637; Jepperson R L (1991) "Institutions, institutional effects and institutionalism", page 145.
24. This is the *ideal type*; the *ideal type* relates to the historic and geographic notion of professionalism and arrives at the notion of a continuum of professions with occupations positioned in relation to one another depending upon their proximity to the *ideal type*. See Vollmer H M and Mills D L (eds) (1966) *Professionalization*, page 481 "a model of occupational structure characterised by certain specific elements"; Siegrist S (1990) "Professionalization as a process: Patterns, progression and discontinuity", "specific socio-historical periods and places", page 193. See also Greenwood 1957 ibid; Barber 1963 ibid.
25. Cogan 1953 ibid; Barber 1963 ibid, page 672.
26. Barber1963 ibid, page 672.
27. Etzioni A (ed) (1969) *The Semi Professions and Their Organization: Teachers, Nurses, Social Workers*, pages 671–672.
28. Etzioni 1969 ibid, page xi.
29. Hodgson 2008 ibid.
30. There is, however, an alternative categorisation for modern occupations: the organisational profession "organisational or managerial professions", see Lewis and Maude 1953 ibid; Reed M and Anthony P (1992) "Professionalizing management and managing professionalization: British management in the 1980s"; Swailes S (2003) "Professionalism: Evolution and measurement" ibid, pages 130–149.
31. Carr-Saunders and Wilson 1933 ibid; Cogan 1953 ibid, page 49.
32. Larson 1977 ibid; Dingwall R (2004) "Profession and social order in a global society", or effects such as power Johnson 1972 ibid, exclusivity and occupational closure; Abbott 1988 ibid and Etzioni 1969 ibid and monopoly, Larson 1977 ibid.
33. Dent and Whitehead 2002 ibid, page 2; Evetts 2003 ibid, page 260.
34. Hodgson 2008 ibid.
35. Adler et al. 2008 ibid, page 359, Craig 2006 ibid, page 13.

36. Scott W R (2008) "Lords of the dance: Professionals as institutional agents", page 227.
37. Scott 2008 ibid, page 227, Leicht 2005 ibid, page 604.
38. Larson 1977 ibid.
39. Barley S R and Tolbert P S (1997) "Institutionalization and structuration: Studying the link between action and institution".
40. Scott W R (2001) *Institutions and Organizations*, page 49.
41. Leicht 2005 ibid, page 604.
42. Abel-Smith B and Stevens R (1967) *Lawyers and the Courts: A Sociological Study of the English Legal System 1750–1965*, law; Marland H (1987) *Medicine and Society in Wakefield and Huddersfield 1780–1870*, medicine; Willmott 1986 ibid, pages 555–580 and Walker 1995 ibid, accounting. Other examples of accounts of the legal profession include Prest W R (1972) *The Inns of Court under Elizabeth and the Early Stuarts 1590–1640*; Prest W R (1986) *The Rise of the Barristers: A Social History of the English Bar 1590–1640*; Duman D (1983) *The English and Colonial Bars in the Nineteenth Century*, and Brooks W R (1986) *Pettyfoggers and Vipers of the Commonwealth: The "Lower Branch" of the Legal Profession in Early Modern England*, Brooks. Similar historical and contextual accounts appeared for medicine in Marland 1987 ibid and for accountancy, Loft A (1988) *Understanding Accounting in Its Social and Historical Context: The Case of Cost Accounting 1914–1975*.
43. Birkett W P and Evans E (2005) "Theorising professionalisation: A model for organising and understanding histories of the professionalising activities of occupational associations of accountants", page 104.
44. Larson 1977 ibid.
45. Burrage M, Jarausch K and Siegrist H (1990) "An actor-based framework for the study of the professions", page 203. There are, according to Faulconbridge and Muzio, four key actors are involved: The practitioners (producers), states (as regulators), academics (as co-developers of the body of knowledge) and users; see Faulconbridge J R and Muzio D (2012) "Professions in a globalizing world: Towards a transnational sociology of the professions", pages 136–152.
46. Faulconbridge and Muzio 2012, ibid, called this "two pillars of professionalization".
47. Abbott 1988 ibid; De Vries R, Dingwall R and Orfali K (2009) "The moral organization of the professions"; Suddaby R and Viale T (2011) "Professionals and field-level change: Institutional work and the professional project", page 428.
48. Selander S (1990) "Associative strategies in the process of professionalization: Professional strategies and scientification of occupations", page 142.
49. Hickson D J and Thomas M W (1969) "Professionalization in Britain: A preliminary measurement"; Greenwood 1957 ibid; Barber 1963 ibid; Millerson G (1964) *The Qualifying Association: A Study in Professionalization*; Wilensky H (1964) "The professionalization of everyone?" and Vollmer and Mills 1966 ibid.
50. Gilmore and Williams 2007 ibid; it is also important to note that the literature and common understandings prevalent in the 1960s coincided with the Institute's first application to the Privy Council for a Royal Charter.
51. Larson 1977 ibid, page 74; Although by 1990 Larson had retreated from that position in which a "professional project" concerned the acquisition of a closed market and monopoly, the idea of a "professional project" as part of "occupational upgrading" (Sciulli 2010 ibid) remains powerful as it carries the meanings of power, prestige and closure.

52. Burrage et al 1990 ibid, page 209.
53. Birkett and Evans 2005 ibid.
54. De Vries et al 2009 ibid.
55. Andrews T M and Waerness K (2011) "Deprofessionalization of a female occupation: challenges for the sociology of professions", page 43. See also MacDonald K M (1985) "Social closure and occupational registration". MacDonald explains the antecedents in the literature and considers three ways in which occupations can achieve social closure. MacDonald considers notions of 'harm'—to people (clients or public); harm to property or wealth rights; and then closure de jure and de facto. I also think that a run-down of professionalisation would be useful and include the literature on modern occupations and the successes or failures. Who has interest in social closure—the practitioner—for status, monopoly—the state to protect its citizens from harm?
56. Krause E A (1971) *The Sociology of Occupations*; Davies C (1983) *The Sociology of the Professions: Lawyers, Doctors and Others*, page 181; Collins (1990) *Professions in Theory and History: Rethinking the Study of the Professions*; Walker 1995, De Vries et al 2009; Suddaby and Viale 2011 ibid, page 428.
57. Willmott 1986 ibid.
58. Abbott 1988 ibid, page 2; Armstrong P (1986) *Managing the Labour Process*; Armstrong P (1988) "The Personnel Profession in the Age of Management Accountancy".
59. Gold and Bratton 2003 ibid; Gilmore and Williams 2003, 2007 ibid.
60. Birkett and Evans 2005 ibid, page 104.
61. Neal M and Morgan J (2000) "The professionalization of everyone? A comparative study of the development of the professions in the UK and Germany".
62. Johnson 1972 ibid; Larson 1977 ibid.
63. Millerson 1964 ibid, page 37.
64. Reader W J (1966) *Professional Men: The Rise of Professional Classes in Nineteenth-Century England*; Perkin H (1989) *The Rise of Professional Society*; Lewis and Maude 1953 ibid; Holmes G (1982) *Augustan England: Professions, State and Society 1680–1730*.
65. Since 2012 there have been thirty-two more Royal Charters counted at the time of writing in March 2019.
66. Chartered   Bodies   https://privycouncil.independent.gov.uk/royal-charters/chartered-bodies/, accessed 15 January 2019.
67. Chartered   Bodies   http://privycouncil.independent.gov.uk/royal-Charters/Chartered-bodies/, accessed 30 November 2012.
68. Larson 1977 ibid coined the term "professional project" to denote the professionalising strategies of occupations to achieve *professionalism*; other scholars also took up the notion in relation to other occupations. In relation to the occupation of human resource management, the idea of closure can be seen in the work of Gilmore and Williams 2003; 2007; Gold and Bratton 2003 ibid.
69. For example, Carr-Saunders and Wilson 1933 ibid; Greenwood 1957 ibid; 1966 "The elements of professionalization", page 9; and Parsons 1939 ibid.
70. Millerson 1964 ibid; Hickson and Thomas 1969 ibid.
71. Kenny T P (1972) "Professional examinations for British training staff"; Seears N (1979) "Can personnel managers deliver?"; Coates in Lawrence S (1979) "Man of the moment: Jack Coates".
72. The Institute's own description on its website describes it as the "professional body for HR and people development", www.cipd.co.uk/, accessed

3 January 2018. The Institute itself features as a professional association in many student textbooks (for example, Marchington M and Wilkinson W (2008) *Human Resource Management at Work: People Management and Development*, pages 128–129; Armstrong M (2009) *Armstrong's Handbook of Human Resource Practice*.

73. Anderson A M (1922) *Women in the Factory: An Administrative Adventure 1893–1921*; Drake McFeely 1988 ibid; Proud D E (1916) *Welfare Work: Employers; Experiments for Improving Working Conditions in Factories*.
74. Niven 1967 ibid.
75. See Anderson 1922 ibid; Drake McFeely 1988 ibid.
76. Niven 1967 ibid—The Institute commissioned and published this book to celebrate the first fifty years. It is interesting to note that by the time Niven got to the archives, much had been destroyed, and this was the case more than fifty years later. Organisations do not care to retain their past unless they can remember it as glorious.
77. Niven 1967 ibid, page 31.
78. Jacques R (1996) *Manufacturing the Employee: Management Knowledge from the 19th to the 21st Centuries*; Kaufman B E (2008) *Managing the Human Factor: The Early Years of Human Resource Management in American Industry*.
79. Niven 1967 ibid.
80. Niven 1967 ibid.
81. Cadbury E (1912) *Industrial Organization*.
82. See Proud 1916 ibid.
83. Proud 1916 ibid, pages 3, 5.
84. See accounts in Niven 1967 ibid and Marks W (1978) *Politics and Personnel Management: An Outline History, 1960–1976*.
85. For examples, see Blackford K M H and Newcomb A (1915) *The Job, the Man, the Boss*; Clarke V M (1949) *New Times, New Methods and New Men*. The early welfare workers were also anxious that their knowledge (individual and collective) would be extended and one of the ways to do this was through research, which was being generated in the field of psychology and human relations. These were applied in organisations, often as a result of national economic emergencies (see for example Clarke 1949 ibid; Baron J N, Dobbin F R and Devereaux Jennings P (1986) "War and peace: The evolution of modern personnel administration in US industry"). The development and the diffusion of practices and discourses for the management and development of people are outside the scope of this thesis, except to highlight the extent to which the Institute used them to build a body of practice, underpinned by the knowledge that had come from a rigorous and 'scientific' background.
86. Cogan 1953 ibid, page 49.
87. Constable J and McCormick R (1987) *The Making of British Managers: A Report for the BIM and CBI into Management Training, Education and Development*; Handy C (1987) *The Making of Managers: A Report on Management Education, Training and Development in the USA, West Germany, France, Japan and the UK*; Williams A P O (2010) *The History of UK Business and Management Education*, pages 4–5; Williams also identified the Chartered Management Institute and the Chartered Institute of Marketing.
88. See for example Fowler A (1987) "When chief executives discover HRM"; Storey J (1987) "Developments in the management of human resources: an interim report"; Torrington D and Hall L (1987) *Personnel Management: A New Approach*; Hall L and Torrington D (1988) *The Human Resource Function: The Dynamics of Change and Development*; Thomason G F (1988) *A Textbook of Personnel Management*.

89. Pitfield M (1979) "Practical and professional: A new look for the IPM's education programme", page 44.
90. Privy Council Papers Set I, I-xv, 5 June 1991.
91. Pitfield 1979 ibid; Seears 1979 ibid; Coates in Lawrence 1979 ibid.
92. The CNAA—the Council for National Academic Awards, responsible for the accreditation of courses and qualification; the Management Charter Initiative (MCI) was established following Constable and McCormick (1987) and Handy (1987); it was responsible for establishing the National Occupational Standards in management.
93. Privy Council Papers Set I-xxii, 29 July 1991, emphasis added, a letter with several enclosures from the Institute's Director–Membership and Education. The enclosures were sample examination scripts. The PMFP comprised four modules—Management Processes and functions; The Corporate Environment; Managing Human Resources; and Managing Information Systems. The second stage remained based around the traditional functional separations of employee resourcing; employee development and employee relations; and the third stage retained the organisationally based project.
94. Investors in People—UK Commission for Employment and Skills *Investment in People—Background.*
95. Fowler 1987 ibid.
96. Reed M I (1996) *Expert Power and Control in Late Modernity: An Empirical Review and Theoretical Synthesis.*
97. Sciulli 2010 ibid; Larson 1977 ibid.
98. This story is illuminating for the light it sheds upon occupational rivalry and status which is often a significant element of a professionalisation. Abbott 1988 ibid; De Vries et al 2009 ibid.
99. Sharpe P H (1979a) "WANTED: A professional organisation for human resources managers", page 231 (see also Sharpe P (1979b) "IPM+ITO=IPTM progress report"; and the Institute's incoming Director-General, interviewed in 2010.
100. Kenny 1972 ibid, page 43; De Vries et al 2009 ibid; Suddaby and Viale 2011 ibid, page 428.
101. Kenny 1972 ibid, page 40.
102. Kenny 1972 ibid, page 43; Finegold D and Soskice D (1988) "The failure of training in Britain: Analysis and prescription", page 43.
103. Sharpe 1979a ibid; In 1993 at the time the two institutes came together, the head of training policy at the Confederation of British Industry (CBI) pointed out that many practitioners belonged to both institutes and that there was often transmigration between the two, *Personnel Management*, page 27; *The Case for Combination*, page 27.
104. Sharpe 1979b ibid; Sharpe had been a member of the unsuccessful IPM/BACIE working party; see note later in Notes.
105. It took the Institute many years of internal professional and academic debate before accepting that HRM was not going away.
106. "The British Association for Commercial and Industrial Education (BACIE) was for many years one of the leading training organisations in the UK. BACIE was founded as the British Association for Commercial Education in 1919 with the aim of ensuring suitable education and training was supported those entering industry and commerce. In 1934 an amalgamation took place with the Association for Education in Industry and Commerce to form BACIE. In 1994 BACIE ceased its operations and its commercial activities were taken over by the Institute of Personnel and Development (IPD)", Institute of Personnel and Development: British Association for

Commercial and Industrial Education (MSS.97/BACIE), Modern Records Centre, University of Warwick.

107. Sharpe 1979b ibid; Sharpe was Chairman of the International Committee of ITOL for six years.

108. ITOL was the organisation which features in the Institute's dealings with the Privy Council Office in 1977, Privy Council Papers, Set I-iii 6 Feb1977, a letter from the Institute's Assistant Director, Training, Organisation and Manpower Planning to the Companies Administration Division at the Department of Trade (carbon copy received at Privy Council.

109. Sharpe 1979a ibid.

110. The event is an important part of the professionalisation process. The jurisdictional conflict came to a resolution in 1994 and the "creation" of the Institute of Personnel and Development in 1994 was one of the first acts of the incoming Director-General.

111. However, at that time, there is no evidence to suggest that a Royal Charter was in the Institute's sights. The Director-General (interview February 2010) indicated that he was unaware of previous attempts.

112. The Institute has "charitable status" under Section 19(1) of the Companies Act of 1948 which gives some concessions for tax purposes in Britain.

113. Swailes 2003 ibid.

114. ACE took place annually in Harrogate, North Yorkshire, a gentile spa town until 2008. The incoming Chief Executive moved the conference to what was considered a much more appropriate, business-like and thrusting venue, in Manchester, across the Pennine Hills, in the North West of England.

115. The Institute's commercial activities became a concern to the Privy Council as the Institute's application for a Royal Charter entered its later phases; the Institute had to give an explanation.

116. CIPD (2013a) "CIPD—Championing better work and working lives—CIPD"; CIPD (2013b) *About us.*

117. Dryburgh G (1972) "The man in the middle", page 3.

118. Legge K and Exley M (1975) "Authority, ambiguity and adaptation: The personnel specialists' dilemma"; Legge K (1978) *Power, Innovation and Problem Solving in Personnel Management*; (1987) "Women in personnel management: Uphill climb or downhill slide"; (1988) "Personnel management in recession and recovery: A comparative analysis of what the surveys say"; (1995) *Human Resource Management: Rhetorics and Realities*; Watson T G (1976) "The professionalization process: A critical note"; (1977) *The Personnel Managers: A Study in the Sociology of Work and Employment*; (2002) "Speaking professionally: Occupational anxiety and discursive ingenuity among human resourcing specialists".

119. Niven 1967 ibid, page 161; Barber D (1979) *The Practice of Personnel Management*, page 90 supported Niven's view.

120. Goldner F H and Ritti R R (1967) "Professionalization as career immobility", page 493.

121. Anthony P and Crichton A (1969) *Industrial Relations and the Personnel Specialists*, page 165.

122. Hanlon G (1998) "Professionalism as enterprise: Service class politics and the redefinition of professionalism", page 50.

123. Clarke 1949 ibid, page 71; The Institute had introduced examinations in 1946.

124. Clarke 1949 ibid, pages 69, 75; Clarke describes how the Select Committee on National Expenditure reported on the way industry should develop for productivity. This said that the human factor of production was just

as important as other aspects of organisation and was the impetus for the progress of personnel management practices.

125. This is how the Institute has recently described the practices. This expression appears many times, as exemplified by the wording on the main web portal shown here CIPD 2013a ibid.

126. For an account, see Delbridge R and Keenoy T (2010) "Beyond managerialism?" page 813.

127. Clarke 1949 ibid; Crichton A and Collins R G (1964) "Personnel specialists—a count by employers"; Barber 1979 ibid; Armstrong M (1977) *A Handbook of Personnel Management Practice.*

128. The Director-General recounted his early encounters with trade unions in the early 1060s in an interview on 20 February 2010.

129. Watson T J (1977) *The personnel managers: A study in the sociology of work and employment*; Legge 1978 ibid; Legge and Exley 1975 ibid.

130. Watson 1977 ibid, page 605.

131. Such as Clarke 1949 ibid; Crichton and Collins 1964 ibid; Barber 1979 ibid; Armstrong 1977 ibid.

132. Personnel Management 1993 ibid; in 1993 on the eve of the combination of the IPM and ITD, contributors to *The Case for Combination,* the series of short articles designed to persuade members of the IPM to vote for the merger with the ITD, wrote about the trajectory of the practices. Seeking a public role was also discussed later by the Director-General and the Chief Economist; it may also suggest a strategy of aggrandisement.

133. Personnel Management 1993 ibid, page 30.

134. Personnel Management 1993 ibid.

135. Personnel Management 1993 ibid, page 27.

136. Personnel Management 1993 ibid.

137. As early as 1979 David Guest reviewed a US textbook for students, which outlined the US approach to managing the human factor in the organisation. He commented upon what the textbook said about the role of the personnel manager, how *he* undertook "a set of multiple roles; and his responsibility is to management not to the workforce". And as for justifying the function, quoting from the book, Guest adds "their justification rests on the value of their programs in contributing to organizational goals and objectives, even if in doing so the employees benefit as well". This idea was powerful for establishing the strategic focus of the function, and therefore its usefulness and status. Guest D (1979) "American perspectives—systematic management of human resources by R B Peterson and L Tracy Addison-Wesley—a review".

138. Sisson K (1990) "Introducing the human resource management journal".

139. As business practices solidified, including those concerned with the management and development of labour, several studies appeared during the 1990s, especially in the US, which suggested a link between the presence of human resource management practices and organisational outcomes (for example, Pfeffer J (1994) *Competitive Advantage Through People: Unleashing the Power of the Workforce*; MacDuffie J P (1995) "Human resource bundles and manufacturing performance: Organizational logic and flexible production systems in the world auto industry"; such studies became influential, and work began to replicate such promising results in a UK context. Some of the notable research programmes with which the Institute were involved included Patterson M G, West M A, Lawthom R and Nickell S (1997) "Impact of people management practices on business performance" (there were others), and output was used extensively within the Institute's qualification programmes. These examples illustrate the Institute's links with other organisations and the growing preoccupation on the

ability of personnel/human resource management to deliver organisational performance. Delivery of organisational performance would enable the practitioner to prove value, and by proxy provide legitimacy reflected on the Institute to an interested public of senior business leaders, politicians and civil servants.

140. The Privy Council Papers (for example, Set I-ii) indicate how the Institute had to sharpen its qualification in order to ensure that it fitted the "degree level" education, but equally compelling was the opportunity afforded to the Institute by the recognition of the need to improve management education (see Williams 2010 ibid).

141. According to the former Institute Examiner in an interview (3 June 2010), the universities wanted to control the Institute's curriculum, but "the Institute said, but if we're the qualifying body, we want to control the curriculum, and the universities basically said, well tough luck, that's the deal . . . so that there was this strained process whereby gradually something that could be academically respectable and labelled human resource management began to emerge as a results of the relationship between universities and IPM".

142. This representation of these professional standards was known as the HR Profession Map and was in development in 2010.

143. Ulrich D (1997) *Human Resource Champions.*

144. This could be a cultural reference to the English Premier League which came into existence on 15 August 1992. Its use expresses an idea of modernity and of belonging to an elite.

145. Armstrong G (2000) "The smarter charter".

146. Director-General interview, 20 February 2010.

147. See Hammond K H (2007) "Why we hate HR", 19 December; Johnson L (2008) "The truth about the HR department". These were two polemics which were current at the time of the interview.

148. These are the words of Gilmore and Williams in 2003, 2007 ibid.

149. For example, Crabb S (1999) "Seal of approval"; (2000) "Major league"; (2007) "Exit interview"; HR Magazine (2001) *We're not Exclusive, Irrelevant, Time-Expired or Elitist.*

## Bibliography

Abbott A (1988) *The System of Professions*, Chicago: University of Chicago Press.

Adler P S, Kwon S-K and Heckscher C (2008) "Professional work: The emergence of collaborative community", *Organization Science* 19(2): 359–376.

Anderson A M (1922) *Women in the Factory: An Administrative Adventure 1893–1921*, London: John Murray.

Andrews T M and Waerness K (2011) "Deprofessionalization of a female occupation: Challenges for the sociology of professions", *Current Sociology* 59(1): 42–58.

Anthony P and Crichton A (1969) *Industrial Relations and the Personnel Specialists.* London: BT Batsford Limited.

Armstrong G (2000) "The smarter charter", *People Management* 6(14): 54.

Armstrong M (1977) *A Handbook of Personnel Management Practice*, London and Sterling, VA: Kogan Page.

Armstrong M (2009) *Armstrong's Handbook of Human Resource Practice*, 11th edition, London and Sterling: Kogan Page.

Armstrong P (1986) "Management Control Strategies and Inter-Professional Competition: The Cases of Accountancy and Personnel Management", in D Knights and H Willmott, *Managing the Labour Process*, Aldershot: Gower.

Armstrong P (1988) "The Personnel Profession in the Age of Management Accountancy", *Personnel Review* 17(1): 25–31.

Barber B (1963) "Some problems in the sociology of the professions", *Daedalus*: 669–688.

Barber D (1979) *The practice of Personnel Management*, London: Institute of Personnel Management.

Baron J N, Dobbin F R and Devereaux Jennings P (1986) "War and peace: The evolution of modern personnel administration in US industry", *The American Journal of Sociology* 92(2): 350–383.

Birkett W P and Evans E (2005) "Theorising professionalisation: A model for organising and understanding histories of the professionalising activities of occupational associations of accountants", *Accounting History* 10(1): 99–127.

Blackford K M H and Newcomb A (1915) *The Job, the Man, the Boss*, Garden City, NY: Doubleday, Page and Company.

Burrage M (1990) "Introduction: The professions in sociology and history", in M Burrage and R Torstendahl (eds) *Professions in Theory and History: Rethinking the Study of the Professions*, London: Sage Publications.

Burrage M, Jarausch K and Siegrist H (1990) "An actor-based framework for the study of the professions", in M Burrage and R Torstendahl (eds) *Professions in Theory and History: Rethinking the Study of the Professions*, London: Sage Publications.

Burrage M and Torstendahl R (eds) (1990) *Professions in Theory and History*, London: Sage Publications.

Cabinet Office (2009a) *New Opportunities White Paper*, www.hmg.gov.uk/media/9102/NewOpportunities.pdf, accessed 14 January 2009.

Cabinet Office (2009b) *Panel on Fair Access to the Professions Announced—New Opportunities White Paper*, www.cabinetoffice.gov.uk/newsroom/news_releases/2009/090113_nopanel.aspx, accessed 14 January 2009.

Cadbury E (1912) *Industrial Organization*, London and New York: Longmans Green and Co.

Carr-Saunders A M and Wilson P A (1933) *The Professions*, Oxford: Clarendon Press.

CIPD (2008) *CIPD Appoints Current Chief Economist John Philpott to Head Up New Public Policy Department*, CIPD Press Office, http://www.cipd.co.uk/pressoffice/_articles/021208Johnphilpottsappointment.htm, accessed 17 March 2009.

CIPD (2013a) *CIPD—Championing Better Work and Working Lives—CIPD*, web page portal, www.cipd.co.uk, accessed 10 May 2013.

CIPD (2013b) *About Us*, www.cipd.co.uk/cipd-hr-profession/about-us/, accessed 21 July 2013.

Clarke V M (1949) *New Times, New Methods and New Men*, London: George Allen and Unwin Ltd.

Cogan M L (1953) "Towards a definition of profession", *Harvard Educational Review* 23: 33–50, Winter.

Collins R (1990) "Market closure and the conflict theory of the professions" in M Burrage and R Torstendahl (eds) *Professions in Theory and History:*

*Rethinking the Study of the Professions*, London: SAGE Publications, pages 24–43.

Crabb S (1999) "Seal of approval", *People Management* 5(16): 42, 19 August.

Crabb S (2000) "Major league", *People Management* 6(5): 52, 2 March.

Crabb S (2007) "Exit interview", *People Management* 13(9): 24–28, 3 May.

Craig J (ed) (2006) *Production Values, Futures for Professionalism*, London: Demos.

Davies, C (1983) "Professionals in bureaucracies: The conflict thesis revisited" in R Dingwall and P Lewis (eds) *The Sociology of the Professions: Lawyers, Doctors and Others*, London: The Macmillan Press Ltd.

Delbridge R and Keenoy T (2010) "Beyond Managerialism?" *International Journal of Human Resource Management* 21(6): 799–817.

Dent M and Whitehead S (eds) (2002) *Managing Professional Identities: Knowledge, Performativity and the "New Professional"*, London: Routledge.

De Vries R, Dingwall R and Orfali K (2009) "The moral organization of the professions", *Current Sociology* 57: 555–580.

Drake McFeely M (1988) *Lady Inspectors: The Campaign for a Better Workplace 1893–1921*, New York: Basil Blackwell.

Dryburgh G (1972) "The man in the middle", *Personnel Management* 4(5): 3, May.

Evetts J (2003) "The sociological analysis of professionalism: Occupational change in the modern world", *International Sociology* 18(2): 395–415.

Faulconbridge J R and Muzio D (2012) "Professions in a globalizing world: Towards a transnational sociology of the professions", *International Sociology* 27(1): 136–152. https://doi.org/10.1177/0268580911423059

Finegold D and Soskice D (1988) "The failure of training in Britain: Analysis and prescription", *Oxford Review of Economic Policy* 4(3): 21–53.

Gilb C L (1976) *Hidden Hierarchies: The Professions and Government*, Westport, CT: Greenwood Pub Group.

Gilmore S and Williams S (2003) *Constructing the HR Professional: A Critical Analysis of the Chartered Institute of Personnel and Development's "Professional Project"*, www.mngt.waikato.ac.nz/ejrot/cmsconference/2003/proceedings/hrmphenomena/Gilmore.pdf, accessed 7 January 2009.

Gilmore S and Williams S (2007) "Conceptualising the 'Personnel Professional': A critical analysis of the chartered institute of personnel and development's professional qualification scheme", *Personnel Review* 36(3): 398–414.

Gold J and Bratton J (2003) *The Dynamics of Professionalization: Whither the HRM Profession?* Paper delivered at the Third Critical Management Studies Conference, Stream 8, Human Resource Management Phenomena—HRM and beyond.

Goldner F H and Ritti R R (1967) "Professionalization as career immobility", *American Journal of Sociology* 72(5): 489–502.

Greenwood E (1957) "Attributes of a profession", *Social Work* 2: 445–450.

Greenwood E (1966) "The elements of professionalization", in H M Vollmer and D L Mills (eds) *Professionalization*, Englewood Cliffs, NJ: Prentice Hall, pages 9–19.

Guest D (1979) "American perspectives—systematic management of human resources by R B Peterson and L Tracy Addison-Wesley—a review", *Personnel Management*: 49, December.

Hammond K H (2007) "Why we hate HR", *FastCompany*, 19 December, www.fastcompany.com/magazine/97/open_hr.htl#, accessed 7 October 2009.

Hanlon G (1998) "Professionalism as enterprise: Service class politics and the redefinition of professionalism", *Sociology* 32(1): 43–64.

Hickson D J and Thomas M W (1969) "Professionalization in Britain: A preliminary measurement", *Sociology* 3: 37–53.

Hodgson D (2008) "The new professionals: Professionalisation and the struggle for occupational control in the field of project management", in D Muzio, S Ackroyd and J-F Chanlat (eds) *Redirections in the Study of Expert Labour-Established Professions and New Expert Occupations*, Basingstoke: Palgrave Macmillan.

Holmes G (1982) *Augustan England: Professions, State and Society 1680–1730*, London: Allen and Unwin.

HR Magazine (2001) *We're Not Exclusive, Irrelevant, Time-Expired or Elitist*, www.hrmagazine.co.uk/hr/news/1013918/were-exclusive-irrelevant-expired-elitist, accessed 8 February 2013.

Institute of Personnel and Development: British Association for Commercial and Industrial Education (MSS.97/BACIE), Modern Records Centre, University of Warwick.

Jacques R (1996) *Manufacturing the Employee: Management Knowledge from the 19th to the 21st Centuries*, London and Thousand Oaks, CA: Sage Publications.

Johnson L (2008) "The truth about the HR department", *FT.com*, http://wwww.ft.com/cms/0/ec6f81e6-ce89-11dc-877a-000077b07658.html, accessed 7 October 2009.

Johnson T J (1972) *Professions and Power*, London and Basingstoke: Palgrave Macmillan.

Kaufman B E (2008) *Managing the Human Factor: The Early Years of Human Resource Management in American Industry*, Ithaca and London: ILR an Imprint of Cornell University Press.

Kenny T P (1972) "Professional examinations for British training staff", *Training and Development Journal*: 40–43, February.

Krause E A (1971) *The Sociology of Occupations*, Boston: Little, Brown and Company.

Larson M S (1977) *The Rise of Professionalism: A Sociological Analysis*, London and Berkeley: University of California Press, pages 99–115.

Lawrence S (1979) "Man of the moment: Jack Coates", *Personnel Management* 11(10): 36–40.

Legge K (1978) *Power, Innovation and Problem-Solving in Personnel Management*, Maidenhead: McGraw Hill.

Legge K and Exley M (1975) "Authority, ambiguity and adaptation: The personnel specialists' dilemma", *Industrial Relations Journal* 6(3): 51–65.

Lewis R and Maude A (1953) *The English Middle Classes*, Great Britain: Penguin Books.

Macdonald K M (1985) "Social closure and occupational registration", *Sociology* 19(4): 541–556.

MacDuffie J P (1995) "Human resource bundles and manufacturing performance: Organizational logic and flexible production systems in the world auto industry", *Industrial and Labor Relations Review* 48(2): 197–221.

Marchington M and Wilkinson A (2008) *Human Resource Management at Work: People Management and Development*, London: CIPD.

Marks W (1978) *Politics and Personnel Management: An Outline History, 1960–1976*, London: Institute of Personnel Management.

Millerson G (1964) *The Qualifying Association: A Study in Professionalization*, London: Routledge.

Muzio D, Ackroyd S and Chanlat J-F (eds) (2008) *Redirections in the Study of Expert Labour-Established Professions and New Expert Occupations*, Basingstoke: Palgrave Macmillan.

Neal M and Morgan J (2000) "The professionalization of everyone? A comparative study of the development of the professions in the UK and Germany", *European Sociological Review* 16(1): 9–26.

Niven M (1967) *Personnel Management 1913–1963: The Growth of Personnel Management and the Development of the Institute*, London: Institute of Personnel Management.

Parsons T (1939) "The professions and social structure", *Social Forces*: 457–467, May.

Patterson M G, West M A, Lawthom R and Nickell S (1997) "Impact of people management practices on business performance", in *Issues in People Management*, London: Institute of Personnel Management.

Perkin H (1989) *The Rise of Professional Society*, London: Routledge and Kegan Paul.

Personnel Management (1993) "The case for combination", *Personnel Management* 25(12): 26–32.

Peterson R B and Tracy L (1979) *Systematic Management of Human Resources*, Reading, MA: Addison-Wesley Publishing Company.

Pfeffer J (1994) *Competitive Advantage Through People: Unleashing the Power of the Workforce*, Boston: Harvard Business School Press.

Proud D E (1916) *Welfare Work: Employers; Experiments for Improving Working Conditions in Factories*, London: G E Bell.

Reader W J (1966) *Professional Men: The Rise of Professional Classes in Nineteenth-Century England*, London: Weidenfeld and Nicolson.

Sciulli D (2010) *Structural and Institutional Invariance in Professions and Professionalism*, Oslo, Norway: Senter for profesjonssudier.

Scott W R (2008) *Institutions and Organisations: Ideas and Interests*, Thousand Oak, CA: Sage Publications.

Seears N (1979) "Can personnel managers deliver?" *Personnel Management* 11(10).

Selander S (1990) "Associative strategies in the process of professionalization: Professional strategies and scientification of occupations", in M Burrage and R Torstendahl (eds) *Professions in Theory and History*, London: Sage Publications, page 139ff.

Sharpe P H (1979a) "WANTED: A professional organisation for human resources managers", *Industrial and Commercial Training* 11(6): 230–232.

Sharpe P H (1979b) "IPM+ITO=IPTM progress report", *Industrial and Commercial Training* 11(9): 386–389.

Sisson K (1990) "Introducing the human resource management journal", *Human Resource Management Journal* 1(1): 1–11.

Smith A (n.d.) *An Inquiry into the Nature and Causes of the Wealth of Nations*, Raleigh, NC: Generic NL Freebook Publisher, HTTP://search.ebscohost.com/

login.aspx?direct=true&db=nlebk&AN=1086046&site=ehost-live,    accessed 28 February 2019.

Storey J (1987) "Developments in the management of human resources: an interim report", *Warwick Papers in Industrial Relations*, No 17, Industrial Relations Research Unit, School of Industrial and Business Studies, University of Warwick, November.

Suddaby R and Viale T (2011) "Professionals and field-level change: Institutional work and the professional project", *Current Sociology* 59(4): 423–442.

Swailes S (2003) "Professionalism: Evolution and measurement", *Service Industries Journal* 23(2): 130–149.

Vollmer H M and Mills D L (eds) (1966) *Professionalization*, Englewood Cliffs, NJ: Prentice Hall Inc.

Walker S P (1995) "The genesis of a professional organization in Scotland: A contextual analysis", *Accounting, Organizations and Society* 20(4): 285–310.

Watson T J (1976) "The professionalization process: A critical note", *The Sociological Review* 24(3): 599–608.

Watson T J (1977) *The Personnel Managers: A Study in the Sociology of Work and Employment*, London: Routledge and Kegan Paul.

Wilensky H I (1964) "The professionalization of everyone?" *American Journal of Sociology* 70(2): 137–158.

Willmott H (1986) "Organising the profession: A theoretical and historical examination of the development of the major accountancy bodies in the UK", *Accounting Organizations and Society* 11(6): 555–580.

# Part 2

# The Institute's Pursuit of Professionalism

# 2    1968–1993: The Play Begins

The year 1968, which begins this chapter, may appear to some as the apogee for the practice of personnel management. The senior experienced practitioner was involved at many levels in the organisation in the conduct of relations between an organisation's management and its workforce. The industrial relations landscape appeared populated by large organisations in the public sector and in nationalised industries. However, retail and other organisations also populated the landscape, but if their industrial relations did not feature as walkouts, strikes or significant pay deals, these organisations did not always occupy the public space to the same extent as public sector or nationalised industries did.

This was the era of the personnel manager who was the industrial relations specialist—they were the essential heroes, with knowledge of the law relating to industrial relations and industrial psychology. These are bodies of knowledge which had developed during the twentieth century and which capitalism had put into the service of capital owners. Some of these heroes had studied the Institute of Personnel Management qualifications and were members. Others became members of the Institute through their organisational position and seniority.[1] Nonetheless, these practitioners were battle-scarred *men*, and their public story is shown in media accounts of industrial unrest. Such accounts, however, have not always recognised other practitioner roles and the development of practice. Furthermore, the public story belies the deep-seated frustration and inferiority felt by many practitioners. A former Institute President, writing in 1972 in the Institute's practitioner journal, voiced this view. He said:

> Nearly always he (sic) is the "man in the middle". For management, who pay his salary, he must argue the company case; from the union viewpoint he is expected to negotiate acceptable terms and conditions for the staff. If the personnel man adopts a progressive policy, management says "slow down". If he goes at the pace of many employers' associations he is accused by the unions of "lagging behind". Equally, what do the staff members think of their personnel man? Is

he a friend or a foe? Frequently the personnel man has a bigger struggle with the attitudes of his own management to change than he does
with the attitudes of those on the shop floor.[2]

The practitioner's problem was that he (sic) was always the "man in the
middle" occupying the organisational chair between management and
the workers. Speaking for many, this writer and Institute member showed
that many practitioners felt undervalued by their organisations. Furthermore, society did not appear to value the practitioner, and as this chapter
will show, efforts to secure a Royal Charter prompted the Privy Council
to see the Institute as an upstart organisation standing for practitioners who were of little significance. These sentiments appear in the Privy
Council Papers which form the basis of the book, and often in handwritten notes and comments on typed pages; the Institute did not see these
observations.

The emerging narrative of the Institute's "professional project" and the
professionalisation of the modern occupation of HR for these purposes
begins in 1968, and only because the Privy Council Papers indicate that
the Institute first made a petition in 1968 . . . and so began the Institute's
charter drama. The narrative plays out in two acts, each with scenes
which broadly coincide with the chronology of the Privy Council Papers.[3]
Other sources also supplement and flesh out this the drama.

## Act One—1968–1991: A Tale of Jurisdictional Wrangling, Respectability and Rejection

This first act concerns a tale of jurisdictional spats, the search for respectability and rejection. It reveals the expectations of the Privy Council in
respect of the conditions for awarding the Royal Charter, and although
the process for awarding a Royal Charter was not at the time made public (thus heightening the mystery and aura of a Royal Charter), it is possible to see a certain trajectory—it begins with an introduction to the Privy
Council through the officers of an existing holder of a Royal Charter.

### Act One, Scene One: A Lunch, a File Note and a Rejection

The President of the Institute of Personnel Management and a colleague, a
Director of the IPM, met a senior representative of the Institution of Production Engineers[4] who was to act in the role of the chosen go-between,
and the Clerk to the Privy Council on 1 February 1968. In advance of the
lunch, the representative of the Institution of Production Engineers wrote
to the Chief Clerk, to confirm arrangements for lunch and enclosed some
"literature about IPM which will help [the Clerk to the Privy Council]
fill this little gap in your knowledge".[5] The communication between the
Institution of Production Engineers and the Privy Council drew attention

to Margaret Niven's newly published book, written to celebrate the 50th anniversary of the Institute.[6] The communication also included the Institute's examination syllabus of the time.

Whatever took place at the lunch on 1 February 1968, the Institute had not impressed the Clerk to the Privy Council. He wrote an extensive file note,[7] expressing doubt as to whether a petition for a Royal Charter from the Institute would be successful at this time. A petition would be "premature", he said, and furthermore the information on the standards and the qualification system "could not strictly be regarded as being professional". The Clerk wrote on the file note:

> There were a number of degree and diploma courses listed in their particulars, which exempted the holders from the Institute's examinations—there was no other profession that I (the Clerk) knew of where this could be done.

The adjective 'professional' appears to create an association with the traditional professional model by focusing on the qualifying criteria for membership of a professional association representing an occupation in the traditional professional model.[8]

The file note also suggests that the Clerk's view had been conveyed to the Institute representatives, but there is nothing to suggest whether they were surprised, or disappointed. This first foray was something of a tentative expedition.

The file note continues with some encouragement to the effect that if the Institute were to:

> establish the profession firmly in the minds of industry and commerce, (and):
>     revise their Memorandum and Articles of Association more closely on the lines of a Chartered body with a Charter and Byelaws. This would ensure the development of the Institute on the right lines and would make it unnecessary to effect any major changes in their constitution, should their application for a Charter in due course prove to be successful.[9]

The Institute's case appeared lost as the file note stated that the Institute should wait for a decade before thinking of applying again to the Privy Council for a Royal Charter.

Although not explicitly said in the papers from this period,[10] the file note reveals certain indicators which mattered to the Privy Council before awarding a Royal Charter; these indicators are recognition on the part of a public, and longevity. The perceptions gained from the first encounters with the Privy Council suggested that the Institute's lack of these attributes would have a bearing on the ability of the Institute to meet the Privy Council's expectations to attain 'professionalism' through the Royal Charter acting as a source of recognition and legitimacy.

The Clerk to the Privy Council had gained the impression from Margaret Niven's book that personnel management "had only really started in 1955".[11] A feature of the traditional professions is that they claim long-establishment, so it appeared more damaging to the Institute's case that, despite being offered Niven's historiography to read to prepare for the meeting, the Clerk had not been able to see the connection between the practices of personnel management, its origins in welfare work and the beginnings of the Institute in 1913 as the Welfare Workers' Association. The Institute was *arriviste*, a recent formation representing an upstart occupation; this position would weaken the Institute's case to claim long establishment.

The contemporary thinking about what constituted professionalism at the time the Institute made this application appears to draw upon the literature of the time.[12] The sources acknowledge the role of the professional association in the development of an occupation towards professionalism. This is *professionalisation*, the process of becoming a profession, and the formation of a collective association is an important signifier of this.

It became an axiom that professionalising occupations sought to mirror key aspects of the traditional western professions of law, medicine and later accountancy. Practitioners coalesced and formed occupational associations, they had recognition and legitimacy among a public, they curated knowledge, and they practised routines as the experts. These occupations engendered trust and set standards for practitioners—standards over practice and standards over conduct and behaviour. In this way, the occupations were able to regulate the member-practitioners and regulate the body of knowledge. Within the British context, they sought the Royal Charter as a badge of recognition and legitimacy.

The Clerk's insistence upon adherence to "professional" academic standards also shows that there were two interpretations of the Institute's approach to the Privy Council for a Royal Charter. First, that the Privy Council had a view of occupations seeking a Royal Charter as being or becoming professional bodies moulded in the traditional professional model as they understood it. Furthermore, they expected that petitioning bodies representing whole occupations were seeking to regulate membership[13] to have the power to say who was fit to be included as a member of the profession. Second, the Privy Council *thought* that the Institute **was** professionalising to regulate the knowledge, practices, practitioners and the production of practitioners. This is what later became known as occupational closure in which a professional body aims to secure a monopoly for the practitioners.[14] The petition for a Royal Charter was a professionalisation.

Finally, the Clerk's file note[15] conveys the impression that the writer thought that personnel management was a transitory activity and that the Institute had to "bed down", and secure the practices as a discipline:

> before it (personnel management) could be regarded as a separate profession.[16]

The Clerk's use of the phrase "separate profession" is noteworthy. It suggests a perception that the practices of personnel management were an organisational function that belonged to another domain of work. The perception of the practices as potentially belonging elsewhere and the reality remains a problem for the Institute and practitioners to this day. The problem concerns the day-to-day practices of the management and development of employees (personnel management or human resource management) and whether they properly belong to the wider function of management and supervision. For this idea to become commonplace would undermine the very reason for the existence of the Institute, given the potential inter-organisational rivalry between the Institute and other bodies representing other functions and disciplines within business and management. The problem accounts for the way the Institute has developed in more recent years.

In the file note, the Clerk suggested that the Institute wait a further ten years before applying again.

### Act One, Scene Two: Nine Years Later

There appears to be no further activity between the Privy Council Office and the Institute until 1977. At the end of the correspondence in 1968, there was much for the Institute to accomplish to make progress in meeting the expectations of the Privy Council Office. There were the academic standards to address and the mode by which practitioners were admitted to membership.[17] The Institute's lack of activity in this area indicates that there were no explicit strategies to strengthen direct control over the membership through educational attainment as a "qualifying association".[18] There were, however, moves to consolidate the territory of work practice as the Institute became embroiled in a rancorous episode and laid claim to the work domain of training. In this way, the Institute could present a unified field of practice and a significant body of members and this is what took place. The Privy Council sources offer a glimpse as to what happened, but the main account comes from lead practitioners themselves.

The Privy Council Papers show that this episode occurred between 6 February 1977 and 22 March 1977. Although it is a brief period, it draws in the jurisdictional rivalry between the domains of personnel management and training, and the extremely vexed issue of the links between the Institution of Training Officers Limited (ITOL) and the Institute (IPM).[19] The inter-occupational rivalry had a bearing upon the Charter application and upon the later progress of the Institute. It left a scar which is still unhealed to this day.

In 1968 the Clerk to the Privy Council had suggested that the Institute make some changes to their constitution in a way which implied compliance with the Privy Council's understanding of how a professional body should organise and conduct its affairs. Specifically, the Clerk suggested that the Institute redraft the Articles of Association as a Charter and Byelaws, but the Privy Council Papers in this episode indicate that the Institute had not addressed this.[20]

The absence of activity on an application for a Royal Charter since 1968 is interesting. There is no way of knowing for certain why the Institute did not appear to take up the suggestion to redraft the constitution to be ready to re-apply; the papers are silent. However, one explanation, found in other contemporary sources, could be that the Institute was looking to make a claim to represent a complete domain of work and was looking to exploit a perceived weakness on the part of bodies representing the field of workplace training, in particular, the Institution of Training Officers Limited (ITOL). In this interpretation, there may have been some overtures to ITOL, and any amendments to the Memorandum and Articles of Association would have been rendered obsolete in the event of the two bodies combining. Other reasons may have been the national and governmental preoccupation with productivity, workplace training and employment law which included several significant pieces of employment legislation concerning the conduct of the employment relationship.

Throughout the 1960s and 1970s, the practitioner's power base had existed in the ability of senior personnel practitioners to star in many high-profile industrial disputes. However, keeping a steady industrial relations brief and a role in the hiring and termination of employees, often in redundancy situations, had become standard fare for many practitioners.

On 6 February 1977, ten years later than the last encounter with the Privy Council Office, the IPM's Assistant Director for Training, Organisation and Manpower Planning wrote to an unnamed official at the Companies Administration Division at the Department of Trade. His purpose: to inquire about the potential effect of an "amalgamation"[21] with the Institution of Training Officers Limited (ITOL), to create a new body to organise the joint activities of the Institution of Training Officers (ITOL) and the Institute of Personnel Management (IPM).

The earlier encounter with the Privy Council in 1968 had concluded with two clear and significant actions that the Institute needed to attend to as far as winning a Royal Charter was concerned. The first action was to erect a secure fence around both the occupational practice domains of training and personnel management to claim and present a unified occupational field to the Privy Council. If the Institute could achieve that level of unification through the mechanism of "amalgamation" of the two institutes, the ITOL and the IPM, then the second task in meeting the expectations for a Royal Charter was to address the qualification and membership structure. In respect of earlier attempts to create a unified field of practice in the 1960s and 1970s, it is unclear whether the Institute's respective leaders remembered the earlier abortive attempt to win a Royal Charter but they did appear more focused upon unfruitful talks with ITOL to combine the two institutes and the domains of training and personnel management.[22]

In the event, the inquiry concerned the effect on the "historical continuity" of the IPM "with particular reference to ambitions for a Royal Charter". This letter also broaches the matter of the charitable status[23] of any new entity and whether there would have to be a new application for charitable status under Section 19(1) of the Companies Act 1948. Both ITOL and the IPM had charitable status which under UK law signalled that the organisation existed for the public benefit and contributed to the perception of the traditional professions of public good, altruism and the furtherance of human progress.

The Institute's letter to the Companies Administration Division at the Department of Trade highlights two sensitivities that the Institute held: first, about the effect that the enclosure of the training field with personnel management might have upon any future application for a Royal Charter, and second, the Institute's concerns that the process is one of "amalgamation", and not a takeover. The Institute's Assistant Director, Training, Organisation and Manpower Planning describes the ITOL as the "smaller and younger body", and any dealings with the IPM that hinted at a 'takeover' would "not win the support of the ITO members".[24]

The Department of Trade, Companies Administration Division responded on 22 February[25] to the effect that the suitable wording in the Memorandum and Articles of Association of the combined body could provide for the "historical continuity". However, the Companies Administration Division at the DTI stated that the new body's representatives would need to apply again for charitable status with the Charity Commission to be registered under Section 19(1) of the Companies Act of 1948.

### Attempts to Secure the Institute's Field of Practice

At this point, an important digression in the Institute's story is called for. Having received assurances that the Institute's claim to longevity would not be compromised by any putative "amalgamation" between the Institute and ITOL, the Institute's Assistant Director Training, Organisation and Manpower Planning wrote to the Privy Council and hinted that there may be some "resistance" to an amalgamation of the IPM and ITOL. The letter explicitly said that the Institute:

> may at some time in the future wish to approach you with regard to securing a Royal Charter.[26]

The Institute's letter is significant for two reasons. First, it once again refers to "anticipated resistance" among the ITOL membership to a conventional "takeover" of the ITOL by the IPM, suggesting inter-occupational rivalry even though some of the practitioners were members of both institutes. Second, the letter suggests a change in the qualifying processes for membership. The Assistant Director, Training, Organisation and Manpower Planning at the Institute proposed that future members of the new body would become corporate members based on examination[27] only. The Institute hoped that the Privy Council Office would respond favourably.

### "A Fairly Borderline Case"

Between 25 February and 10 March 1977, an exchange of internal notes within the Privy Council Office took place.[28] One file note is handwritten and the signature undecipherable[29] and appears to be in response to the Institute's earlier letter which acted as a reminder of the soundings already taken in 1968. The writer of this handwritten note claimed not to know about the ITOL or "to what extent the IPM has improved its standards since 1968". Whilst the file note suggested that the question of historical longevity would not necessarily be of great concern, the qualification and entry standards remained a problem. The Privy Council Office was expecting additional information about an enhanced qualification scheme and corresponding curriculum.

At issue were the perceived lower standards of the ITOL, to which the Institute's earlier letter had alluded. The writer of the file note indicates that he does not want to deal with this matter by correspondence but suggests a meeting with the Institute.

There appear to have been internal discussions within the Privy Council Office about this Institute's overtures, or at least the exchange of notes (not all of which are extant). On 10 March 1977,[30] the Clerk wrote:

> These people would still seem to be a fairly borderline case. Do you wish to see them as (Name) suggests and obtain some material beforehand?

There is a degree of irritation in the tone of the scribbling, and there are no encouraging signs for the Institute, other than the prospect of a meeting. On the very same day, 10 March 1977,[31] the Clerk of the Council wrote to the Institute proposing a meeting, and added that "the proposed amalgamation" of the ITOL and IPM would not:

> adversely affect the Privy Council's view of the period of existence of your Institute.

What remained an issue for the Privy Council Office were the entry qualifications required for membership of the putative profession, and the letter to the Institute continued that it was the question of *new* qualifications following any amalgamation which was:

> a rather more difficult one (than the "period of existence") especially if the standards of the Institution are lower than those of your Institute.

The papers from the Privy Council reveal that the entry qualifications at ITOL were even lower than those at the IPM, and therefore the Privy Council was concerned about the effect the lower standards would have on the Institute's own standards.

The Privy Council Office explicitly requested:

> information about examinations and entry qualifications etc for both bodies, and the level of management at which members are employed.[32]

The Institute sent the information requested and the meeting took place at 3 pm on 22 March 1977.

Immediately after the meeting on 22 March 1977, the Clerk to the Privy Council wrote a file note, dated and signed it.[33] The file note outlined the substantive content of the meeting which concerned the discussion about the potential amalgamation between the ITOL and the IPM. The file note showed that the Institute had acknowledged the lower entry standards at ITOL and that the IPM "itself was by no means 'respectable' (the quotations appear in the original document)" to be granted a Royal Charter. The view of the Privy Council Office reflected in the file note was that the Privy Council Office would examine the combined qualifications and entry standards at the time of an application for a Royal Charter.

The note suggests that a:

> slight dilution of standards would be compensated for by the new body being able to claim to cover the whole field (of personnel management and training).[34]

The file note of the meeting of 22 March 1977 appears to close this episode, with the Institute and ITOL seemingly in talks about combining the fields of personnel management and training. From the perspective of the

Privy Council Office, however, the issue affecting any outcome as it might apply to the award of a Royal Charter remained the nature of member-ship and the qualifying processes for members to become full members.

There is a long gap in the correspondence between the Institute and the Privy Council Office, and the records appear to show that there was no contact between them. Neither did the merger between the Institute and ITOL happen. This is marked in the account provided by a founding member of ITOL[35] writing in the *Journal of Industrial and Commercial Training* in 1979, an event which I will come to later.

### Over-Academic, Too General and Lacking in Relevance: Qualifications

The Institute's qualifications had been a concern to the Privy Council,[36] but after the initial inquiries, the Institute did revise its qualification struc-ture in 1979/1980.[37] It is a matter of interpretation as to the precise rea-son, but one of the factors is likely to be the developments in practice.[38] But it is noticeable that the Privy Council had made the academic and intellectual credentials of the Institute's qualification a cause of concern, and an excuse for not awarding the Royal Charter when the Institute first began to petition for a Royal Charter.

The main source for the revision of the Institute's qualification struc-tures is the Institute's Assistant Director of Membership and Education writing in the Institute's journal *Personnel Management*.[39] He opened his article with a criticism of the existing scheme. It was, he said, "over-academic, too general and lacking in relevance". The charge of the qualification being "over-academic" contradicts what the Privy Council would have expected given the status of the university degree and the practices "founded upon an understanding of the theoretical structure of some department of learning or science".[40] Nevertheless, the Institute's 1979/1980 revision of the qualifications and standards are significant in the Royal Charter story.

The revised curriculum shows both the development of practice and practitioner preoccupations and reflects the socio-political background, and elements of the qualification and membership structure remain extant to the present day. The field of training acquired the additional moniker ". . . and development", and in some organisations (and certainly within the academic field) became the field of "learning and development" and sometimes human resource development (HRD). Developments in prac-tice and the revisions to the curriculum were taking place against the backdrop of the neoliberal takeover of many fields of social life, includ-ing government and business, and in this theatre, a different focus for the Institute's practices emerged.

In earlier years, there had been few opportunities for the student practitioner to study for the Institute's qualification but with the new arrangements, the Institute was now offering educational institutions the opportunity to be flexible. This had the effect of widening access to a greater variety of study options "ranging from full-time courses giving exemption to full-time IPM courses, under—or post-graduate courses, courses linked to BEC Highers or the DMS".[41] Furthermore, depending upon earlier academic attainment, students were able to apply for exemptions from parts of the Institute's qualification and still receive the award. The Institute kept control of the first part of the qualification and students sat the IPM National Examinations.

The Assistant Director of Membership and Education justified the move in this way:

> This is felt to be entirely appropriate—the Institute regulating entry to the profession by examining those areas where it was a work-based project, in the form of "a report to senior management".

The new qualification structure addressed the critical area of the assessment of professional competence. Practitioners working towards the final stage of the qualification were, according to the Assistant Director:

> personnel practitioners who (had) reached a point in their personnel and professional development where the opportunity to apply, rather than acquire, knowledge and skills is more appropriate . . . the individual will be expected to diagnose human resource problems, devise and evaluate alternative solutions, and produce realistic recommendations for action.

The development of the new qualification structure and content shows, inadvertently, an attempt to meet the Privy Council's expectations, despite the focus upon credentialing senior practitioners without the qualification and the focus on the practical application of knowledge rather than theory. The new qualification, therefore, strengthened the Institute's focus on practitioner experience; however, it remained anathema to the Privy Council.

### Human Resource Management and the Arrival of "American Perspectives"

Within the political sphere, the Conservative government which began in May 1979 followed a neoliberal agenda and it had a profound effect on Britain. There was considerable reform of the legislation governing the activities of trades unions, and actions to privatise industries, open state-run monopolies to private enterprise and deregulate in the name of the market.

The strategic management of employees as human resources had been known as human resource management in the US for some while and the practices had evolved and matured within a neoliberal context and culture; they were not unique practices[42] but any maturity of thinking came to prominence beyond the US in the mid-1980s with a number of textbooks about the strategic importance of employees.[43] This trend had begun somewhat earlier. Showing interest in the way the US dealt with the practical aspects of managing a workforce, in 1979, one UK academic in the field wrote a review of a student textbook from the US for the Institute's journal *Personnel Management*. It was called *Systematic Management of Human Resources*.[44] The writer warned early on of the limited usefulness of such texts because the book was naturally grounded in the American context and the legislation and industrial relations frameworks were different. He might have gone on to say that the history and trajectory of the function in the US context would not be readily associable to the British context. Whilst saying that there was much to admire about the textbook, the writer did suggest that those British readers wanting a textbook would be better "stick(ing) to the UK choices", but those readers interested in "American perspectives" would find the book valuable.

But, interest in American perspectives did accelerate in the middle of the 1980s as the idea of the strategic focus for the management and development of workers was appealing to a function which appeared to have struggled in the 1970s. The reading of the US textbooks had a permanent but querulous effect upon the practices of people management and development in the UK.[45] Experience in Britain was somewhat different from the US experience.

Nevertheless, there was less of a sense of evolution and maturation, but more by way of irruption causing many larger organisations to rename their Personnel functions as "the Human Resource Department" (often overnight). This had the effect of creating space and opportunity for practitioners of personnel management and their spokespeople to improve the status and standing of the practitioner and the practices because of the named importance of the strategic management and development of employees. The main advocates of this so-called new way of managing people at work and the employment relationship were not necessarily mainstream practitioners, but often the most senior people in the organisation who encountered the US material in their travels and in their dealings with other senior business figures. Ordinary practitioners viewed the practices and the very idea of humans as resources as problematic. In Britain, human resource management appeared to transform from the chrysalis of personnel management into an organism which was capable of shapeshifting, depending upon the textbooks or learned journal articles read and the perspective from which it was experienced. Although the activities appeared broadly the same (although wrapped in over-embellished packaging), the focus of the employment relation-ship and the problematising of the employee as a resource was different. These were opinions which corresponded with the individualised view of labour and the primacy of the market both of which underpinned current political and economic thinking.

### The Movement Behind the Scenes

The interaction between the Institute and the Privy Council Office resumed in the late winter of 1991 and this episode began on 21 Febru-ary 1991 and ended in August 1993. By this time, the main actors at the Institute and at the Privy Council Office had changed. A new Director-General of the Institute began in 1992 and ITOL had broken apart and become the Institute of Training and Development (ITD). This reflected the change in practice from "training" to "learning and development" and the oncoming practices under human resource management.

There had also been an attempt to form another organisation, the Institute of Personnel and Training Management, which would, accord-ing to one of those who were involved, provide "a service to the many personnel and/or training managers who need national representation and down-to-earth support in their day to day jobs".[46] This is less than veiled criticism of the Institute of Personnel Management for the way the actors had conducted themselves during the talks . . . and so to return to the activity between the Institute and the Privy Council Office.

## Act One, Scene Three—1991–1993: Persistence Begins to Pay Off But Still Ends in Rejection

On 21 February 1991, the Institute Secretary met the new Clerk to the Privy Council at the Privy Council Office. A letter confirmed this.[47] Fol-lowing the meeting, the Clerk wrote a file note[48] confirming that the meeting had concerned:

> the possibility of the Institute petitioning for a Royal Charter.

On the file note, the Clerk admitted that he was "generally impressed", but said that the Institute's Secretary had agreed to undertake some:

> research on the status of the IPM qualification and the proportion of members admitted by examination.[49]

He continues, noting that the Institute and the Institute Secretary were "unaware apparently of the existence and implications of the European Directive on the mobility of professionals".[50]

## The European Dimension and Professionals

This file note is illuminating and significant because it suggests that the Privy Council believed that the Institute *was* petitioning for a Charter to become a profession following the traditional professional model. If this were the case, the EU Directive 89/48/EEC would include the occupation of personnel management. At the time of the correspondence, Directive 89/48 EC appears to have been the latest word about the mobility of "professionals". It only becomes clear in the later directives that only certain types of professionals were included, and these were those who fulfilled the traditional model. The directive in its original form shows the close association in public and elite beliefs about the link between the institution of the Royal Charter and the traditional model of professionalism which was found in the literature in the English language.[51] The Directive as interpreted in this file note shows the persistence of the model as a social structure far wider than Britain, as all EEC member states would need to ensure that institutional arrangements offered parity and comparability.

Because of the stipulations of the EU Directive, therefore, the Privy Council were still concerned about the Institute's standards and qualifications. Article I (d) of this Directive laid out the conditions on which members of an occupation could qualify for inclusion under the Directive. The Privy Council thought that for the occupation represented by the Institute to be a *profession* and appear on the list then the Institute would need to address the problem seen in the qualifications too.

Directive 89/48 EEC defined "professional activity" in this way:

> a regulated professional activity (. . .) pursued by the members of an association or organisation the purposes of which is to promote and maintain a high standard in the professional field concerned and which, to achieve that purpose, is recognised in a special form by a Member State and:
>
> - Awards a diploma to its members
> - Ensures that its members respect the rules of professional conduct which it prescribes and confers on them the right to use a title or designatory letters, or to benefit from a status corresponding to that diploma.

Since February 1991, the Institute must have kept some communication with the Privy Council Office, even though the papers do not say anything explicitly, because the Clerk accepted a lunch engagement at the Institute's premises. The Institute Secretary confirmed that "the Director-General and his Management Team" would entertain representatives from the Privy Council Office at the Institute offices in Wimbledon, London, on 8 May 1991.[52]

On the same day, 1 May 1991, the Institute Secretary wrote an expansive letter directly to the Clerk to the Privy Council.[53] This letter was responding to an earlier letter[54] and looked to respond to the concerns of the Privy Council concerning standards and qualifications.

The Institute's letter of 1 May 1991[55] reveals more about the process to apply for a Royal Charter. A body representing an occupation that was petitioning for a Royal Charter needed a sponsor from a relevant government department. In the case of the Institute, the Department of Employment was that sponsoring department of state. This contrasts with the first attempt in 1968 in which the Institution of Production Engineers, a body Chartered since 1954 eased introductions.[56]

To alleviate the concerns of the Privy Council concerning academic standards, the Institute Secretary asserted that the IPM qualification in effect since 1980[57]:

> was recognised as one of degree standard by the Burnham Further Education Committee.[58]

According to the Institute Secretary, in 1987 the Institute's Professional Education Scheme met postgraduate diploma standards set out by the Council for National Academic Awards (CNAA)[59]—the Scheme was awarded 70 points under the UK's Credit Accumulation and Transfer Scheme (CATS) and only 120 were needed for a postgraduate degree at master's level.

The Privy Council had also been concerned about the entry of candidates to the Institute who were experienced practitioners but without the qualification. The Institute Secretary said that the Institute assessed 10% of applicants for membership through the oral examination.

The Institute's letter also tried to address the question of the Directive 89/45/EEC; however, the writer may have missed the Privy Council's point entirely. The letter assures the Privy Council that EU Directive 89/45/EEC on professional mobility would not be a problem, saying:

> There are no barriers to our members working in Europe neither are there barriers to personnel managers from France, Germany or other members of the Community working in the UK. Directive 48(?) would not appear to present us with any problem.[60]

The 1989 EU Directive[61] was part of the preparations for the EU Single Market in 1992, and it concerned the mobility of professional occupational groups. The Annexe to the 1989 Directive held a list of UK bodies to which this Directive EC89/48/EEC applied. The Institute did not appear, however it was "a non-exhaustive list". The text of the Directive continues:

> Whenever a Member State grants the recognition . . . it shall inform the Commission, therefore, which shall then publish this information in the official Journal of the European Communities.

One interpretation of the relevance of this Directive in the Institute's Charter application was that the Royal Charter was a form of state recognition, and the Privy Council had been trying to ensure that an award of a Royal Charter would mean that the Institute had not only met the Privy Council's conditions but would also meet the stipulations of the Directive. In this way, the Institute's members and practitioners would be classed as *professionals* under the traditional model of professionalism as the Privy Council Office understood it.

### Persistence Despite Resistance

Undaunted by the continuing tepid encouragement at the Privy Council Office, the Institute pressed ahead and organised an Extraordinary General Meeting at the Institute on 17 May 1991 to seek member support for a Charter application. The intention to do this is in the correspondence between the Institute Secretary and the Privy Council.[62] What characterises the Institute's dealings with the Privy Council Office at this time (1991) is the continuous pleading as to whether a petition for a Royal Charter would be likely to succeed or not. These pleas for reassurance fall upon, if not 'deaf' ears, but certainly unyielding, and circumspect 'ears'.

On 5 June 1991, the Deputy Clerk to the Privy Council approached the Department of Employment, the Institute's sponsor, about the approaching application.[63] The letter reiterated the basis on which a Royal Charter is granted to an occupational association. These are:

1.  the body counts among its members the major proportion of the practitioners of a distinct profession;
2.  most corporate members are qualified, by the body's own examinations, or in a relevant discipline, at least to the level of a first degree;
3.  the sphere of activity of the body can be distinguished from existing chartered or other significant organisations;
4.  the body is financially sound; and
5.  the public interest would be served by the grant of a Charter.

The threads of the traditional professional model remain persistently woven into the materiality of the Institute's hopes: the association must represent members of a "distinct profession", the educational attainment must be at least of degree level, and the organisation must be unique and must pay attention to the 'public interest'.

Variations of this letter were sent to the Department of Education and Science, the Cabinet Office and the Department of Trade and Industry,[64] and all recipients were invited to comment on "how the Institute is regarded . . . in terms of its standards of practice".[65]

In the version of the letter sent to the Department of Education and Science, the Deputy Clerk's concern was whether the Institute's qualification really was equivalent to degree level.[66] The letter contains a rehearsal of the factors which the Privy Council found disconcerting in the Institute's arrangements. One important detracting factor was the Institute's policy of including practitioners, "senior personnel managers without formal qualification", as full members based on position and experience.

A second and equally principal factor was the recognition that personnel management was:

> a wide discipline with an area of overlap with other bodies such as the BIM (British Institute of Management) which also harbours Charter ambitions.[67]

The Deputy Clerk indicated that he thought that the first "*problem*" (italics in the text) could be resolved "by narrowing or even closing, the route in question", that is, closing the experience-only route to full membership.

Making the case that personnel management was "at least as distinct a discipline as marketing"[68] could address the second identified "*problem*".

The organisational specialisms of management and marketing had also been agitating for recognition by a Royal Charter.[69] The activities of these organisational functions appear as other examples of "professional projects" or "occupational upgrading",[70] and what is most interesting and relevant is the idea of struggle for recognition among these occupational and organisational groups, which they considered deliverable through the acquisition of a Royal Charter; it also is an expression of inter-occupational rivalry.

The Deputy Clerk's letter added that the Privy Council would decide whether to invite the Institute to make a "formal application" "in the light of comments received". Furthermore, if that invitation were made, then the relevant Secretaries of State would be required to approve the Charter. From the length and complexity of such a process, requiring the approval of key state actors, it would be difficult to argue that a Charter in Britain's 'old school' and traditional structures does *not* constitute a form of state recognition, and therefore close to professionalisation in the traditional model.

Between 10 July 1991 and 27 September 1991, there were exchanges between the Institute, the Privy Council Office and various state departments[71] and the previous Institute Secretary wrote to say she was leaving to take another post.[72]

On 29 July 1991, the Institute's Membership and Education Director sent a document *The Submission of the Professional Education Scheme of the Institute of Personnel Management to the Privy Council* to accompany the information which had been requested.[73] There were nineteen appendices which included twenty-four examination scripts and six management reports. The document talks about the Institute's objectives, which were:

- To provide an association of professional standing for its members through which the widest possible exchange of knowledge and experience can take place
- To develop a continuous evolving professional body of knowledge to assist its members to do their jobs more effectively in response to changing demands and conditions
- To develop and maintain professional standards of competence
- To encourage investigation and research in the field of personnel management and the subjects related to it
- To present a national viewpoint of personnel management and to establish and develop links with other bodies both national and international concerned with personnel

The submission outlined three mechanisms for achieving the objectives:

a. Making the continuously developing body of information and knowledge available to members and management generally through an active information service, conferences, courses, publications and by any other available means
b. Providing high standards of training for the profession and entry into Corporate Membership of the Institute by means of exams conducted by the Institute and by objectively assessed experience
c. Taking positive steps to encourage investigation and research in the field of personnel management and subjects related to it

The submission focuses on the emphasis the Institute has always placed on 'professional training' since 1913 and acknowledged the increasing professionalisation of management and the intention to take part in that.

The consultation over the summer of 1991 prompted the Deputy Clerk to declare to a new Institute Secretary that the position was "not altogether encouraging" and the chance of a successful petition was "at best borderline".[74]

So, what contributed to so discouraging an outcome? The Further and Higher Education Branch of the Department of Education and Science requested sight of examinations from recent years for both stages of the qualification, and the relevant scripts across a range of achievement to "assess standards", as the Privy Council had asked them to do.[75] The Institute forwarded as much of the required material in two consignments.[76]

The opinions of the departments of state invited to comment were not helpful to the Institute's cause, ranging from critical to lukewarm.

The Cabinet Office who represented the Civil Service said it had "no strong views on the IPM".[77] The Cabinet Office was, however, "keen to encourage greater professionalism within personnel management" in the Civil Service. So far, so encouraging. Unfortunately, the letter continued to say that the Civil Service had itself been running IPM qualifications and did not find the information the Institute disseminated to be of a high standard. The "published research" that the Institute had undertaken was described as "somewhat patchy".[78]

The contributions from the Department of Education and Science, the Department for Trade and Industry, and the Cabinet Office made it clear too that much of the IPM provision was found in the Further Education (FE) and not the Higher Education (HE) sectors, that is, not of degree standard. This was not an encouraging statement concerning the status of the qualification and the expectation of meeting the Privy Council Office requirements. The critique continued to the effect that there was overlap in the curriculum and the descriptors the Institute used for the classification of awards, such as "pass degree level" and "good pass degree level" did not help matters.[79] The Further and Higher Education branch of the Department of Education and Science criticised the content of both the examination questions and the responses seen in the sample scripts sent in July 1991[80].

A less critical, but equally unhelpful, view came from the Department for Trade and Industry (DTI) who argued that Chartered status would make the Institute "too inflexible",[81] a statement which is tantalisingly vague. What kind of a role did the Department for Trade and Industry expect the Institute to play? Helpfully, however, and in support of the Institute's recognition of the experience of practitioners, and reflecting trends in management education, the Department for Education and Science and the DTI pointed out that the trend in vocational education was towards more open access and competence-based Accreditation of Prior Learning (APL).[82] This shows the Privy Council Office to have a lack of awareness about the trends, but it did lend legitimacy to the Institute's practice of admitting senior practitioners on experience alone, which had appeared distasteful to the Privy Council in earlier correspondence.

Three terse letters[83] precipitated a pause in the project: the Deputy Clerk at the Privy Council Office wrote to the Institute Secretary with the discouraging news and the suggestion to wait a further two to three years. The Privy Council Office returned the scripts to the Institute, which the Institute Secretary acknowledged on 27 September 1991.

At the end of this period, there are several observations to make. The period coincided with a different and more critical set of writing about the traditional professional model. These writings recognised the monopolistic nature of the traditional professional model and its exclusionary and privileged effects in society. The first tranche of papers reveals several important waypoints on the road to the Privy Council eventually award-ing a Royal Charter to the Institute. There are also important things to note concerning the persistence of the traditional model at the Privy Council Office. The Privy Council Office had articulated their expecta-tions of a profession and these broadly follow the characteristics of the model found in the literature. There was a sense of elitism and exclusion-ary privilege. However, there are the beginnings of a process and enough clues for the Institute to evolve and develop so that it mimicked the pro-fessions in the traditional professional model.

The stage is set anew for the arrival of a new leader at the Institute in 1992, the completion of the enclosure of training into the ambit of the Institute, and eventually the award of a Royal Charter. The award of a Royal Charter *was* a signifier of a profession in the traditional profes-sional model; however, the stage scenery and props had shifted and the professionalisation was still incomplete.

After the Institute and the Privy Council had exchanged the corre-spondence in which the Institute had sent copies of their examination papers, and the Privy Council, following comments from other interested parties about the possibility of the Institute receiving a Royal Charter[84] this period of activity ended and there were no dealings between the Insti-tute and the Privy Council until 1993.

The next episode, if judged by the correspondence between the Insti-tute and the Privy Council, suggests that little happened. During this hia-tus, a new Director-General joined the Institute and he addressed one of the most long-standing sores for the Institute, the relationship with the domain of training and development and the enclosure of the domain of personnel/human resource management *and* training and development within the purview of the Institute.

*"Let's Create a New Institute"*[85]: *A Successful Predatory Raid*

The new Director-General joining the Institute in 1992 came from an employee relations background in the car industry. The Director-General is a key informant in the Institute's story and his remembered account is important in filling the holes left by the Privy Council Papers. It is also fortunate that some of this event is recorded publicly in the Institute's contemporary journal, *Personnel Management*, and later *People Man-agement*. It is possible to stitch together a coherent narrative from the Institute's own practitioner journals.

The new Director-General was a new broom, and in giving his account he claimed that he was not aware of the Institute of Training and Devel-opment (ITD)[86] until he joined the Institute of Personnel Management. He was also without the baggage of organisational memory of the failed attempt to win the Royal Charter and to merge the two fields of training and personnel management.[87] However, and this is a crucial point, he was very aware of the changing field of practice and very aware of contemporary discourses within the field of practice.

In an interview[88] the Director-General stated that he had always:

> had this view that there was an artificial schism in the profession between the learning and training people and the personnel/HR people . . . no sense in that and I'd never heard of the ITD until I went to the IPM—and so we started discussing in the IPM the possibility of coming together.

In an interview, he also made observations on the size of the ITD ("23,000 members") but most damningly of all, he claimed that:

> they had no credible research, they had nothing very much.[89]

In saying this, the Director-General was comparing the ITD unfavourably with the IPM. The IPM was a professional body in the shape of the traditional professions of medicine, law and accountancy—learned bodies whose purpose was to advance knowledge in the field; the ITD was not. However, there was an even greater case for combining the two fields of practice and that concerned the developments taking place in Vocational and Educational Training (VET), and the rise of the National Vocational Qualification (NVQ). The NVQ could have provided a challenge for the Institute to be able to claim primacy and dominance over the knowledge associated with a field of practice and retain the marker of a "qualifying association"[90] which was essential if the Institute was to receive a Royal Charter.

What was to happen next was framed publicly as the "creation" of a new institute:

> let's create a new Institute, let's not merge the two institutes, let's not take over.[91]

By this, the Director-General meant that there was a possibility that any interested parties would see any action of this nature as a takeover of a smaller occupation by a larger, predatory one. Aware also of the changes in the field of practice, he felt that the two fields should be united because there were also dangers in having "a divided professional body". If the Director-General had been familiar with earlier correspondence between the Institute and the Privy Council, which no source indicates he was at this point, the remarks would have been apt, not least because internecine pettiness would prevent either body presenting a unified and significant mass of members and knowledge to any onlooker.

With a stated desire to create a new Institute to represent the fields of training and personnel/human resource management, the

Director-General's declared intent accomplishes two purposes when expressed in this way: first, the idea of "creation", of creating something new, is a post-hoc rationalisation of the way in which the events were seen by members of the ITD, which was indeed a takeover.

The second purpose suggests a view that the field of people management and development should be considered as one, especially so, if the field and the occupations associated with the practices were to advance in legitimacy, desirability and social standing. The idea of a unified field reflects the position that training developed into training and development, and the notion of learning and continuous and life-long learning were prevalent discourses, especially under human resource management practices.

So, the talks between the Institute and the ITD, the training body, began again. Briefing documents for members were distributed with the Institute's journal in November 1992 and June 1993. A month later in July 1993, the Director-General authored an article entitled *A new Institute for a changing profession* in *People Management*, in which he rehearsed the changes to the practice[92] which acted as justification for the act of combination.

In his oral remembered account of events, the Director-General's insistence of a fresh slate, a new beginning, a new institute, is laden with fragments of past unsuccessful talks.[93] He explained all the effort expended personally in making the case for two institutes to come together as one and to unite the two fields of practice, and two bodies of knowledge. He visited various branches of both the IPM and ITD, as he declared "two or three times a week and trying to encourage people to think more strategically and more ambitiously".

In November 1993, there was a compelling double page in the Institute's journal[94] called *The Case for Combination*. Contributors included eighteen senior practitioners from across the training and personnel management fields and included key figures from both the IPM and the ITD as well as personnel and human resource directors from organisations across the public and private sectors. These contributors wrote short opinion pieces in *The Case for Combination* which gave the impression of supporting the case for the merger. A close reading of the article, however, shows important aspects of the event which played out.

From *The Case for Combination*, there are several key themes which give further clues to how this event evolved. For example, there were members of both institutes who were discontent at the prospect of any form of change to their own institute. On the one hand, recently qualified IPM members were concerned about "the dilution of their qualification", because of the perceived lack of rigour and low status of ITD members, whilst on the other, ITD members feared a loss of individuality "if their institute is gobbled up by 'big brother', IPM".[95]

Some of the articles highlight the perceived relative status of both occupations, the development of human resource management practices, and the depth of feeling the prospect of "combination" aroused. Even though contributors tended to use the language of "combination", not "merger" or "amalgamation", they seem aware of the sensitivities of the members of both institutes.

Other aspects which emerged concern the public perception of both occupations, the extent to which they should be involved in public policy, the moribund nature of old practices and the new emerging fields of practice, the devolution of practices to the line manager, and an appreciation of the nature of learning (not training) in the workplace. The article's main purpose, however, was to discuss the key themes which would unite readers around a single institute and a unified, integrated set of practices.

In the field of public policy, one comment piece argued that it was important for a new institute to be strong enough to influence national policy on workplace matters. This implied that neither institute had done that previously and that such inertia was diminishing the credibility of both occupations. The Director of Personnel at one of Britain's leading supermarkets said:

> From the perspective of government and boardroom, as well as in the interests of members throughout the country, a co-ordinated voice on important national issues is critical.

This commentator continued:

> the idea of a joint institute to represent all human resource professionals and to ensure their views are put forward with credibility to government departments and ministers and to the top management of companies.

Other commentators also hinted at a changed occupational world and therefore the new institute, to be relevant in this new world, needed to assimilate human resource management and human resource development, and therefore *The Case for Combination* had to be made. For example, one commentator drew upon a recent survey of human resource management practices[96] and expressed the choice facing practitioners and the Institute:

> We can seek a pivotal role, with a highly respected HR department exerting a powerful policy—making influence. We can become professional mechanics with limited skills, interests and scope.
>
> I know which future I'd prefer. I support the merger because it will give us all the opportunity to see the new exciting role that's on offer. I don't want to be a member of the future "Institute of Personnel Mechanics" or the future "Institute for Training Drudges".

Comments by senior practitioners in *The Case for Combination* indicate that a unified field of practice under a combined institute would create increased influence on a wider social stage and to greater social standing for the practitioner. One commentator observed that "a new institute that can capture and disseminate all that is best in managing people and organi-sations would be a great national asset", but, she added, this could only be achieved by widening access to non-members, encouraging line managers to accept that training and personnel is part of the line manager's "career pathway". "Widening access to non-members" was a strategy which the Privy Council had not found acceptable in the earlier discussions with the Institute. This was also a dangerous line of thinking if the Institute was to receive a Royal Charter because the Privy Council in 1991 had said that a holder of a Royal Charter had to represent a unified field.[97]

The comment pieces recognised that both fields of practice were chang-ing. This had not been the case the last time potential merger talks had failed in the late 1970s. At that time, training was associated with 'blue collar' instruction and apprentices, whilst personnel management was associated with compliance and record keeping. A contributor to *The Case for Combination* explained:

> That is perhaps why many middle-aged personnel managers think of ITD members as instructors, and many middle-aged training manag-ers think of IPM members as sitting in smoke-filled rooms and keep-ing the records in order.[98]

This contributor foregrounds changes and alludes to trends in human resource development, especially to senior management commitment to "management development, career development, reward and contract structures, and organisational flexibility".

The contributor continued by reminding readers that:

> Forward thinking organisations regard the management of human resources as a critical and integral part of the strategic planning process.

Other contributions focused on the increasing requirement for practi-tioners to become involved in strategies to improve organisational capa-bility and the motivation of the workforce and, therefore, "(t)he isolation of training from this complex mix both at the organisational and profes-sional level is a nonsense".[99]

The Director of Training and Development at a British bank summed up the recognition that a wider and combined field of practice had evolved and as he added:

> The proposal to merge the two institutes is quite simply a recognition of the reality that both the personnel management and the training

professional have each been converging on total human resource management.[100]

Human resource issues know no such boundaries.[101]

The December 1993 issue of *Personnel Management*, in which *The Case for Combination* appeared, was the last one edited by the incumbent editor.[102] At the end of the article, the outgoing editor observed that there was a real sense that government and business had ignored both institutes; she claimed this was due in no little part to their earlier failure to agree.[103]

> The last attempt to merge the two institutes failed largely through apathy. This time it really matters. Government and chief executives say: "A plague on both your houses" and ignore us because we can't get our act together. This time let's make it happen. A new combined institute is the only logical way forward for the professional. VOTE for the IPD!

The outgoing editor's partisan observation is interesting as it was an editorial and used the term and idea of 'merger', and whether deliberately or accidentally, she released the proposed name of the new institute, the Institute of Personnel and Development, the IPD.

In the following New Year issue of *Personnel Management*, there was one lone voice of complaint about the article *The Case for Combination*:

> The 18 representatives of the "great and the good" were unanimously in favour of the proposed merger. How were the 18 selected? Is it significant that the training and development specialists among them outnumbered by two to one those with wider HR responsibilities, or is this just a coincidence?[104]

Underneath the letter, the editor rebutted the complaint:

> we approached a range of top HR people with no prior knowledge of their stance on this issue. No contributions were omitted or doctored. We deliberately chose people with fairly strong training and development interests or responsibilities, as they seemed most likely to have a case for the continuation of a separate training institute; in the event, they didn't.

There were two letters in support of the merger.

The article itself, *The Case for Combination*, had never used the language of 'takeover', and the abstemious attempts to avoid even a sniff of that prospect were aided by the use of terms such as "amalgamation" and "combination". The Institute's Director-General indicated[105] that the Institute regarded the ITD as weaker and to all intents launched a predatory raid on the field of training and development to secure dominance over the field. It is a matter of interpretation as to whether the move was designed to make the Institute more fitting to receive a Royal Charter by seeking to claim a unified domain of occupational practice or whether it was a pragmatic response to the evolving practices. However, the Director-General speaking of the successful eventual "combination" of the Institute of Training and Development and Institute of Personnel Management said:

> I've always been a great believer in the change management field because you've got to be able to pull the ladder behind you so people can't backslide and so we used the creation of IPD very much to do that—if you hold my feet to the fire, truth to tell, it was an IPM takeover of an organisation that wasn't going anywhere really.[106]

The Director-General suggested that events leading to the new institute were far from easy and alluded to earlier attempts to address the issue of training, the role of trainers and their occupational association for many years. The fears of some of the ITD members of obliteration and takeover by the IPM were well-founded. Over ten years later, a chartered member of the Institute and learning and development specialist corroborated these events. She had been a member of the ITD, and she said that she personally viewed the possibilities very favourably as the combination of the two fields of practice "would increase the professional status" of those working in the training field, promote a shift of thinking and practice from training to development. She also confirmed that the interested public regarded the IPM as "elite" and the ITD was "the poor relation". So, according to this learning and development practitioner, the event:

> "was sold as a merger of professional bodies dealing with people in work situations".

She hoped that the occupational snobbery would pass, however in the end, she acknowledged that "it did feel more like a takeover". She also suggested that it was the Institute (IPM) membership who kept the historic elitism and snobbery.

The public pronouncements of combination and merging two fields of practice concealed the prevailing view from the top of the IPM, that the creation of the new Institute was indeed a takeover. Far from the achievement of equal parties, this was a rapacious grab of a piece of organisational practice from another set of practices.

The Director-General said[107] that once the Institute had secured the enclosure of the field of training and development into the ambit of the Institute of Personnel Management, he ensured that the name of ITD was expunged. There are few references of any significance to the ITD on the internet.[108]

Following the successful vote in February 1994 to create the Institute of Personnel and Development, the Director-General wrote a comment piece[109] in which he talks about the tasks ahead. He uses the language of the traditional model of professionalism without referring to the Royal Charter but recognising the changing practice of devolving people management practices to the line manager.[110] The comment piece continues with the urge for practitioners to share "the highest standards of people management" with others; only that will lead to "greater organisational effectiveness". The Director-General explicitly said that the Institute would not be "inwardly focused or restrictive".

The formation of the body to represent the field of training, development and personnel management had a considerable impact upon the ability of the Institute to be able to claim authority over a complete domain of practice, which had been an explicit concern of the Privy Council Office, that of creating the distinctiveness expected.[111]

*Moving on to the Royal Charter*

Once the IPM/ITD affair had been settled, the Director-General turned his attention to several matters affecting the new organisation, the IPD. These were the commercial activities, the journal, and the qualification and its underpinning body of knowledge.

In his oral account the Director-General had said that once the long-running sore of the division between the two domains of practice of personnel management and training and development had been settled, the next obvious project was to seek a Royal Charter.[112] The Director-General was fully aware of the significance of a Royal Charter and what was needed to get one.

Through the *combination*[113] of the two former institutes of the ITD and the IPM, the new Institute achieved a significantly increased membership.[114] This was useful as far as the Institute (IPD) could claim to represent not only a unified field of practice, but most practitioners in a combined field of practice.

The next goal was to show the body of knowledge in a way which aimed to prove parity with other bodies of knowledge. The body of knowledge had to be "learnable" and capable of extension and development. Much of the writing about the traditional professions saw the body of knowledge as a key indicator of professionalism,[115] a theoretical knowledge domain that was based on scientific principles, was tested rigorously and could be applied in professional work. The university is the site where 'scientific' knowledge emerges, and therefore, professions and by extension, occupations aspiring to professionalism tended to forge greater links with them through research programmes and the provision in the higher education sector of the Institute's qualification programmes.[116] The universities developed and purveyed the profession's knowledge and produced the practitioners, a symbiotic if an incestuous relationship.

The status of the practitioner, now a practitioner who could be performing roles in human resource management which did encompass training and personnel management roles, had been a long-standing concern. The Director-General had felt that one of the reasons for this was the difficulty many practitioners had in convincing their employers of their value to the organisation. In his interview, the Director-General said that the Royal Charter would represent:

> a removal of a negative that they needed . . . because they were sitting alongside Chartered engineers, Chartered accountants . . . and they weren't chartered.[117]

On this occasion, the Director-General engaged a firm of solicitors to act on the Institute's behalf in the dealings with the Privy Council Office; this was a strategy which was quite different to that pursued in previous encounters with the Privy Council.[118]

So, the narrative turns to the end game—the bringing of the Institute's pursuit of the Royal Charter to a close.

## Notes

1. This became a point which exercised the Privy Council in relation to the Royal Charter and which will emerge later in the narrative.
2. Dryburgh G (1972) "The man in the middle", page 3.
3. The chronology appears material to the narrative and suggests a line of events; however, it is important to recognise that the papers are unformed and incomplete and show the Privy Council's cataloguing of correspondence between the PCO and the Institute. There is little context—other sources must give context.
4. Privy Council Papers Set I-I, 15 January 1968 a letter between the Institution of Production Engineers and the Privy Council. The Institution of Production Engineers received a Royal Charter in 1954 and was to act as intermediary at this early state of the Institute's application.
5. The fact was, the Institute, despite its claim to longevity, was not known to the Privy Council Office; this was an institute representing actors within the economic domain of social life, and therefore appeared of little interest to an administrative elite.
6. Niven M (1967) *Personnel Management 1913–1963: The Growth of Personnel Management and the Development of the Institute.* The forward to Margaret Niven's book was given by HRH Prince Philip who hailed the book important in gaining "a proper understanding of the practice and profession of Personnel Management".
7. Privy Council Papers Set I-ii, 1 February 1968—a file note written by the Clerk to the Privy Council who had attended the meeting.
8. There is no explicit statement of what the criteria for a professional body would be, to satisfy the Privy Council Office, until 1991. It is, therefore,

possible to interpret the Privy Council's note only using literature such as Carr-Saunders A M and Wilson P A (1933) *The Professions*; Millerson G (1964) *The Qualifying Association: A Study in Professionalization*.

9. Privy Council Papers, Set I-ii, 1 February 1968 ibid.
10. The conditions under which a Royal Charter was awarded were explicitly stated in the Privy Council Papers in 1991; there is no explicit statement of what the criteria for a professional body would be, to satisfy the Privy Council Office, until 1991; Privy Council Papers Set I-xv, 5 June 1991. This is a letter from the Deputy Clerk to the Privy Council to an official at the Department of Employment as part of the Privy Council process for determining whether the Institute should receive a Royal Charter. This letter explains the circumstances under which charters are given:

    1. "The body counts among its members the majority of the practitioners of a distinct profession."
    2. Most corporate members are qualified, by the body's own examinations or in a relevant discipline, at least the level of a first degree.
    3. The sphere of activity of the body can be distinguished from existing chartered or other significant organisations.
    4. The body is financially sound.
    5. The public interest would be served by the grant of a Charter." As late as 1991, it was clear that the Privy Council associated a profession and the Royal Charter with conceptions of a profession modelled upon the traditional model, see Carr-Saunders and Wilson 1933 ibid; Millerson G (1964) *The Qualifying Association: A Study in Professionalization*.

11. Privy Council Papers Set I-ii, 1 February 1968 ibid.
12. Carr-Saunders and Wilson 1933 ibid; Millerson 1964 ibid.
13. This became known as occupational closure; see Larson M S (1977) *The Rise of Professionalism: A Sociological Analysis*.
14. Larson 1977 ibid.
15. Privy Council Papers Set I-ii, 1 February 1968, ibid.
16. Privy Council Papers Set I-ii, February, ibid.
17. However, in 1975 Institute members could still progress through the Institute's hierarchy of membership based on experience, rather than other academic qualifications, a practice which the papers indicate was anathema to the Privy Council Office. Timperley S R and Osbaldeston M D (1975) "The professionalization process: A study of an aspiring occupational organization", page 612.
18. "Qualifying association", Millerson 1964 ibid.
19. ITOL later became the Institute of Training and Development (ITD); however, the two fields remained separate until 1994. The Institute's Director-General, who was at the helm when the Charter was awarded, spearheaded the formation of a new institute, the Institute of Personnel and Development (IPD); this body represented both training and personnel/human resource practitioners.
20. Privy Council Papers Set I-ii, 1 February 1968 ibid; the Privy Council Papers are silent as to why the Institute had not taken the advice from the Privy Council Office and the Institute papers or sources that might have dealt with this were not available. Although there *appears* to have been an absence of activity on the part of the Institute, this may not be the case and it is important to remember the limitations of the sources used to track the Institute's professionalisation and the question of what is missing.
21. Privy Council Papers, letter Set I-iii, 6 February 1977, a letter from the Institute's Assistant Director, Training, Organisation and Manpower Planning

to Companies Administration Division at the Department of Trade (carbon copy received at Privy Council Office) A Letter concerning the potential effect of an amalgamation with the Institution of Training Officers Ltd (ITOL). This letter indicates the suspicion that if the amalgamation of the "smaller and younger body" with the IPM were in fact seen to be a 'takeover', then this "will not win the support of the ITO members". If there were to be a new body to spearhead the activities of the ITOL and IPM, then what effect would there be on the "historical continuity" of the IPM "with particular reference to ambitions for a Royal Charter". There was also a concern about the two charitable statuses, and whether if the two bodies became one there would have to be a new application for charitable status.

22. Sharpe P H (1979a) "WANTED: A professional organisation for human resources managers".

23. The Institute has "charitable status" under Section 19(1) of the Companies Act of 1948 which gives some concessions for tax purposes in Britain.

24. In 1994 ITOL and IPM did combine the two occupational domains and many training practitioners did fear that the Institute as the larger body would submerge the training officers. There were other issues of concern too relating to the perceived disparity in status between training officers and personnel management practitioners.

25. Privy Council Papers, Set I-iv, 22 February 1977, letter from the Department of Trade and Industry to the Institute in response to the letter of 6 February 1977.

26. Privy Council Papers Set I-v, 25 February 1977, letter from the Institute to the Privy Council which proposes the possibility of an amalgamation between the IPM and the ITOL. The Institute seeks comments and refers to the "anticipated resistance of the membership to a conventional "takeover"". The letter also contains the idea would be that members of the new body would be admitted to corporate membership on the basis of examination only.

27. This appeared to be a strategy towards meeting the requirements of the Privy Council for a Royal Charter. According to Margaret Niven (1967), the IPM operated such an entry requirement from 1955, but some practitioners were still being admitted based on experience; ITOL did not have such a requirement.

28. Privy Council Papers Set I-vi, between 25 Feb 1977 and 10 March 1977. File note—This appears to be a file note prompted by the receipt of the earlier letter (Set I-v) that acted as a reminder of the soundings already taken in 1968. The writer of the note claims not to know about the Institution of Training Officers (ITOL) or "to what extent the IPM has improved its standards since 1968". The file note suggests that the historical longevity issue would not necessarily be of great concern—the entry standards, through the qualification, was an issue. There is an issue with the perceived lower standards of ITOL to which the Assistant Director of Membership and Education's earlier letter had pointed. The writer does not want to deal with this matter by correspondence but suggested a meeting with the IPM.

29. The later file note of 10 March Privy Council Papers Set I-vi suggested the name of the official; however, I am not able to disclose it.

30. Privy Council Papers Set I-vi 10 March 1977; a file note on which the signature is undecipherable—the writer is a Privy Council official and is an internal note between officials. This last file note suggested the name of the official who had taken part in the exchange of file notes; however, I am not able to disclose it at the request of the contact at the Privy Council Office.

31. Privy Council Papers Set I-vii, 10 March 1977; a letter from the Clerk to the Privy Council to the Institute's Assistant Director, Training, Organisation and Manpower Planning. The letter is a carbon copy and proposes a meeting, and requests "information about examinations and entry qualifications etc for both bodies, and the level of management at which members are employed".

32. Privy Council Papers, Set I-ix, 15 March 1977, a letter from the Institute's Assistant Director, Training, Organisation and Manpower Planning to the Clerk of the Privy Council. The letter encloses the information requested and confirms a meeting set for 3 pm on 22 March 1977.

33. Privy Council Papers Set 1-x, a file note, typed and signed by the Clerk to the Privy Council on 22 March 1977, following the meeting which was called to discuss the effect, if any, that the amalgamation of ITOL and IPM would have.

34. Privy Council Papers Set I-x, 22 March 1977 ibid.

35. Sharpe 1979a ibid.

36. File note, Privy Council Papers Set i-ii, 7 February 1968 ibid.

37. Pitfield M (1979) "Practical and professional a new look for the IPM's education programme".

38. More pressing, perhaps to practitioners was the perceived lack of power and usefulness of the function Watson T J (1977) *The Personnel Managers: A Study in the Sociology of Work and Employment*; Legge K (1978) *Power, Innovation and Problem Solving in Personnel Management*; Legge K and Exley M (1975) "Authority, ambiguity and adaptation: The personnel specialists' dilemma".

39. Pitfield 1979 ibid.

40. Cogan M L (1953) "Towards a definition of profession", pages 33–50.

41. Pitfield 1979 ibid.

42. In their discussions of HRD O'Donnell et al observed that both HRD and HRM were products of a postmodern economic thinking, which they said was "not really unique or a major break with the past but rather a special case of culture in a line of development that can be traced back to its genesis in the industrial revolution" O'Donnell D, McGuire D and Cross C (2006) "Critically challenging some assumptions in HRD", page 7.

43. Fombrun C J (1983) "Strategic management: Integrating the human resource systems into strategic planning"; Fombrun C, Tichy N and Devanna M (1984) *Strategic Human Resource Management*; Beer M, Spector B, Lawrence P R, Mills D Q and Walton R E (1984) *Managing Human Assets*; Beer M and Spector B (1985) "Corporate wide transformations in human resource management".

44. Guest D (1979) "American perspectives—systematic management of human resources by R B Peterson and L Tracy Addison-Wesley—a review"; Peterson R B and Tracy L (1979) *Systematic Management of Human Resources*.

45. Keenoy T (1990a) "HRM: A case of the wolf in sheep's clothing"; (1990b) "Human resource management: Rhetoric, reality and contradiction"; (1997) "Review article: HRMism and the languages of re-presentation"; (1999) "HRM as hologram: A polemic"; (2009) "Human resource management", Chapter 22, page 454–472.

46. Sharpe 1979 ibid, page 231; Chapter One gives greater detail on this putative organization.

47. Privy Council Papers Set I-xi, 22 February 1991, letter from the Institute Secretary to Deputy Clerk to Privy Council.

48. Privy Council Papers Set I-xii, 22 February 1991, handwritten file note of 22 February 1991.

49. Privy Council Papers Set I-xii, ibid; the Institute has a policy of admitting senior practitioners to membership based upon seniority in the occupation and the role they were performing.
50. In 1991, Directive 89/48/EEC concerned the preparation of member states for the creation of the European Single Market in 1992 and contained "a general system for the recognition of higher-education diplomas awarded". In 1992, Directive 92/51/EEC was issued which concerned "a general system for recognition of professional education and training to supplement Directive 89/48/EEC". The European Directive on Mobility of Professionals currently stands as Directive 2005/36/EC—The Free Movement of Professionals and the two directives referred to here are precursors of that.
51. See Carr-Saunders and Wilson 1933 ibid; Parsons T (1939) "The professions and social structure"; Wilensky H I (1964) "The professionalization of everyone?"; Hickson D J and M W Thomas (1969) "Professionalization in Britain: A preliminary measurement".
52. Privy Council Papers Set I-xiii, 1 May 1991, letter from Institute Secretary to the Deputy Clerk at the Privy Council Office confirming arrangements for lunch at IPM House, on the 8 May 1991.
53. Privy Council Papers Set I-xiv,1 May 1991, letter from Institute Secretary to the Deputy Clerk at the Privy Council; this letter reveals important information about the process for petitioning for Royal Charter. There has to be a "Central government sponsoring Department". In the case of the Institute this was the Department of Employment.
54. Privy Council Papers Set I-xii, mentioned in a file note at the Privy Council Office, 22 February 1991.
55. Privy Council Papers Set I-xiv, ibid.
56. Privy Council Papers Set I-i, 15 January 1968, letter from the Institution of Production Engineers to the Clerk at the Privy Council.
57. These are the new standards and qualifications; see Pitfield 1979 ibid.
58. Privy Council Papers Set I-xiv, letter 1 May 1991, Institute Secretary to the Clerk to the Privy Council. The Burnham Further Education Committee is a long-standing body whose original focus dealt with teachers' pay and conditions in the school and college sector. In 1972 it published the document *Grading of Courses*, which tried to list courses and qualifications in Britain according to a points system to allow cross comparisons, particularly with degrees awarded by the Higher Education sector.
59. The CNAA—the Council for National Academic Awards handled the accreditation of courses and qualification.
60. Privy Council Papers Set I-xiv, ibid; the question mark is in the original.
61. European Directive EC89/48/EEC. Neither the Institute (IPM) nor the Institute of Training and Development (ITD). These two bodies combined in 1994 to form the Institute of Personnel and Development (IPD).
62. Privy Council Papers, Set I-xiv, ibid.
63. Privy Council Papers, Set I-xv, 5 June 1991, Deputy Clerk at the Privy Council Office to Department of Trade and Industry.
64. Privy Council Papers, Set I-xv ibid.
65. Privy Council Papers Set I-xv ibid.
66. Privy Council Papers Set I-xv ibid; the letter specifically asks recipients: "whether the IPM qualification (could) be regarded as equivalent to a first degree."
67. Privy Council Papers Set I-xv, ibid. This also indicates the issue with the practices as they had evolved—the practices evolved from several other disciplines—management practice, sociology economics and industrial relations.
68. Privy Council Papers Set I-xv, ibid.

69. The Institute of Marketing received a Charter on 7 February 1989 and became the Chartered Institute of Marketing. The British Institute of Management received a Charter in 2002 and became the Chartered Management Institute (CMI). This was two years after the Institute of Personnel and Development had received the Royal Charter, and before the Institute was able to confer chartered status on qualifying members. This event appeared to rankle with the Director-General when I interviewed him (interview, 20 February 2010), as he admitted, ruefully:

"Subsequently they (the Privy Council) gave the Institute of Management a one-step process, they went straight to (individual Charter) . . . having learned the lessons of what we had done, because they did a deal with government and (gained) a Royal Charter after we did, but we (did it) the proper way and the hard way . . . the ability to award individual status a couple of years later—it was a big deal, very important psychologically".

70. Larson 1977 ibid; Sciulli D (2010) "Structural and institutional invariance in professions and professionalism".

71. Privy Council Papers Set I-xvi, 10 July 1991, a letter from an official of the Enterprise Initiative Division (Education and Training branch) of the Department of Trade and Industry (DTI), to the Clerk at the Privy Council Office. The letter confirms that DTI are making internal inquiries and "a substantive response" will come in due course"; Set I-xvii, 9 July 1991, a letter from an official in the Further and Higher Education Branch of the Department of Education and Science to the Clerk at the Privy Council Office. The letter seeks more information, namely "copies of the examinations set over the past two or three years at Stages 1 and 2 and, to assess standards, examples (say, two each of student scripts adjudged to be of lower, middle and upper levels"; Set I-xviii, 11 July 1991, a letter from an official at the Employment Department(ED) to the Clerk at the Privy Council. This letter is important in two ways. Firstly, the ED was not particularly 'enthusiastic'. The letter referred directly to two of the criteria set out in the Clerk's letter of 5 June 1991—the members are part of a "distinct" profession and the "sphere of activity" does not overlap with the domain of other bodies, probably meaning the British Institute of Management and the Institute of Training and Development (ITD). However, the ED letter does suggest that the Privy Council should recognise the trend toward assessment of competence rather than knowledge through examination. This reflects the change in a National Vocational Qualification system which recognised experience and the accreditation of prior learning; Set I-xxi, 31 July 1991, having received the scripts and information, a Clerk at the Privy Council Office forwards them to the Further and Higher Education Branch at the Department of Education and Science; Set I xxiii, 20 August 1991 a letter from the DTI responding to the Privy Council Office inquiry; Set I-xxiv, 22 August 1991, a letter from the Cabinet Office for the Civil Service to the Privy Council; Set I-xxv 11 September 1991, a letter from the Further and Higher Education branch of the Department of Education and Science to the Privy Council Office.

72. The Institute Secretary had left in late July to join the Chartered Institute of Marketing (letter Institute's Secretary to the Clerk at the Privy Council Office, 23 July 1991, Set I-ixx), highlighting the extent to which knowledge and expertise gained in one professional association may be equally valuable in another.

73. Privy Council Papers Set I-xxii, 29 July 1991, a package from the Institute's Director of Membership and Education enclosing nineteen appendices including twenty-four examination scripts and six management reports. The document talks about the Institute's objectives also.

74. Privy Council Papers Set I-xxvi, 18 September 1991.
75. Privy Council Papers Set I-xvii, 9 July 1991, the Further and Higher Education Branch of the Department of Education and Science to Privy Council Office.
76. Privy Council Papers Set I-xx 30 July 1991. The Institute Secretary to the Privy Council, and Set I-xxii, 29 July 1991 Institute Director–Membership and Education to the Privy Council; the letter stated that scripts older than the two diets in that current year had been destroyed as a matter of custom.
77. Privy Council Papers Set I-xxiv, the Cabinet Office for the Civil Service to the Deputy Clerk at the Privy Council, 22 August 1991.
78. No source that I could find shows whether the Institute was aware of this matter; however, according to the Director-General of the Institute (interview, 20 February 2010), the Institute had begun to undertake some research, of higher quality. This was in response to the views expressed and was important to show that as a profession the Institute could develop the body of knowledge.
79. Privy Council Papers Set I-xxv, 11 September 1991, letter from the Further and Higher Education branch Department of Education and Science to the Privy Council.
80. Privy Council Papers Set I-xxv ibid.
81. Privy Council Papers Set I-xxiii, 20 August 1991, a letter from the DTI to the Deputy Clerk at the Privy Council Office.
82. Privy Council Papers Set I-xxiii 20 August 1991 ibid.
83. Privy Council Papers Set I-xxvi, 18 September 1991, letter from Privy Council to the Institute Secretary; Privy Council Set I-xxvii, 23 September 1991, letter from Privy Council Office to Institute Secretary returning the scripts; Set I-xxviii Letter 27 September 1991, letter from Institute acknowledging receipt.
84. Privy Council Papers Set I-xxvi 18 September 1991, the Privy Council to the Institute's Secretary, a letter in which stated that the position was "not altogether encouraging"; Set I-Xxvii 23 September 1991, a letter from the Privy Council returning the scripts; Set I-xxviii 27 September 1991, a letter from the Institute to the Privy Council acknowledging receipt.
85. Director-General, interview February 2010.
86. The Institute of Training and Development was the successor name of the main organisation for training practitioners; in 1979 this had been the Institution of Training Officers Limited (ITOL); see Sharpe 1979a.
87. Sharpe 1979a ibid.
88. Director-General Interview, February 2010.
89. Director-General ibid; there was a general view that a profession in the traditional model should undertake research to push the boundaries of human knowledge in pursuit of improving society, and during the period, the Institute's practice was increasingly turning to academic institutions for research to prove the importance of human resource management practice for organisational progress.
90. Millerson 1964 ibid.
91. Director-General, interview ibid.
92. This relates to the different focus of practice within the field, which could be attributed to the advent of human resource management; Personnel Management (1993) "The case for combination", page18.
93. There had been earlier discussion shown in Privy Council Papers about the effect of any merger or amalgamation of the IPM and IPD in case members thought that it was a takeover of a larger body of a weaker one—but it was. Privy Council Papers Set I-vi, between 25 February 1977 and 10

March 1977, Set 1-viii, 10 March and Set I-x, 22 March 1977; Sharpe 1979a ibid.

94. Personnel Management 1993 ibid, pages 26–32.
95. Personnel Management 1993 ibid.
96. The Price Waterhouse Cranfield survey was "an international comparative survey of organisational policies and practices in human resource management in Europe"; it took place between 1989 and 1992. See Brewster C and Hegewisch A (eds) (2017) *Policy and Practice in European Human Resource Management: The Price Waterhouse Cranfield Survey*, page 230.
97. Privy Council Papers Set I-xv 5 June 1991 ibid.
98. Personnel Management 1993 ibid, page 27.
99. Personnel Management 1993 ibid, page 30.
100. Personnel Management 1993 ibid.
101. Personnel Management 1993 ibid. The editor was leaving; the language of "human resources" is interesting here, and the references to the evolving field among practitioners first, and the Institute later, may indicate the tendency of the Institute to be cautious in changing practice; there was also a sensitivity to the language in terms of the use of "humans" as "resources", when "personnel management" was perceived as more benevolent and dignified.
102. Personnel Management 1993 ibid.
103. Sharpe 1979a ibid.
104. Personnel Management 1993 ibid, page 23.
105. Director-General, interview February 2010.
106. Director-General interview 2010.
107. Director-General interview 2010.
108. This statement occludes the difficulty with oral testimony from anyone, and particularly elites with a legacy to preserve. There are issues with over-aggrandisement and memory.
109. Armstrong G (1994) "Comment: A sound foundation for the IPD".
110. Devolution of practices to the line manager was increasing in popularity; in theory the practices created the possibility for the practitioner to become more involved with loftier matters such as organisational effectiveness and strategic issues. See Torrington D and Hall L (1998) "Letting go or holding on: The devolution of operational personnel activities". The models of HRM which had come from the US increasingly discussed and advocated this practice; see Ulrich D (1990) *Delivering Results: A New Mandate for Human Resource Professionals*; (1997) *Human Resource Champions: The Next Agenda for Adding Value and Delivering Results* and Ulrich D and Brockbank W (2005) *The HR Value Proposition*.
111. Privy Council Papers Set I-xv, ibid q letter of 5 June 1991 which stated: "The body counts among its members the major proportion of the practitioners of a distinct profession", and "The sphere of activity of the body can be distinguished from existing chartered or other significant organisations."
112. Director-General, interview February 2010 ibid.
113. Personnel Management 1993 ibid.
114. Query Membership Numbers.
115. See Cogan 1953 ibid; Wilensky 1964 ibid; Hickson and Thomas 1969 ibid.
116. Larson (1977 ibid, page 17) recognised this phenomenon as did Burrage et al 1990.
117. Director-General interview February 2011.
118. Privy Council Papers Set II-i, 16 September 1996—a solicitor's letter to the Clerk of the Privy Council.

## Bibliography

Beer M and Spector B (1985) "Corporate wide transformations in human resource management", in R E Walton and P R Lawrence (eds) *Human Resource Management, Trends and Challenges*, Boston: Harvard Business School Press.

Beer M, Spector B, Lawrence P R, Mills D Q and Walton R E (1984) *Managing Human Assets*, New York: Free Press.

Brewster C and Hegewisch A (eds) (2017) *Policy and Practice in European Human Resource Management: The Price Waterhouse Cranfield Survey*, London: Taylor & Francis.

Carr-Saunders A M and Wilson P A (1933) *The Professions*, Oxford: Clarendon Press.

Cogan M L (1953) "Towards a definition of profession", *Harvard Educational Review* 23: 33–50, Winter.

Dryburgh G (1972) "The man in the middle", *Personnel Management* 4(5): 3, May.

Fombrun C J (1983) "Strategic management: integrating the human resource systems into strategic planning", in *Advances in Strategic Management*, Vol. 2, Greenwich, CT: JAI Press.

Fombrun C J, Tichy N and Devanna M (1984) *Strategic Human Resource Management*, New York: John Wiley and Sons.

Guest D (1979) "American perspectives—systematic management of human resources by R B Peterson and L Tracy Addison-Wesley—a review", *Personnel Management*: 49, December.

Hickson D J and Thomas M W (1969) "Professionalization in Britain: A preliminary measurement", *Sociology* 3: 37–53.

Keenoy T (1990a) "HRM: A case of the wolf in sheep's clothing", *Personnel Review* 19(2): 3–9.

Keenoy T (1990b) "Human resource management: Rhetoric, reality and contradiction", *International Journal of Human Resource Management* 1(3): 363–384.

Keenoy T (1997) "Review article: HRMism and the languages of re-presentation", *Journal of Management Studies* 34(5): 825–841.

Keenoy T (1999) "HRM as hologram: A polemic", *Journal of Management Studies* 36(1): 1–23.

Keenoy T (2009) "Human resource management", in M Alvesson, T Bridgman and H Willmott (eds) *The Oxford Handbook of Critical Management Studies*, Oxford: Oxford University Press, Chapter 22, pages 454–472.

Larson M S (1977) *The Rise of Professionalism: A Sociological Analysis*, London and Berkeley: University of California Press.

Millerson G (1964) *The Qualifying Association: A Study in Professionalization*, London: Routledge.

O'Donnell D, McGuire D and Cross C (2006) "Critically challenging some assumptions in HRD", *International Journal of Training and Development* 10(1): 4–16.

Parsons T (1939) "The professions and social structure", *Social Forces*: 457–467, May.

Personnel Management (1993) "The case for combination", *Personnel Management* 25(12): 26–32.

Peterson R B and Tracy L (1979) *Systematic Management of Human Resources*, Reading, MA: Addison-Wesley Publishing Company.

Pitfield M (1979) "Practical and professional a new look for the IPM's education programme", *Personnel Management*: 42–45, December.

Sciulli D (2010) *Structural and Institutional Invariance in Professions and Professionalism*, Oslo, Norway: Senter for profesjonssudier.

Seears N (1979) "Can personnel managers deliver?" *Personnel Management* 11(10).

Sharpe P H (1979) "WANTED: A professional organisation for human resources managers", *Industrial and Commercial Training* 11(6): 230–232.

Timperley S R and Osbaldeston M D (1975) "The professionalization process: A study of an aspiring occupational organization", *The Sociological Review* 23(3): 607–627.

Wilensky H I (1964) "The professionalization of everyone?" *American Journal of Sociology* 70(2): 137–158.

# 3  1993, 1996–2003: The Institute's Drama Continues

Despite the fragmenting traditional British model of professionalism under neoliberal and new public management reforms, the Royal Charter stayed the epitome of professionalism, status, esteem and legitimacy. In the autumn of 1991, any hope that the Institute elite still held of achieving a Royal Charter remained unfulfilled, hanging in sight but tantalisingly out of reach.[1] The Privy Council Papers do not shed any light on the Institute's progress until the paper trail resumes briefly in 1993 and then again in 1996. The apparent gap in the Institute's activity between 1991 and 1993 towards achieving a Royal Charter did not signify, however, that the project had dissipated. Interest in the Royal Charter had not, in fact, waned and like an untreated boil, continued to erupt as a project for the Institute.

The Institute, between 1980 and 1991 had much to occupy it as practitioner members tried to reconcile identity and the body of knowledge and practice with the shifting practices of human resource management. The socio-political environment of the Thatcher decade provided a fertile plot for such reconciliation struggles to take place. Identity projects in the practitioner field in the 1980s suggested that the emergent paradigm of human resource management and the discourses which had taken root would create opportunities for practitioners to strengthen claims to legitimacy and status—discourse such as 'talent', 'performance', 'strategy' and 'creativity' acquired an urgency in the practitioner's work. In the early part of the twentieth century, the practitioner had been primarily concerned firstly with the welfare and wellbeing of the employee, and secondly with administration and industrial relations. However, the new practices and thinking peddled by academics and practitioners suggested rethinking the practitioner's role. The practitioner became the visible handmaid or valet of the organisation, of management and of capital. This had always been the case, but this time and under the primary discourse of human resource management, employees noticed.

In the autumn of 1991, the Privy Council suggested that the Institute wait another two to three years before applying again.[2] Each time the Privy Council had rejected the Institute's overtures, correspondence did provide clues as to how the Institute could win a Royal Charter. The criteria for an award of a Royal Charter had been clearly articulated in papers and file notes passing within the Privy Council and between the Privy Council and their advisers.[3] Among these criteria were that a petitioning professional body must represent members of a "distinct profession", the educational attainment must be at least of degree level, and the organisation must be unique and must pay attention to the 'public interest'.

The correspondence between the Institute and the Privy Council might suggest that little happened between the autumn of 1991 and 1993. However, this was not the case as the Privy Council Papers reveal that in August 1993 an internal memo between an official who later handled the successful Royal Charter and the Deputy Clerk at the Privy Council Office[4] reveals that the Institute (IPM) had asked the Permanent Secretary of the Department of Employment to sponsor a petition for a Charter and he (or she) turned to the Privy Council for advice.

Unsurprisingly, the official at the Privy Council Office was unaware of the Institute's history with the Privy Council and recorded that he had responded to the official at the Department of Employment by giving what appears to be a standard response:

> If and when a Charter was referred, the fact would be gazetted[5] and anyone who wished to express a view would be free to do so. In the first instance, however, the Institute would be well advised to get in touch with the Privy Council Office.

At this point, the Privy Council documentation ceases until 1996; however, there are some important activities which the Institute undertook which fills the gap left by the hiatus in the Privy Council documents. The activities may be interpreted as contributing to a continuing professional project. The activities were purposeful and had the appearance to the Privy Council and other interested onlookers of an end goal of the type of professionalism exhibited by the Royal Charter: a regulated profession, with powers to regulate practitioners, in which the occupation, through the Institute, could repel the unregistered. An alternative view, however, is that the Institute just did what was necessary to win the Royal Charter and notions of regulation and occupational closure were not part of the plan. The onlooker has only the context and a reconstructed record to help decide.

## The Institute Takes the Initiative

Between 1991 and 1993, a new Director-General had taken office and eventually settled the issue of the joint domain of practice of personnel management, and training and development, or at least, through the "creation" of the new Institute of Personnel and Development, had been instrumental in bringing the domain of training and development within the purview of the Institute.[6] This made a considerable impact upon the ability of the Institute to claim to have authority over a complete domain of practice, which had been an explicit concern of the Privy Council Office and which was set out in a letter of 5 June 1991 which stated:

> The body counts among its members the major proportion of the practitioners of a distinct profession,
> and
> The sphere of activity of the body can be distinguished from existing chartered or other significant organisations.[7]

The act of combination in the creation of the new Institute would swell the membership of the new organisation, and neutralise the threat posed by a rival organisation who could claim a field of practice and knowledge. In 1994, once the two institutes had combined, the Institute of Training and Development (ITD) disappeared along with its name, its members and practices subsumed by the Institute of Personnel and Development (IPD).[8] Afterwards, in 1994, the Director-General wrote a comment piece for the practitioner journal, *Personnel Management*.[9] In it, he talks about the tasks ahead to build and consolidate the new Institute: the commercial activities (to build the finances), the practitioner journal, and the qualification and its underpinning body of knowledge. The language used in the comment piece is redolent with meaning reminiscent of the traditional model of professionalism. The commentary talks of "the comprehensive body of knowledge which underpins [the] profession", that "it is a systematic learnable discipline, with a wider range of explicit competencies which need to be applied appropriately by everyone who has responsibility for other people"; in other words, this aligns with the changing practice of devolving day-to-day practices to line managers.[10] The comment piece continues with the urge to for practitioners to share "the highest standards of people management" with others; only that will lead to "greater organisational effectiveness". The Director-General explicitly said that the Institute would not be "inwardly focused or restrictive"; this is a use of language which portends a modern organisation which did not look to regulate its members by license to practice, a significant contrast with the traditional model of professionalism which was prevailing at the Privy Council.

In the comment piece, the Director-General does not explicitly mention the Royal Charter but speaking later in 2010, he said that once the long-running sore of the division between two domains of practices had been settled, the next obvious project was to seek a Royal Charter.[11]

Underpinning the traditional professional model is the idea of a theoretical knowledge domain that is derived from scientific principles, tested rigorously, that can be applied in professional work. Much of the writing about the traditional professions saw the body of knowledge as a key indicator.[12] The university is the site where 'scientific' knowledge emerges, and therefore, professions and, by extension, occupations aspiring to professionalism tended to create links with them.[13] The universities develop and purvey the profession's knowledge and produce the practitioners, a symbiotic if incestuous relationship. The Director-General was fully aware of the significance of a Royal Charter and what was required to get one.

Through the *combination*[14] of the two former institutes of the ITD and the IPM, the new Institute achieved a significantly increased membership.[15] This was useful in so far as the Institute (IPD) could claim to represent not only a unified field of practice, but most practitioners in the field. The next goal was to establish the body of knowledge in a way which aimed to establish parity with other bodies of knowledge which was "learnable" and capable of extension and development.

With these thoughts, I return to the Institute's Charter drama, with a resumption of material from the Privy Council Papers.

### Act Two, Scene One: "The Institute of Personnel and Development wishes to pursue an application for a Royal Charter"[16]

By 1992, a practitioner could be performing roles in human resource management encompassing training, employee development and personnel management, and yet the status of the practitioner was still a concern to many involved in the field. Reflecting upon this period in 2010, the Director-General said that he had felt that one of the reasons for this was the difficulty many practitioners had in convincing their employers of their value to the organisation; a Royal Charter would make a difference in that it would represent:

> a removal of a negative that they needed . . . because they were sitting alongside Chartered engineers, Chartered accountants . . . and they weren't chartered.

The Director-General had made the acquisition of a Royal Charter a goal and the zeal with which he pursued this is indicated by the fact that, when he took on the goal of acquiring a Royal Charter, the Institute had engaged a firm of solicitors to act on the Institute's behalf in the dealings with the Privy Council Office; this was not the case in the period between 1968 and 1991.[17]

On 16 September 1996, the firm of solicitors acting on behalf of the Institute wrote to the Clerk to the Privy Council Office. The letter acknowledges earlier dealings on the matter of an earlier application for a Royal Charter.[18] The tone of the letter is altogether different from earlier correspondence. In the first attempts between 1968 and 1993, the Institute's correspondence was directed towards finding out whether it was worthwhile putting in an application; this time, the Institute through the solicitors approached the Privy Council more in the positive expectation that there would be an application.

The letter of 16 September 1996[19] provides a catalogue of the achievements of the Institute, details of governance, and the Institute's contributions to society and at the end in a more deferential tone and asks whether the solicitors could attend the Privy Council Offices:

> to come to discuss the application (for a Royal Charter) in order to progress it.

The letter encloses a copy of an interview which had appeared earlier that year for *People Management*[20] in which the Director-General talked about setting a "wider role" for the Institute. The letter also enclosed the Institute's financial statements indicating that the Institute's finances were strong.

There was no response and three weeks later the solicitors telephoned the Privy Council Office and found that the Privy Council Office had not received the first letter. Accordingly, the solicitor promptly sent another.[21]

Ignoring the ebullient tone struck by the solicitors in their earlier letter, the response from the Privy Council Office is cautious[22] and states that the Privy Council would consult their advisers:

> with a view to advising you, in due course, on a personal basis, as to whether a Petition would be likely to be successful.

## A Meeting and Two File Notes

Among the Privy Council Papers is an anonymous and undated file note which reports on a telephone call the solicitors made to the Clerk at the Privy Council Office on behalf of the Institute in advance of a meeting on 14 November 1996 at the Privy Council Office.[23] The telephone call sought an early view as to whether there was any likelihood of success. The writer of the file note consulted the file and responded on 22 October to say that he could not "give any kind of preliminary view before the meeting".[24]

The file note continues:

> However, I said that I thought the discussion was likely to centre very much on *what the institute thought was* the public interest case for granting the Institute a Charter. Other *major* issues were likely to be the academic qualifications for entry to the Institute, how far

the Institute covered the majority of practitioners in the field, and the extent of the Institute's contact with Government. I said I thought another issue for advisers was likely to be the extent to which personnel management continued to be regarded as a specialism as opposed to a function which was increasingly dispersed within organisations.[25]

The importance of this file note[26] is that it displays the main and recurring problems for the Institute concerning the success of a petition for a Charter, namely the academic standards and the distinctiveness of the occupation.[27] Although these were problems for the Institute, the file note also indicates that the Privy Council were still adhering to the perceived links between the Royal Charter and the traditional professional model concerning the public benefit ethos, academic standards and distinctiveness. There appeared to be little understanding of the practices in the field and the trends towards continuing professional development and lifelong learning, which forged a greater connection between employment and education, resulting in a trend towards the accreditation of prior learning and experience (APL). This was something both the Department of Education and Science and the Department of Employment had noted in earlier correspondence from August 1991.[28] The inference is, therefore, that the Privy Council Office was still of the mind that the Institute's application for a Charter was directed towards closing off the occupation as in a traditional "professional project" as Larson observed and described the phenomenon in 1977.[29]

The second meeting took place on 14 November 1996[30] and the Institute's Director-General, the Institute Secretary, the Director of Membership and Education and the Institute's solicitors were present. The meeting included a presentation by the Director-General which he then sent on after the meeting.[31] The letter concluded:

> We look forward to hearing further from you when you have been able to take your soundings and give consideration to our wish to proceed with a formal application when you judge appropriate.

Following the meeting, a representative from the Privy Council Office present at the meeting wrote a file note.[32] The file note is expansive about the Institute, following the creation of the new body in 1994 and comments that the Institute had given a presentation at the Privy Council Office; this is the presentation which the Director-General of the Institute had enclosed in a letter on 18 November 1996.[33] The file note summarised the substantive content of the meeting on 14 November 1996 when the topics had included the "merger" between the IPM and ITD in 1994, membership numbers, the Institute's aims, its governance, routes to membership and educational routes, its activities including dissemination of information, research, public profile and its financial position.

The file note summarises the Director-General's view of the reasons for seeking a Royal Charter:

> (The Director-General) said that the membership had voted, in the context of the merger that the IPD should aim to obtain a Charter. The Institute was a unique body whose important contribution to the economy should be recognised. Personnel aspects were increasingly central to the success or failure of organisations, and recognition of the IPD by means of a Charter would help bring home the importance of the discipline. In other words, it was not seen just a matter of status for members of the Institute.[34]

This extract from the Privy Council Office file note is noteworthy since it corroborates what the Director-General had maintained in an oral account[35] that the Institute was not seeking a Royal Charter to raise the status of practitioners but because it was an important body for safeguarding the integrity of important organisational routines upon which organisations depended. But although the Director-General sought to assure the Privy Council that the application for a Royal Charter was not for the purpose of status,[36] but was for the public good, he showed remarkable fleetness of rhetoric in other outlets aimed at a practitioner audience.

This file note also commented upon the purposes of the Institute which would appear as Objects in any future Charter and Byelaws were a Royal Charter to be granted:

> (The Director-General) said that the objects of the Institute are for the public benefit, to promote and develop the science and practice of the management and development of people (including the promotion of research and publication of the useful results of such research). More specifically, the Institute aims to advance continuously the management and development of people for the benefit of individuals, employers and the community at large, to be the professional body for those specialising in advancing this process; and to be recognised as the leading authority and influence in the field.
>
> To this end, the Institute has as its mission to lead in the development and promotion of good practice, for application both by professional members and by their organisational colleagues; to serve the professional interests of members, and to uphold the highest ideals in the management and development of people. The Director-General emphasised that the Institute is thus directed both at the professionalism of its own members and at the greater good of Britain at large. The Institute is primarily an educational charity and does not seek a regulatory role or a closed shop arrangement. Much emphasis is place(d) on helping non-professionals to improve their

own performance in the field, at a time when the management of organisations is undergoing a major change.[37]

The file note reports that at the end of the meeting on 14 November 1996, the Clerk to the Privy Council undertook to consult the Privy Council's advisers as to the success of an application. Based on the consultation, the Clerk would then give a "*personal* view"[38] whether it was worth making a formal application.

Over six months elapsed following the meeting of 14 November 1996, and in the interim, the Privy Council consulted their advisers about the Institute.[39] This correspondence is missing; however, a letter from the Clerk at the Privy Council Office to the solicitors indicated that the Privy Council were still concerned about the number of graduates who were full members of the Institute; it was "a point of particular relevance".[40] In an earlier engagement with the Institute's putative application,[41] the Institute's qualification had long been chief among the Privy Council's concerns that the qualification had to be equivalent to first-degree level at least.[42] Not only did the Institute need to represent a sizeable proportion of practitioners working in the field, who were also members, but the corporate (full) voting members of the Institute had to have a qualification of graduate level. This would show that the Institute represented enough practitioners of the occupation as outlined in earlier Privy Council Office papers.[43]

The Clerk to the Privy Council proposed a meeting "to discuss the issues bearing on a prospective Petition by the Institute for a Charter of Incorporation".[44] The letter acknowledged that the Institute had indicated a rise in the number of graduates among the full membership, so on that basis and:

> without being able to pronounce authoritatively on the eventual reaction of the Privy Council, the prospects of a successful application are sufficiently encouraging for the Institute to submit a Petition.[45]

The Institute, at the invitation of the Privy Council, sent a draft Charter and Byelaws and a draft petition to the Privy Council.[46] The solicitors would no doubt have drafted these documents and on receipt of the draft documentation, the Privy Council sent them on to several of the Privy Council's advisers for consultation, a process which took from November 1997 to February 1998.[47]

Although some of the advisers were still consulting, on 17 February 1998 the Clerk to the Privy Council wrote to the Institute's solicitors with signs of progress.[48] The letter concludes, however, with the dispiriting observation that there were still some "issues of substance" which had arisen from the first draft Charter and Byelaws which the Privy Council had forwarded to its advisers on 5 November 1997. The advisers had raised observations which amounted to three main issues—the Institute's longevity, its public good and regulation and disciplinary matters—all issues which have resonances in the traditional professional model (see Appendix II).

### Issue 1: Longevity

The letter to the solicitors[49] on 17 February 1998 indicated that the draft Charter had given "the impression that the Institute came into being from scratch in 1994". The traditional professional model tended to support occupations that could show how long it had been in existence[50] and this issue had been a concern already raised by the Institute in 1977 when the doomed 'merger' talks between the ITOL and IPM were still in play.[51]

### Issue 2: A Public Good—Commercial Activities, a Library, and Confusion

Hidden in Article 3[52] of the draft Charter and Byelaws was the second issue; this had alerted the Privy Council Office to the commercial activities of the Institute. Article 3 implied the promotion of a profession, rather than the promotion of altruistic purposes of a profession in the traditional model. The Institute had "charitable status" under Section 19(1) of the Companies Act of 1948 which gives some concessions for tax purposes in Britain. This status interested the advisers to the Privy Council and there was a concern that not all the Institute's activities were "wholly charitable" to receive tax concessions under Section 19(1) of the Act and the Privy Council view was that:

> Chartered bodies tend to confine trading activity to wholly-owned subsidiaries.[53]

In earlier representations to the Privy Council Office shown in a file note,[54] the Institute had boasted of their library facilities, declaring:

> The library is the largest, most comprehensive collection of personnel and training and development material in Europe. Steps are being taken to make it accessible on the Internet.

It was two years later before the Privy Council Office picked this up and asked whether "the library (would) be open to the public".[55] The Institute's library is for members only, and its mention by the Institute was for undergirding the claim that the Institute curated a body of knowledge, an essential element of the traditional professional model, and a link to raising the status of the practices to a science. This illustrates yet another misunderstanding between the parties in this drama: by raising the subject of the library, the Institute was attempting to demonstrate how it kept its knowledge base, however the Privy Council Office appeared to think that the facilities were part of the traditional professional model of promoting the public good.

## Issue 3: Regulation and Discipline

An important feature of the traditional professional model is autonomy, measured by the profession's ability to regulate itself and its members without external interference. The mechanising for accomplishing that is through internal governance procedures such as the register of members, codes of conduct and disciplinary procedures. Draft Byelaw 13 in the Institute's correspondence[56] had suggested that the Institute had the right to expel a member (assumed to be male) who became bankrupt. However, the writer at the Privy Council Office observed in his considered response that[57]:

> such a provision would normally be appropriate only when a person was offering professional services to the public, whereas the Institute presumably includes a large number of people working as employees.

This last query highlights the Institute's Achilles' heel—the site of practice, which was in organisations where organisational constraints governed the practitioners' autonomy and freedom to act not by practice and code. Such constraints may have also come from other organisational professionals with greater power and status.[58]

The Privy Council expected the Byelaws to explicitly address the Institute's process for disciplining errant members, and the letter of 17 February 1998 specifically asked:

> Can you say how your clients would propose to regulate disciplinary matters?[59]

If the Institute were able to disbar members who transgressed this would demonstrate the autonomy of the Institute in the matter of regulating the occupation in the way found in the traditional professional model. The regulated professions had codes of conduct by which members self-governed and were governed; there was an expectation on the part of the Privy Council that the Institute would fall into line. It was a happy chance that the Institute had a Code of Conduct and had had a Code of Conduct since 1979[60] but its purpose was, as the Institute's Director-General said in 2010 in an interview, as a statement of "standards of behaviour".

## New Drafts of the Petition and Charter

On 26 August 1998, the Institute, through the solicitors, responded to the Privy Council's letter of 17 February 1998, addressed the advisers' comments and gave revised drafts of the petition and Charter.[61] These sources illustrate how this petition for a Royal Charter was composed.[62]

In the Institute's case, the draft petition covers the Institute's recent history following the combination of the ITD and IPM. The draft petition declared the "objects" of the Institute to be:

> to promote and develop the science and practice of the management and development of people (including the promotion of research and publication of the useful results of such research) for the public benefit.[63]

It explained how "experienced practitioners" became corporate (full voting) members, which was "through professional assessment and accreditation of prior certificated learning",[64] achieved "without compromising the Institute's high standards through rigorous quality assurance and systematic competence assessment".[65] Whether or not the Privy Council had conceded the point about the admission of some practitioners without examination, which had been of concern earlier, the Institute appeared to have won this point of permitting suitably senior and experienced individuals to be members without having the qualification. However, once again, the Institute tried to show its compliance with the Privy Council's expectations of a Chartered organisation.

The handwritten annotations on the Privy Council Office copy indicate that the Institute's response did not satisfy the Privy Council, and the Clerk at the Privy Council sent the annotated documents back to the Institute's solicitors.[66] The Clerk also addressed the power of the Executive Board, and member qualifications and experience as a requirement for full membership of the Institute and the occupation:

> At the moment, too much discretion is vested in the Executive Board. A professional body which aspires to Chartered status should require applicants for corporate membership to hold a first degree or equivalent in the discipline in question. Many Chartered bodies, meanwhile, have a minimum experience requirement.[67]

Although irksome to the Clerk of the Privy Council, the Institute's drafting had implied a desire for beneficial accruals to itself and recognition through the Royal Charter; nevertheless, this time the Privy Council Office appeared content to let it by. The Privy Council also ignored the statement that the Institute was *not* looking for self-regulation which they might still have if the Royal Charter was to confer a state of professionalism in the traditional sense but looked for something else to focus upon—in this case, the criteria for full membership. In other words, the Privy Council Office may not have liked what the Institute was proposing about the beneficial accruals to the Institute, but they ignored that point and threw another obstacle in the way. This illustrates the way in which both parties, with divergent goals and understandings, had to reach accommodation so that matters could progress to a conclusion.

The draft Byelaws are interesting in appearing to name the occupational practices as "science", and the "management and development of people",[68] rather than either personnel management or human resource management. Practice as "science" was an important device to bolster claims to rigour and objectivity and enhance the status of both the practices and the practitioner. Furthermore, drawing attention to the term "management" could have represented a hidden danger to the Institute's search for a Royal Charter. "Management" and its organisational focus would not make the practices constitute a "distinct profession" which "can be distinguished from existing Chartered or other significant organisations", as the guidance had originally set out back in 1991.[69]

## Issues of Substance

Between September and December 1998 there is silence according to the Privy Council Papers, but the account shows that the Institute's solicitors had telephoned the Privy Council Office.[70] On 7 December 1998, the Clerk to the Privy Council advised that they were still waiting for the advisers' comments on the revised draft,[71] but he did say:

> I am reasonably confident of bringing this stage of the process to a conclusion shortly and expect to have a small number of points of substance to discuss with you before the drafts are finalised.

Matters were not finalised with any great speed, however, as two months later in February 1999 the Clerk wrote to the Institute's solicitors apologising for the delay.[72] The Clerk said that "the few remaining points of substance" needed to be resolved "rigorously at this stage, to avoid difficulties in the wake of the submission of a formal petition".

The letter of February 1999 to the Institute's solicitors also reveals that the Charity Commission had made comment upon the drafts sent by the solicitors in the papers of the previous August; those comments were of enough concern and could "delay grant of a Royal Charter".[73] This was the problem. The Charity Commission objected to the wording in the draft Memorandum and Byelaws that suggested the promotion of an occupational practice; this was "inconsistent with the Institute's charitable status" and this matter remained unresolved until after the correspondence of November 1999.[74] The Charity Commission suggested that the word "practice" be excised and replaced with:

> the promotion of the art and science of the management and development of people . . . for public benefit.[75]

The Deputy Clerk was quite clear on the Charity Commission's view that unless the word "practice" was removed the Commission would not support the Institute's Royal Charter "whilst retaining its charitable status", which was important to the Institute.

Interest fell upon the Institute's boast about the library and the Privy Council asked whether:

> the library be open to the public? This bears on the question of whether the Institute's activities are wholly charitable.

The Commission questioned the Institute's trading activity which in the case of a chartered body should be a subsidiary company.

The documentary evidence which might tell what happened between February 1999 and the award of the Royal Charter in 2000 is silent; however, the Institute's petition was placed in the *London Gazette* in late 1999. Even though there was a possibility that the Institute's charitable status might be in jeopardy because of the Charity Commission's objection to some of the wording in the draft documents, the episode appears to close without resolution. At this point, the Privy Council adhere closely to the characteristics of the traditional professional model completely unaware of the developments within the field of organisations. The Institute, however, pressed on with communication with members and justification for the application.

## The Institute Makes a (Premature) Announcement and a Charm Offensive

The Report for the Institute's conference for 1998 announced that the Annual Conference and Exhibition in Harrogate for 1998 might just be the Institute's last annual conference as the Institute of Personnel and Development—the last because:

> the application for a Charter had now been lodged with the Privy Council and is proceeding as expected.

It was not, however, the last conference for the Institute, as the Institute of Personnel and Development as matters trundled on while the advisers were still consulting on the draft documents which the Institute had sent.

The conference report also reported that the Institute was setting aside funds to cover the activities necessary to undertake the petition for a Royal Charter, and afterwards if the application was successful. The report of the conference also revealed that the Institute, in anticipation of a successful application for a Royal Charter, had already commissioned "design and branding experts" so that the Institute's identity would represent the new aims and objectives of a chartered professional body.

In May 1999, *Personnel Management* announced that the Institute's Council had approved "plans that could lead to the institute gaining chartered status" in 2000.[76] The article continued to outline the events and assure readers of *People Management* that they would be kept informed of the "Royal Charter process", and what a successful outcome would mean and that there would be a postal ballot in August 1999.[77]

While the Institute's petition was still the subject of consultation among the Privy Council Office and its advisers, the Director-General gave another optimistic view of the Royal Charter to members in August 1999 in the Institute's journal *People Management*.[78] This too was a piece of preparation and persuasion. In the article,[79] the Director-General looked to head off concerns about rising costs to members due to the application for the Royal Charter, and a reduction in member services. He stated that the Institute had established a fighting fund; he was less forthright about where the money had come from, presumably member subscriptions and income from the Institute's commercial enterprises.

Referring to the communication activity that the Institute was undertaking, the Director-General added:

> More importantly, I think that our members expect to be communicated with in a professional fashion—we are not some "hole in the wall" institute operating out of a back street.

On the 'eve' of the membership ballot, the Director-General explained the significance of the Royal Charter.[80] He said that it was:

> recognition that the profession has arrived—that people management and development is a coherent profession, based on a body of knowledge, understanding and competence that is capable of being defined, promoted, taught and learned, and continually developed.[81]

He looked for the occupation's place alongside other organisational functions. He spoke in terms of 'prestige' to be gained and an opportunity for practitioners to lose their felt "second class" place, and to be in the "premier league".[82] Then, according to the Director-General, there were the benefits that would accrue to the Institute itself—this would be an institute that was "an example for professional bodies in the twenty-first century".[83]

Throughout the interview for *People Management*, the Director-General highlights the desire to show to a "consuming public"[84] that "the practices were as important as other management functions". He also focuses upon the role of the Institute as a purveyor of essential services to members rather than a regulating body. On this, he specifically says:

> We are not backward looking; we are not interested in restrictive practices of demarcation lines; regulation or granting licenses to practice. We have set out to be a professional Institute that adds value to its members in the performance of their jobs, whatever stage of career they are in.[85]

This view of the reformed Institute as a professional body *without* occupational closure means that it is not acting as a professional body for a profession in the traditional model, and this is a view that is like that espoused by senior members of the Institute earlier.[86]

The appeal to contemporary discourses of the knowledge economy and competitiveness as a further justification for the charter is revealed in the appeal to the discourse of the knowledge economy and competitiveness. The Director-General says:

> As we move into the knowledge economy, it's increasingly going to be people who make the sustainable difference between winning and losing. Chartered status would recognise that and give us additional clout in making it happen.

He does not elaborate on how the Institute or its members would be able to accomplish this. However, this text does resonate with key slogans attached to various pieces of research and policy documents begun in 1994 with the *People Make the Difference* policy paper (1994) that the Institute had begun to promote at conferences.

Throughout the interview, the Director-General foregrounded the idea that:

> people management and development . . . (had) . . . equal weight to the other dimensions of management.[87]

This is a shot across the bows of those who would seek to say that the practices were not unique to this group of practitioners (as the Privy Council had wondered in the Institute's early engagement with them). The statement also justifies the petition to the Privy Council being for the *Institute* alone to receive the Charter. In this respect, the Charter would have no significant effect on practitioners, other than their occupational association being a Chartered body.

The interviewer for *People Management* asks directly about the influence a chartered IPD could bring among policymakers, to which the Director-General remarked that it would:

> be a level of recognition that the institute and its members have not previously enjoyed. It would confirm us as the only credible professional membership body focusing on the people dimensions of enterprise.

Again, and echoing earlier Institute spokespeople, the Director-General firmly links the status of practitioners among their organisations with their effectiveness, and the:

> contribution they make to continuously improving performance and to developing the potential of people.[88]

In this statement, the Director-General is aiming to strengthen claims made in 1994 about the expertise of the training and development practitioners.

The interview for *Personnel Management* concluded with the admission that the charter would not:

> catapult us into the boardroom, or into the inner circle of public policy. We are getting there already through the value of our members' contributions to organisational effectiveness and the good of society.

The 1999 interview is full of the language of the traditional professions, except for language that speaks of the occupation as being closed to non-members and regulated. In fact, the position is quite the reverse, with the idea that what is at stake here is the potential of people at work, the good of society and, in achieving this, the previously separate functions of training and development and personnel/human resource management are united. The Institute, furthermore, had been consistent in its view about what *professionalisation* would mean.

## Engaging the Membership

Before the successful petition, with carefully positioned and targeted communication to the recalcitrant membership in mailings, and through the pages of *People Management*, the Institute attempted to not only explain the benefits of the Charter but to encourage graduate members of the Institute to 'upgrade' their membership.[89] The article in *People Management* explained that not only would new corporate members secure voting rights for themselves, but also demonstrate a critical and more convincing mass of collective will to the Privy Council. The piece in *Personnel Management* in 1990 suggests a concern that some 20,000 members of the Institute[90] had not 'upgraded' their membership. The Director of Education and Membership recognised this situation as arising for a "variety of reasons".[91] She announced an "upgrading" initiative. Perhaps it was the issue of subscription cost in return for member services that were not always valued, but perhaps chief was the reality that the Institute's qualification by itself had secured the graduate member their first recognisable role in personnel/human resource management in an organisation and the employing organisation did not insist upon their employee (the Institute's member) climbing the Institute's grade hierarchy.

The upgrading initiative announced in advance of the final stages of the process to attain a Royal Charter was significant, and not just for the individual practitioner, but for the Institute as well:

> In our latest upgrading drive which involved writing to all graduate members, we highlighted the benefits of moving up to corporate level. One of the practical benefits is the higher earning potential. Survey results have shown that those at MIPD level earn up to 12.5 per cent more than their graduate counterparts.

The article continued:

> Being a full member also means that you will be able to have your say in the institute's future and the Royal Charter. We are keen that all those members who have put in a lot of work with the institute should get a vote.[92]

In an important article for *People Management*, the Director-General also explained the significance of the upgrading exercises to the Privy Council:

> But that's quite a small step. The big one is to secure the overwhelming support of members for our initial application to the Privy Council. A huge vote in favour would demonstrate that the membership is behind this application, and that would be particularly important to the Privy Council. It would also be consistent with what our members have told us.[93]

The Institute's exhortation for members to upgrade their membership to corporate full voting membership[94] is clearly important in the light of this statement—that an application would only be considered to succeed if the membership wanted it. The Director-General continued:

> We have had an endorsement from the institute's governing council, from the executive board and from individual members at branch

meetings, courses and conferences that I have attended all over the UK and Ireland. Members are constantly asking me how we are progressing.[95]

This passage appears constructed to lend weight to the endeavour and generate excitement and promise. It also conveys the sense that the Royal Charter is all but granted. The Director-General continued to talk in terms of:

> an overwhelming wish among personnel and development professionals that they should be part of a chartered body.

He relayed the story of a letter received from a former member in Australia who:

> wrote to say how pleased she was that, after more than 40 years in the profession, her institute was now in a position to make this application credibly.[96]

The interviewer in the *People Management* article asked the Director-General about the potential for members to be reluctant to join a chartered institute, to which the Director-General expounds, a view later expressed in his interview with me, that:

> The Institute would still be a broad church, with open access and a variety of "pick and mix" routes of progression to the various levels of professional standards. We would still present ourselves in a totally modern, forward-looking way—we aim to be a pathfinder for professional institutes in the 21st century. . . . I believe that we are at the leading edge of creating the 21st century, so I don't see any reason why the charter should get in the way of people wanting to belong to the institute. In fact, we want people to feel that we are a "must belong" institute, because we help people to do their jobs much better.

Here the Director-General is alluding to the professional standards and that IPD membership should be considered:

> as a criteria (sic) to recognise that the institute's standards are the standards of professionalism and excellence to which anyone in people management and development must aspire.[97]

The Director-General said he believed that "chartered status will help [. . .] in the cause".

## The Institute's Project Completed?

The obstacles that had been placed in the Institute's way did not deter the Institute or halt the endeavour. The Privy Council Office records do not show what measures the Institute set in motion to address these last concerns, but the Institute's petition was finally declared in the *London Gazette* in November 1999 and became "the subject of formal consultation within government".[98] The Institute received the Royal Charter which was awarded in the spring of 2000 and announced it to the membership through *People Management*.[99] The Royal Charter came into effect from July 2000, and the Institute became the Chartered Institute of Personnel and Development (CIPD).

The Director-General spoke rarely about the earlier dealings with the Privy Council Office; however, in an interview for *People Management* in March 2000[100] when asked about the news about the Royal Charter, he did convey a sense of the earlier difficulties:

CRABB: You must have been very relieved when you heard that the institute had got its charter.

THE DIRECTOR-GENERAL: Absolutely. It's taken us four years this time round, and then there's the time that our predecessors spent pursuing chartered status—the Institute of Personnel Management certainly applied and got knocked back, for example. So, we're really pleased that it went so smoothly this time. We had to go through a very rigorous process to satisfy the Privy Council that we are a profession, with a distinctive body of knowledge, competence and practice that underpins what we do, and that our professional standards are at the highest level.

We had to satisfy the most demanding scrutiny that you could imagine, and we came through with flying colours. That's particularly pleasing for our members; getting this charter was important to them. After all, every time we asked them what they thought, more than 99 per cent were in favour of pursuing the charter.

The interview sets a tone of satisfaction and optimism infused with the pain of the earlier attempts.

### *Act Two, Scene Two—"The Man in the Middle" Comes Out on Top and Receives a "Stamp of Quality"*[101]

With the Royal Charter won, the final scene in the Institute's charter drama, the narrative turns to the end game—the bringing of the Institute's professional project to what appears to be a complete close with the granting of Chartered status to individual members.

## The End Game(?)

Although the Privy Council Papers reflecting the awarding of chartered status to individuals begin in 2002,[102] the drama really begins in 1999. In an interview with *Personnel Management* in 1999[103] before the Institute received the Royal Charter, the Director-General had indicated to members that once a Charter had been granted the Institute would seek approval to award chartered status to individual members.

The announcement was premature, given the Privy Council's continuing concerns and the conditions placed on the Institute; however, in the interview the Director-General had explained that there was a "two-stage" process, in so far as it would be the Institute itself that would receive the Royal Charter; there would be another stage before members could be individually chartered. He added:

> You can't move straight to individual chartered status. To begin with, all of our members will be members of the Chartered Institute of Personnel and Development. Once we have some track record as a chartered body, we'd fully intend to move forward to the next stage and seek the approval of the Privy Council to grant chartered status on individual members.[104]

Although the Director-General had already made this statement to members in 1999, in November 2002, the Director-General wrote to the Clerk to the Privy Council.[105] The letter indicates that there had already been some preliminary discussions. The matter at hand was, indeed, the Institute's "plans to apply for full members to use the chartered title on an individual basis" and this time there were no solicitors to act as an intermediary.[106]

The Director-General outlined the support for the proposal among the governing body and attached the draft Byelaws which the Institute had drawn up dealing with individual chartered status. The Director-General added that those of the members who attended a recent Annual General Meeting greeted the proposal "with enthusiasm". The Director-General had outlined a proposal[107] which was that everyone who was a full member of the Institute would become a chartered member and entitled to use the designation Chartered MCIPD. Anyone else would become chartered once they met:

> the CIPD's regulations in respect of our professional standards (qualifications), experience, and continuing professional development.

Professional standards, qualifications, experience and demonstration of commitment to continuing professional development are the institutionalised characteristics of professionalism in the traditional model and indicate an association between the Institute's ability to regulate its own members, traditional professionalism and the institution of the Royal Charter.

In addition to outlining the proposal, the Director-General sought to determine whether the proposal was "likely to be acceptable to the Privy Council".[108] He looked for a positive outcome before the end of 2002 and before the Institute put the proposal out to postal vote among existing full members eligible to vote on this matter.

The Privy Council remained silent on the Institute's desire for an answer before the end of 2002.

## Change at the Privy Council

In February 2003, the *dramatis personae* had changed once again. Dealings took place by telephone between a different official at the Privy Council Office and the Institute's Secretary.[109] The Privy Council had already circulated the draft and revised Byelaws (in the Director-General's letter of 21 November 2002) to the advisers and they had commented. Although the advisers had "no objection in principle", the Privy Council's letter of 4 February[110] outlined some issues of concern to them.

These issues of concern reflect the pre-occupations of the time, particularly equal opportunities. The amended Byelaws proposed that only practitioners with a first degree in "a relevant discipline" would be admitted to chartered status; this shows how keen the Institute was to meet the conditions which they thought the Privy Council would require, because it had been such a persistent condition throughout the Institute's pursuit of the Royal Charter. The advisers had been concerned about unintended "barriers which could act against the interests of certain groups" because the Institute could set its own admission requirements in regulations which they had not seen. The writer concludes:

> Advisers would need to be reassured that the arrangements made for Chartered status includes robust safeguards for equal opportunities.[111]

This intervention is significant: by appearing to support the membership of practitioners who had experience but not a first degree, the letter reflected a slippage in the thinking of the Privy Council and of fissures opening in the traditional professional model. The traditional professions had always been gendered; however, here, and later than the first equality legislation in Britain, the Privy Council Office had woken up to the issue of equal opportunities and the recognition that the stipulation of a first degree in a relevant discipline might unintentionally disadvantage certain groups.

The Institute's Secretary responded on 7 February 2003,[112] assuring the Privy Council that the concerns "raised in your 4 February 2003 letter can be satisfied easily". She explains the Institute's longstanding practice of providing access to membership through non-academic or non-traditional routes and their focus on equal opportunities. The response conflated access and equal opportunities, saying:

> There is no requirement to hold a first degree in a "relevant discipline" in order to become a full member and therefore a Chartered member. This is not a requirement now and there is no intention to change this with the introduction of the Chartered title. We seek to make the profession as open access as possible and it is possible to qualify (i.e. meet the professional standards) through a number of routes which test both knowledge and competence.
>
> This allows individuals to chose (sic) a route which suits them and has been particularly effective in achieving a very high percentage of women in the profession. Over 80% of the people currently registered on our professional development scheme (PDS) are women.[113]

## The Institute Mobilises the Membership

In line with the occupations cast in the traditional model of professions, the Institute has a hierarchy of membership. At the time just before the successful petition to the Privy Council for a Royal Charter in 2000, student members who had undertaken part of the qualification were licentiates of the Institute.[114] On their attainment of the qualification, the member 'upgraded' to become a graduate member. Graduate membership conferred few rights, and so to become a fully vested member of the Institute, entitled to vote to alter the constitutional arrangements, the graduate needed to show through their continuing professional development (CPD) that they had an "appropriate level of management experience".[115]

Whilst the Privy Council Office was still deliberating the issue and consulting with their advisers, the Institute engaged in work of persuasion to encourage members who were not yet full, voting members of the Institute, to apply to be upgraded to full members, become eligible to vote on the issue of individual chartered status and, if the affair was successful, become chartered members. The organ of choice was the journal, *People Management*.

There had been a considerable drive to persuade graduate members to officially 'upgrade' their membership to become full (voting) members in preparation before the award of the Royal Charter and these initiatives continued after 2000.[116]

## Parallel Activity at the Privy Council

On 13 March 2003, the Privy Council Office responded.[117] The correspondence indicates that the Institute Secretary's letter had reassured the Privy Council and the advisers were satisfied with the assurances and were "content with the proposals in [the Director-General's] letter of 21st November".[118] There was one final suggestion, however, that the wording "university degree" also be followed by the words:

> or other qualification recognised by the Qualifications and Curriculum Authority or the Scottish Qualifications Authority as equivalent to a degree.

This was confirmation from the Privy Council that there was now no outstanding reason for not pursuing the application for individual Chartered status "in the expectation of a fair wind".[119]

The Institute Secretary wrote to say that this was "encouraging news",[120] but the Institute was concerned about the phrase: "or other qualification recognised [. . .] as equivalent to a degree". The Secretary said[121]:

> We fully endorse the need to ensure the widest access to the profession and will continue to ensure that there are a range of qualification and competence based/assessed routes to membership.

The reason for the concern was that the amendment which the Privy Council's advisers had suggested would cause "practical difficulties", such as redrafting other documents. The reason was the phraseology "at least at the level of a university degree" suited the international context in which the Institute's members were increasingly engaged. She continued:

> We are increasingly operating within a wider international sphere, and of course within Europe, the existing phraseology relates well to the terms of the Bologna[122] declaration.

Furthermore, the Institute Secretary declared that the Privy Council had required this wording when the Charter was granted in 2000. She added:

> Since this is relatively recent in members' minds to seek to amend it now might seem odd to them.
>
> Our current professional standards are at M level (that is, above the level of a first degree) but may be met by following a range of qualification and other routes, including many within the remit of the QCA and SQA.[123]

The Institute's Secretary wrote on 5 June 2003[124] to the Privy Council Office to make a formal request that the Privy Council agree to a new Byelaw:

> to allow the Institute to grant individual full members the right to use the Chartered title on an individual basis.

In order to reassure the Privy Council even further, the Institute's Secretary's letter outlined the range of routes to full membership "which test both knowledge and competence" and she proposed the post-nominal letters which chartered members would be able to use.[125]

The Institute's Secretary,[126] in outlining the range of routes to full membership, introduces the flexibility of the Institute's programmes in that many practitioner members combine several routes to meet the full professional standards.

The letter also proposes the post-nominal letters which chartered members could use. In parenthesis, the Institute's Secretary adds "there is no generic word for entry into full membership".

The Institute indicated that they wanted to implement the change by October 2003 for reasons relating to the collection of subscriptions.

The objections from the Charity Commission appear to have been resolved satisfactorily (although there are no papers in this bundle to confirm this).

## An Extraordinary General Meeting

As with the application for a Royal Charter, the Institute had to gain the agreement of the membership[127] and so on 4 June 2003 at an Extraordinary General Meeting (EGM) the Institute's membership approved that the Institute should seek to change the Byelaws permitting the Institute to award individual chartered membership.[128]

The editorial pages of *People Management* and general press releases announced the likelihood of individual Chartership.[129] A press release of 5 June 2003[130] announced to the general public and to members that the process to seek individual Chartered status was well underway:

> At the Extraordinary General meeting held in London yesterday, the full members of the Chartered Institute of Personnel and Development (CIPD) voted overwhelmingly in favour of making a formal application to the Privy Council to give the Institute power to permit all its full members to use the titled "Chartered".

The press release of 5 June 2003 also carried the Director-General's observation about the reasons why the Charter had been awarded in 2000—it was, he said:

> in recognition of our contribution to people management.

The result of the vote at the EGM was announced in *People Management* on 12 June 2003.[131] The vote, described as "overwhelming", represented the delivery of "an important promise—"to seek approval to award individual Chartered title".

The Director-General outlined the process which the Institute had endured, the implications for practitioners and the significance for employers. The press release reported that the:

> new Chartered status will act as a trigger to encourage an even greater commitment to continuing professional development (CPD). CPD will be a key requirement for Chartered members and the CIPD will continue to sample the development activity of members on a regular and random basis.

Furthermore, the press release continued, once the change to the Institute's Byelaws was approved by the Privy Council, full members of the Institute would be able to call themselves chartered members and use the designation "Chartered MCIPD"[132] from 1 October 2003.

*People Management*[133] carried the announcement of the award of the individual Chartered status. The award immediately affected 37,000 members out of approximately 119,000.[134]

The Director-General said in the editorial:

> The new Chartered status will show employers and other stakeholders in the workplace that a Chartered member of the CIPD is an experienced and qualified professional who is constantly updating his or her knowledge and skills and, importantly, that they can understand and contribute to the wider business environment in which they are working. . . .
>
> We want chartered membership to be the aspiration for all those who are working towards, or have met our professional standards. It will provide great advantage to both individual members and their organisations and it is an important benchmark which shows true professionalism.

These words carry reflections of the practitioner as both expert and skilled practitioner, continuing the sense of practical vocation, which many had feared lost in the over-academic curricula of the Institute in the 1970s and 1990s. The words also continue the theme of the role of the practitioner as the Business Partner,[135] an aspirational identity which continued to underpin the Institute's professional standards up to 2010.

In the Institute's Annual Report for 2002–2003 following the award of the individual Chartership, the Group Human Resources Director of Vodafone Group plc was quoted: He said:

> Now the CIPD has gained authority to confer individual status on its members, the organisational people specialists can fully achieve

credibility and consequential authority on a par with those in other individually Chartered professions.[136]

Mr Dryburgh, former Institute Vice President, writing in 1972 might have found the award of individual Chartered status to qualified practitioners a remedy to the lack of recognition from his organisational colleagues he described in *Personnel Management*:

> The competent personnel "professional" is now backed by considerable expertise, knowledge and numeracy which is frequently not recognised or used by his company.[137]

Reflecting upon the Charter events in his interview with me in 2010, the Director-General indicated that the Charter was important, but in terms of making a difference to members in terms of their standing with their employers represented by their remuneration and their influence in the organisation, it carried less weight.

The Director-General spoke of his involvement in the application for a Royal Charter as a "campaign" and described it as "an uphill battle", and the reason for that, he admitted was:

> because it isn't self-evident that personnel/HR people are a coherent profession.[138]

Those words underpin the Institute's problem in professionalisation in the traditional model because of the mongrel nature of the practices and the underpinning disciplines. The episode and indeed the Privy Council Papers indicate that with the ability of the Institute to confer individual chartered status on qualifying members the "professional project" and the professionalisation of HR as measured by comparison with the traditional model was in fact *in*complete.

## Sic Transit Gloria Mundi[139]

The Royal Charter had granted a veneer of legitimacy and status to practitioners and the practices to a point, but to all intents and purposes, it was a hollow victory. Line managers were increasingly undertaking the day-to-day tasks of applying organisational policies for managing a workforce, often unwillingly as hitherto they had been able to rely upon the practice knowledge and skill of the personnel or human resources practitioner. Practitioners, however, encouraged and persuaded by the rhetoric advancing from the United States, and in their study for the Institute qualification, were increasingly looking up the organisation for a strategic connection to find status and legitimacy. But professionalism in the traditional sense was ceasing to matter as the model of traditional professionalism was already cracked. The Institute had to look for other ways to maintain the shiny but transparent and transitory legitimacy and recognition it had won.

## Notes

1. Privy Council Papers Set 1-xxvi, 18 September 1991, the Privy Council to the Institute's Secretary, a letter in which stated that the position was "not altogether encouraging"; Privy Council Papers Set 1-xxvii, 23 September 1991, a letter from the Privy Council returning the scripts; Set I-xxviii, 27 September 1991, a letter from the Institute to the Privy Council acknowledging receipt.
2. Privy Council Papers Set I-xxxvi, 18 September 1991 ibid.
3. Privy Council Papers Set I-xv, 5 June 1991, a letter from the Deputy Clerk to the Privy Council to an official at the Department of Employment. The letter outlines how the Institute has approached the Privy Council concerning a Royal Charter. The Privy Council explains the circumstances under which charters are given that: "The body counts among its members the majority of the practitioners of a distinct profession" and "The sphere of activity of the body can be distinguished from existing chartered or other significant organisations."
4. Privy Council Papers Set I-xxix, 11 August 1993, a file note between officials at the Privy Council Office. The IPM had asked the Employment Department, the Permanent Secretary to sponsor a petition. The unknown person from DE had clearly been asked for advice and he, in turn, was asking the Privy Council Office for advice.
5. In this case, the term "gazette", means to appear in the *London Gazette*. This source is also important in uncovering the processes for Royal Charters.
6. The new Institute of Personnel and Development came into being in 1994; activity recorded in the Privy Council Papers suggests that nothing formal in relation to the Royal Charter happened for two years. This is unlikely. Chapter 2 gives an account of these events.
7. Privy Council Papers Set I-xv ibid. As late as June 1991, it is clear that the traditional model of the professions and its meaning to institutions such as the Privy Council persisted and was still dominant. Privy Council Papers Set I-xv ibid.
8. See Chapter 2; the *creation* of the Institute of Personnel and Development took place in 1994 after many abortive attempts to combine the domains of training and personnel management. See also Personnel Management (1993) "The case for combination".
9. Armstrong G (1994) "Comment: A sound foundation for the IPD". This article appeared following the successful vote in February 1994 among members of the Institute of Personnel Management and the Institute of Training and Development to create the Institute of Personnel and Development.
10. Devolution of practices to the line manager was increasing in popularity; in theory the practices created the possibility for the practitioner to become more involved with loftier matters such as organisational effectiveness and strategic issues. See Torrington D and Hall L (1998) "Letting go or holding on: The devolution of operational personnel activities". The practice was increasingly seen in the models of HRM which had come from the US; see Ulrich D (1990) *Delivering Results: A New Mandate for Human Resource Professionals*; (1997) *Human Resource Champions: The Next Agenda for Adding Value and Delivering Results* and Ulrich D and Brockbank W (2005) *The HR Value Proposition*.

11. Director-General, interview February 2010.
12. See Cogan M L (1953) "Towards a definition of profession", page 49; Wilensky H I (1964) "The professionalization of everyone?"; Hickson D J and M W Thomas (1969) "Professionalization in Britain: A preliminary measurement".
13. Larson M L (1977) *The Rise of Professionalism: A Sociological Analysis*, page 17, recognised this phenomenon as did Burrage M, Jarausch K and Siegrist H (1990) "An actor-based framework for the study of the professions".
14. Personnel Management (1993) "The case for combination".
15. Privy Council Papers Set II-vii, anonymous file note, after 14 November 1996; this indicates that "at the time of the merger the IPM had numbered some 53,000 and the ITD some 20,000, making a total membership of 70,000 when account was taken of an overlap of about 2,000"—this corroborates a view that many members of the ITD were also members of the IPM.
16. Privy Council Papers Set II-i, 16 September 1996—a solicitor's letter to the Clerk of the Privy Council. The Institute had put the matter into the hands of a solicitor. The solicitor's letter encloses an interview with the Director-General which appeared in *People Management* and explains the earlier contact with the Privy Council, but states clearly that the Institute (of Personnel and Development, IPD, an event which happened in 1994) now wanted to pursue the Royal Charter. The Institute's solicitors outline the Institute's mission:

- "To lead in the development and promotion of good practice in the field of the management and development of people, for application both by professional members and by their organisational colleagues.
- To service the professional interests of members; and
- To uphold the highest ideas in the management and development of people".

The solicitor is appealing on the grounds of the Institute's position as the only body "which services specialists in the management and development of people". The solicitor outlines the Institute's size and geographical coverage, the pre-eminence of some of its members—"Senior members of the Institute are invited to speak at international conferences and gathers, and are able to disseminate UK best practice around the world." The letter explains where the Institute's members work and ensures that the recipient of the letter understands that the Institute's standards "are at the level of a post-graduate diploma", coupled with practitioner experience. This accumulation of resource would give a member full (voting) membership. The letter discusses the importance set by the Institute of the contemporary practice (found in the traditional professions) of continuing professional development (CPD). By August 1996, the Institute had 79,000 members of whom 29,000 were full voting members, 19,000 who were graduates of the Institute working to provide the relevant CPD for full voting membership, and 31,000 associates and affiliates some of whom were "working towards meeting the standards of the Institute".

The solicitor's letter provides one of the Institute's objectives, which "is to promote the management and development of people for the public benefit". This is achieved by the qualification scheme, research, "development of professional policy, including the publication of guidance notes on best practice and the provision of library and information and legal advisory services". The letter also draws attention to the conferences and the fortnightly journal, *People Management*. Finally, the letter states how the Institute's finances are sound.

17. Privy Council Papers Set II-i, ibid.

18. Privy Council Papers Set II-i, ibid.
19. Privy Council Papers Set II-i, ibid.
20. MacLachlan R (1996) "Institute focusing on a wider role (interview with Institute of Personnel and Development Director-General, Geoff Armstrong".
21. Privy Council Papers Set II-ii, 3 October 1996, a letter from the Institute's solicitor.
22. Privy Council Papers Set II-iii, 7 October 1996, a letter from the Clerk to the Privy Council to the solicitor.
23. Privy Council Papers Set II-iv; a file note due to the sequencing of material inside the Papers received from the Privy Council, this note was dated after 21 October 1996 and it refers to a proposed meeting on 14 November 1996. Privy Council Papers Set II-v is a letter between the Institute's solicitors and the Clerk to the Privy Council confirming the arrangements and the attendees of the meeting on 14 November 1996.
24. Privy Council Papers; due to the sequencing of Papers inside the Papers received from the Privy Council, this note was dated after 21 October 1996.
25. The italics represent a handwritten amendment in the facsimile copy of the original.
26. Privy Council Papers Set II-iv ibid.
27. The Director-General admitted, albeit several years after the event, that it was not clear to him that the practices were coherent and circumscribed (interview 20 February 2010).
28. Privy Council Papers Set I-xxiii, 20 August 1991; APL is a "range of activity and approaches used formally to acknowledge and establish publicly that some reasonably substantial and significant element of learning has taken place. Such learning may have been recognised previously by an education provider, (. . .) or it may have been achieved by reflecting upon experiences outside the formal education and training systems, described for the purposes of the *Guidelines* as 'prior experiential learning', Quality Assurance Agency for Higher Education (2004).
29. Larson 1977 ibid, pages 99–115.
30. Privy Council Papers Set II-v 10 October 1996 ibid; Set II-vi 18 November 1996, a letter of thanks from the Director-General to the Clerk to the Privy Council. The letter encloses the material which the Institute had presented at the meeting on the 14 November 1996.
31. Privy Council Papers Set II-vi, 18 November 1996 ibid.
32. Privy Council Papers Set II-vii, undated and anonymous, but it was after the meeting on 14 November 1996.
33. Privy Council Papers Set II-vi, 18 November 1996 ibid.
34. Privy Council Papers Set II-vii, anonymous file note, after 14 November 1996. The file note also talks about governance and membership grades—graduate, licentiate, associate and affiliate (studying and non-studying). Associates —certificate holders and S/NVQ level 3. Licentiate—"signified that an individual has met the requirements of one or two fields of the Institute's professional standards". The file note adds: "(for example, Training and Development specialists may prefer to remain at a licentiate grade, rather than gain a wider qualification.)" Three fields (Core management, core P and D, and Generalist/specialist personnel and developments of the professional standards needed to be completed for an individual to become a graduate.
35. MacLachlan 1999 and reiterated in Crabb S (1999) "Seal of approval"; (2000) "Major league"; (2007) "Exit interview", and in interview, 20 February 2010.
36. Other senior IPM protagonists had expressed doubts about the usefulness of attaining professionalism in the sense understood by the traditional

professional model Jack Coates in Lawrence S (1979) "Man of the moment: Jack Coates", page 40 and Seears N (1979) "Can personnel managers deliver?". Both Coates and Seears were former Presidents of the Institute.

37. Privy Council Papers Set II-vii, after 14 November 1996 ibid.
38. The emphasis is in the original.
39. The Privy Council had done this before during the earlier and unsuccessful dealings between the Institute and the Privy Council between 1968 and 1996.
40. Privy Council Papers Set II-viii, 26 June 1997. This is over six months after the last correspondence from the Clerk to the Privy Council to the Institute's solicitors explaining that the consultation with the advisers is over and proposing a meeting.
41. Privy Council Papers Set I-xv, 5 June 1991 ibid.
42. The qualification had been of degree standard for some years, but this was not the only obstacle thrown in the way of the Institute.
43. Privy Council Papers Set I-xv, 5 June 1991, this letter to the advisers sets out the Privy Council's conditions for a Royal Charter awarded to a professional body.
44. Privy Council Papers Set II-viii, 29 July 1997, the Clerk to the Privy Council to the Institute's solicitors.
45. Privy Council Papers Set II-viii, 29 July 1997 ibid.
46. Privy Council Papers Set II-xi 17 February 1998. This is a letter from the Clerk to the Privy Council to the Institute's solicitors regarding the outcome of the circulation of the Institute's draft Charter and Byelaws.
47. Privy Council Papers Set II-x, 5 November 1997, a letter from the Clerk to the Privy Council to the Institute's solicitors regarding the outcome of the circulation of the draft Charter and Byelaws. Some of the advisers were still consulting.
48. Privy Council Papers Set II-xi, 17 February 1998, Privy Council Office to the Institute's solicitors.
49. Privy Council Papers Set II-xi, 17 February 1998, ibid.
50. Wilensky H I (1964) "The professionalization of everyone?"; Hickson and Thomas 1969 ibid; Brundage J A (1994) "The rise of the professional Jurist in the thirteenth century".
51. The Institution of Training Officers Limited (ITOL) became the Institute of Training and Development (ITD) in 1978. Privy Council Papers Set I-iii, 6 February 1977, Set I-iv 22, February 1977 and Set I-v, 25 February 1977.
52. Privy Council Papers Set II-xi, 17 February 1998.
53. Privy Council Papers II-xi, 17 February 1998; CIPD Enterprises operates as a subsidiary of the CIPD; it was incorporated in 1994, www.bloomberg.com/research/stocks/private/snapshot.asp?privcapId=46606268, accessed 1 February 2019.
54. Privy Council Papers Set II-vii, anonymous file note, after 14 November 1996 file note: "The library is the largest, most comprehensive collection of personnel and training and development material in Europe. Steps are being taken to make it accessible on the internet." It is also important to note that the internet was in its infancy, and what the Institute meant about accessibility referred to Institute members and not the public.
55. Privy Council Papers Set II-xi, 17 February 1998.
56. Privy Council Papers Set II-xi, ibid.
57. Privy Council Papers Set II-xi, ibid.
58. Armstrong P (1985) "Changing management control strategies: The role of competition between accountancy and other organisational professions"; (1986) "Management control strategies and inter-professional competition: The cases of accountancy and personnel management".

59. Privy Council Papers Set II-xi, 17 February 1998.
60. On introducing the Institute's 2012 Code of Conduct, an Institute President claimed that the Institute "always had a code of conduct", see Wright V (2012) "View from the CIPD: Accountable to all". This may not have been the case as a predecessor President was charged with "steering though the first ever code of professional conduct", see Lawrence 1979 ibid.
61. Privy Council Papers Set II-xii, 26 August 1998: The Byelaws among the Privy Council Office papers have been annotated with revisions to address the advisers' concerns.
62. Privy Council Papers Set II-xiii 7 September 1998; a letter from the Deputy Clerk to the Privy Council to the Institute's solicitors acknowledging receipt of the documents. The writer specifically asked for a response to particular points which had already been raised in the letter of 5 June 1998, but which was missing from the bundle.
63. Privy Council Papers Set II-xiii, 7 September 1998 ibid.
64. APL is a "range of activity and approaches used formally to acknowledge and establish publicly that some reasonably substantial and significant element of learning has taken place. Such learning may have been recognised previously by an education provider, (. . .) or it may have been achieved by reflecting upon experiences outside the formal education and training systems, described for the purposes of the *Guidelines* as 'prior experiential learning'", Quality Assurance Agency for Higher Education 2004 ibid.
65. Privy Council Papers Set II-xiii, 7 September 1998 ibid.
66. Privy Council Papers Set II-xiii, 7 September 1998 ibid.
67. Privy Council Papers Set II-xiii, 7 September 1998 ibid.
68. The phrase "management and development of people" and not "human resource management" appears to derive from the Director-General's avowed dislike of the term, despite its growing currency within organisations and within the Institute itself.
69. Privy Council Papers Set I-xv, 5 June 1991 ibid; distinctiveness and overlap with other organisational functions had appeared significant during the lead up to the creation of the combined field of people management and development as shown in "The case for combination" in the Institute's journal *Personnel Management* in 1993.
70. Privy Council Papers Set II-xiii, 7 September 1998 and Set II-xiv, 7 December 1998; a letter from the Clerk to the Privy Council to the Institute's solicitor who had followed up the petition by telephone.
71. Privy Council Papers Set II-xiv, 7 December 1998, ibid.
72. Privy Council Papers Set II-xv, 9 February 1999 in which a letter of 3 February 1999 was mentioned; this letter appears to be missing, but it could be a follow-up inquiry from the Institute's solicitors; progress was slow and modern management organisations are not used to such tardiness. The Clerk writes that the "position remains as indicated in (his) letter of 7 December (1998)", Set II-xiv ibid.
73. Privy Council Papers Set II-xii, 26 August 1998, the Institute's solicitors to the Clerk to the Privy Council.
74. Privy Council Papers Set II-xvi, letter 11 November 1999.
75. Privy Council Papers Set II-xvi, letter 11 November 1999 ibid; the wording suggested by the Charity Commission was a fudge, but the wording continues to appear in the Institute's constitution; it is a throwback to the days of traditional professionalism.
76. Williams C (1999) "Corporate ascent".
77. Williams 1999 ibid.

78. Crabb S (1999) "Seal of approval", page 42.
79. Crabb 1999 ibid.
80. Crabb 1999 ibid. Watson has already undertaken analysis of the text of this interview from the perspective of the discursive resource of "professionalism" as a topic for analysis, rather than as a social process, as analysis of "professional projects" or professionalisations tend to be, see "Speaking professionally: Occupational anxiety and discursive ingenuity among human resourcing specialists" (2002), pages 99–115.
81. Crabb 1999 ibid.
82. In this, the Director-General is particularly resonant with Dryburgh's view from 1972 (see Dryburgh G (1972) "The man in the middle"). In his interview with me in 2010, the Director-General referred to the award of the Royal Charter as the "removal of a negative".
83. Crabb 1999 ibid.
84. "consuming public" is a phrase used by Johnson T (1972) "The truth about the HR department", which aptly sums up the array of audiences there are for the professional body, its practitioner members and the practices.
85. Crabb 1999 ibid, page 42.
86. Lawrence 1979 ibid and Seears 1979 ibid.
87. Crabb 1999 ibid, page 42.
88. Crabb 1999 ibid, page 42.
89. Williams C (1999) "Corporate ascent"; Initiatives to persuade an inactive non-corporate membership to upgrade were, and continue to be, a frequent event.
90. According to the first Annual Report and Accounts following the Royal Charter (2000–2001), there was a total membership of approximately 110,000 members.
91. Williams 1999 ibid, page 1. The concern over the lack of conversion from graduate to corporate member was manifest when I attended the Branch Policy Advisers' Day, held at the CIPD's, Central London premises in October 2008, and the phenomenon is borne out by interview data from two practitioners, who commented that there was incentive from the organisation's perspective for a graduate member with the qualification to convert to being a full member.
92. Williams 1999 ibid, page 1.
93. Crabb 1999 ibid.
94. For example, Williams 1999 ibid.
95. Crabb 1999 ibid.
96. Crabb 1999 ibid. It was a little premature given the objections that the Charity Commission to whom the draft petition had been circulated now raised a matter which is discussed later Privy Council Papers II-xvi, 11 November 1999.
97. Crabb 1999 ibid, page 42.
98. Privy Council Papers Set II-xvi, letter 11 November 1999 Deputy Clerk to the Council to the Institute's solicitors, with a copy to another person in the Privy Council Office whose role is unclear. This is the letter in which the Institute learns of the Charity Commission's concerns. The Charity Commission objected to the word "practice" in the Institute's draft documents; they wanted the following wording for the objects "the promotion of the art and science of the management and development of people [. . .] for public benefit".
99. PM Editorial (2000) "Institute gets its charter".
100. Crabb S (2000) "Major league", page 52.

101. Dryburgh 1972 ibid; PM Editorial (2003) "CIPD launches individual chartered membership".
102. Privy Council Papers Set III-i, 21 November 2002. This is a letter from the Director-General to the Privy Council which enclosed proposed changes to the Charter and Byelaws.
103. Crabb 1999 ibid.
104. Crabb 1999 ibid.
105. Privy Council Papers Set III-i, 21 November 2003 ibid. There is reference to some preliminary discussions "a few weeks ago" concerning proposals for the Institute to confer chartered status on individual members. The Director-General outlines the current requirements for entry to full (voting) membership and sets the focus on Continuing Professional Development (CPD). The Director-General says he would like a response before the end of the year so that the Institute can put the proposition out to the membership for a vote.
106. Later in this short process, the Institute's Secretary took over the correspondence between the Institute and the Director-General paid tribute to her "for her sterling work" (interview, 20 February 2010).
107. Privy Council Papers Set III-i, letter 21 November 2002 ibid.
108. Privy Council Papers Set III-i, ibid.
109. Privy Council Papers Set III-ii, 4 February 2003, a letter from an official at the Privy Council to the Institute Secretary outlining the advisers' comments.
110. Privy Council Papers Set III-ii, ibid.
111. Privy Council Papers Set III-ii, ibid.
112. Privy Council Papers Set III-iii The date on the letter is 7 January 2003, but it may be an error as the letter explicitly states that it is responding to a letter of 4 February 2003. The Institute's Secretary is responding to the questions posed in the previous letter.
113. Privy Council Papers Set III-iii ibid. This observation by the Institute's Secretary says more about the gendered nature of the occupation than illuminates the Privy Council's question.
114. For an account of the membership grades, see Appendix I, Privy Council Papers Set II-vii, Undated but after 14 November 1996, ibid.
115. Williams 1999 ibid; the application for a Charter itself had to demonstrate the agreement of the corporate members, and therefore, the proportion of the Institute's full members who could vote on the proposals and agree to the petition was important to the enterprise. Not only did the Institute's Memorandum and Articles of Association need full members to agree, but the Privy Council decision-making processes needed this condition. An official at the Privy Council Office had written to the Department of Employment concerning the Institute's application and had outlined some general requirements; Privy Council Papers Set I-v, 5 June 1991.
116. PM Editorial (2003) "Upgrade campaign is on".
117. Privy Council Papers Set III-iv, 13 March 2003, a letter from the Clerk to the Privy Council to the Institute Secretary.
118. Privy Council Papers Set III-iv, letter 13 March 2003 ibid.
119. Privy Council Papers Set III-iv, ibid.
120. Privy Council Papers Set III-v, 18 March 2003, a letter from the Institute's Secretary to the Clerk to the Privy Council. There are copies to the Director-General and the Director of Membership and Education.
121. Privy Council Papers Set III-v, 18 March 2003 ibid.
122. The Bologna declaration, a product of the Bologna Process whose objectives include member states to adopt a "common framework of readable and comparable degrees" (European Commission 1999, page 4).

123. QCA, Qualifications and Curriculum Authority; SQA, Scottish Qualifications Authority.
124. Privy Council Papers Set III-vi, 5 June 2003 ibid.
125. Licentiate, Chartered Member and Chartered Fellow, terms which were in use until the introduction of new Professional Standards in 2010. In her letter of 5 June 2003, Privy Council Papers Set III-vi ibid, the Institute's Secretary added in parenthesis "there is no generic word for entry into full membership".
126. Privy Council Papers Set III-vi, 5 June 2003; the Institute Secretary states:
    "As part of our open access arrangements we offer associate and licentiate membership to those who have completed the professional standards in part. This is thus inclusive of those who do not wish to study for the full qualification and provides a stepping-stone for entry into full membership."
127. PM Editorial (2003) "Vote for individual chartered status", 3 April; "Status of affairs", 1 May 2003a.
128. Privy Council Papers Set III-vi, 5 June 2003, a letter from the Institute Secretary to the Clerk to the Privy Council "to formally request the Privy Council to agree to a new byelaw to allow the Institute to grant individual full members the right to use the chartered titled on an individual basis". In the same letter, the Institute's Secretary referred to the EGM which had taken place the day before and said: "98.9% of those voting were in favour", adding that it was "an overwhelming indication of support" and "significantly more than the 75% required by the byelaws".
129. PM Editorial 2003a ibid; (2003b) "Individual status gets 'yes' vote"; (2003c) "Upgrade campaign is on"; (2003d) "Privy council backs new title".
130. CIPD Press Office (2003) "CIPD members vote "yes" to individual chartered status". The press release of 5 June 2003 also carried a comment by the Director-General in which he gave the reasons for which the Charter had been awarded in 2000—it was, he said: "In recognition of our contribution to people management."
131. PM Editorial 2003b ibid. The Privy Council Office papers conclude showing the Schedule with effect from 8 July 2003 amending the Byelaws, Privy Council Papers Set III-vii, 8 July 2003, an amendment to the Byelaw granting the Institute the power to confer chartered status on individual members.
132. M is "Member" of the Institute and was the grade that graduates (licentiates) of the Institute achieved after 'upgrading'.
133. PM Editorial (2003e) "CIPD launches individual chartered membership".
134. CIPD Annual Report 2002–2003 (CIPD).
135. Ulrich 1997 ibid.
136. CIPD Annual Report 2002–2003, page 3.
137. Dryburgh 1972 ibid.
138. Director-General interview 20 February 2010.
139. A phrase used in papal coronation ceremonies which is taken to mean that earthly things pass away. It is considered to be borrowed from Thomas à Kempis, *The Imitation of Christ*: "O quam cito transit gloria mundi."

## Bibliography

Abbott A (1988) *The System of Professions*, Chicago: University of Chicago Press.
Andrews T M and Waerness K (2011) "Deprofessionalization of a female occupation: Challenges for the sociology of professions", *Current Sociology* 59(1): 42–58.

Armstrong G (1994) "Comment: A sound foundation for the IPD", *Personnel Management* 26(7): 20.

Armstrong P (1985) "Changing management control strategies: The role of competition between accountancy and other organisational professions", *Accounting, Organizations and Society* 10(2): 129–148.

Armstrong P (1986) "Management control strategies and inter-professional competition: The cases of accountancy and personnel management", in D Knights and H Willmott (eds) *Managing the Labour Process*, Aldershot: Gower.

Brewster C and Hegewisch A (eds) (2017) *Policy and Practice in European Human Resource Management: The Price Waterhouse Cranfield Survey.* London: Taylor & Francis.

Brundage J A (1994) "The rise of the professional Jurist in the thirteenth century", *Syracuse Journal of Law and Commerce* 20: 185, Spring.

Burrage M, Jarausch K and Siegrist H (1990) "An Actor-based framework for the study of the professions", in M Burrage and R Torstendahl (eds) *Professions in Theory and History: Rethinking the Study of the Professions*, London: Sage Publications.

Carr-Saunders A M and Wilson P A (1933) *The Professions*, Oxford: Clarendon Press.

Chartered Institute of Personnel and Development (2003) *Annual Report 2002–2003.*

CIPD Press Office (2003) *CIPD Members Vote "Yes" to Individual Chartered Status*, Press release 5 June, www.cipd.co.uk/pressoffice/_articles/05062003083008.htm?IsSrchRes=1—accessed 24 November 2010.

Cogan M L (1953) "Towards a definition of profession", *Harvard Educational Review* 23: 33–50, Winter.

Crabb S (1999) "Seal of approval", *People Management* 5(16): 42, 19 August.

Crabb S (2000) "Major league", *People Management* 6(5): 52, 2 March.

Crabb S (2007) "Exit interview", *People Management* 13(9): 24–28, 3 May.

Dryburgh G (1972) "The man in the middle", *Personnel Management* 4(5): 3, May.

Finegold D and Soskice D W (1988) "The failure of training in Britain: Analysis and prescription", *Oxford Review of Economic Policy* 4(3): 21–53.

Hickson D J and Thomas M W (1969) "Professionalization in Britain: A preliminary measurement", *Sociology* 3: 37–53.

King D S (1993) "The conservatives and training policy 1979–1992: From a tripartite to a neoliberal regime", *Political Studies* XLI: 214–235.

Larson M S (1977) *The Rise of Professionalism: A Sociological Analysis*, London and Berkeley: University of California Press, pages 99–115.

Lawrence S (1979) "Man of the moment: Jack Coates", *Personnel Management* 11(10): 36–40.

Macdonald K M (1985) "Social closure and occupational registration", *Sociology* 19(4): 541–556.

MacLachlan R (1996) "Institute focusing on a wider role (interview with Institute of Personnel and Development Director-General, Geoff Armstrong", *People Management*, 27 June 1996.

Mazza C and Strandgaard Pedersen J (2015) "Good reading makes good action: Nothing so practical as a managerial panacea?" in A Örtenblad (ed) *Handbook* of *Research on Management Ideas and Panaceas: Adaptation and Context*, Cheltenham: Edward Elgar, Chapter 19, page 349.

Millerson G (1964) *The Qualifying Association: A Study in Professionalization*, London: Routledge.

Niven M M (1967) *Personnel Management 1913–1963: The Growth of Personnel Management and the Development of the Institute*, London: Institute of Personnel Management.

Örtenblad A (ed) (2015) *Handbook of Research on Management Ideas and Panaceas: Adaptation and Context*, Cheltenham: Edward Elgar Publishing.

Parsons T (1939) "The professions and social structure", *Social Forces*: 457–467, May.

Personnel Management (1993) "The case for combination", *Personnel Management* 25(12): 26–32.

Pitfield M (1979) "Practical and professional a new look for the IPM's education programme", *Personnel Management*: 42–45, December.

PM Editorial (2000) "Institute gets its charter", *People Management* 6(4): 13, 17 February

PM Editorial (2003a) "Status of Affairs", *People Management* 9(9): 49, 1 May.

PM Editorial (2003b) "Individual status gets 'yes' vote", 9(12): 7, 12 June.

PM Editorial (2003c) "Upgrade campaign is on", *People Management* 9(13): 62, 26 June.

PM Editorial (2003d) "Privy council backs new title", *People Management* 9(15): 7, 24 July.

PM Editorial (2003e) "CIPD launches individual chartered membership", *People Management* 9, 1 October, online only.

The Quality Assurance Agency for Higher Education (2004) *Guidelines on the Accreditation of Prior Learning*, www.qaa.ac.uk/docs/qaa/quality-code/accreditation-prior-learning-guidelines.pdf?sfvrsn=edadf981_12, accessed 6 November 2018.

Seears N (1979) "Can personnel managers deliver?" *Personnel Management* 11(10).

Sharpe P H (1979) "WANTED: A professional organisation for human resources managers", *Industrial and Commercial Training* 11(6): 230–232.

Torrington D and Hall L (1998) "Letting go or holding on: The devolution of operational personnel activities", *Human Resource Management Journal* 8(1): 41–55.

Ulrich D (ed) (1990) *Delivering Results: A New Mandate for Human Resource Professionals*, Boston, MA: Harvard Business School Press.

Ulrich D (1997) *Human Resource Champions: The Next Agenda for Adding Value and Delivering Results*, Boston, MA: Harvard Business School Press.

Ulrich D and Brockbank W (2005) *The HR Value Proposition*, Boston, MA: Harvard Business School Press.

Watson T J (2002) "Speaking professionally: Occupational anxiety and discursive ingenuity among human resourcing specialists", in M Dent and S Whitehead (eds) *Managing Professional Identities: Knowledge, Performativity and the "New Professional"*, London: Routledge, Chapter 6, pages 99–115.

Wilensky H I (1964) "The professionalization of everyone?" *American Journal of Sociology* 70(2): 137–158.

Williams C (1999) "Corporate ascent", *People Management* 5(8): 1–2.

Williams C (2003) "How to . . . be a chartered CIPD member", *People Management* 9(20): 52–53, 8 October.

Wright V (2012) *View from the CIPD: Accountable to All*, http://blog.peoplemanagement.co.uk/2012/04/view-from-the-cipd-accountable-to-all/#more-983, accessed 25 April 2012.

# 4  Beyond the Institute's Royal Charter

After the long search for a Royal Charter for status and legitimacy, Mr Dryburgh, "the man in the middle",[1] had triumphed after over thirty years of trying. However, by the time that the practitioner's star reached its zenith, the game had changed.

Whether through realism about the prospects of personnel/human resource management as a *profession*, or a search for legitimacy, it is within the final phase of the Institute's Charter drama that the personnel/human resource management practitioner begins to re-form from professional in the traditional model to a businessperson. It was the context of neo-liberal thinking which made this possible, as the practitioner became responsible for self-making and becoming self-made.[2] The Institute choreographed this re-formation in a series of revisions to the curriculum and professional standards in which the Institute delineated the practices and behaviours which constituted a professional practice.

The traditional professional model had occupational control at its heart; however, with the privileging of management and organisation, the organisation had been emerging as a site of practice for the expert professional.[3] Some expert professionals whose professional body already exercised *de jure* regulatory occupational control found themselves having to negotiate the tensions between managerialism and professionalism. However, the Institute never had succeeded in achieving *de jure* control, despite the Royal Charter, and therefore any occupational control continued to be difficult. It was an age-old problem. A claim to be the voice for all practitioners in the field of personnel/human resource management, "a distinct profession",[4] could only be achieved if the legitimacy won by the Royal Charter was maintained and extended in the context of the organisation, where the practitioner exercised their knowledge. A project of a different order was required to maintain that legitimacy which the Royal Charter might have conferred, and in this later phase, the Institute clung to that legitimacy by clinging on to the malleable surfaces of the traditional professional model. Instead of occupational closure through state regulation, de jure, the "license to practice", the Institute exercised a different form of occupational control through the qualifications and membership hierarchy and created a market for a certain kind of labour. Therefore, this later phase demonstrates a search for occupation control and occupational legitimacy through achieving certain attributes of organisation, that is, the way in which the Institute organised itself in terms of its structure, the offering to members and the conduct of its affairs through the relationships with other influential actors, most significantly, knowledge and practice expertise, and attention to the public good. These embody the three anchors of the traditional professional model—organisation, knowledge and values (see Appendix II).

The Institute, as a body representing the practitioner as an expert professional, used the knowledge and values derived from the traditional professional model as organising principles. Instead of being an organiser of members and practitioners, the Institute began to move away from the production and regulation of regular member practitioners towards closer relationships with other key agents with the resources to confer legitimacy. The relationship between the practitioner and their organisational seniors, or other agents with a willingness to confer legitimacy, became overtly important to successful practice, even though this had long been the case. The practitioner's ability to adapt the delivery of practice and contribution to the organisational context became essential to success.

This chapter begins with the Director-General's reflections upon his time in office and on the achievement of the Royal Charter. This is a precursor to what happened next in the equally significant period following his retirement when the Institute appointed a new Chief Executive and the Institute needed to keep practices relevant to the changing needs of organisations under the human resource management discourses.

## Reflections on the Award of the Royal Charter

In March 2007, after fifteen years, the Director-General of the Institute announced his intention to step down. In the Institute's journal, *People Management*, he reflected upon his time in office and spoke of the objectives he had set for the Institute. The first objective was:

> to create an institute that adds distinctive value at every stage of a member's career, and which provides a body of knowledge on people management and development that both members and their colleagues in other disciplines can and do use.[5]

The second of the Director-General's objectives was to argue that the practices that the Institute claimed belonged to its sphere of influence were indeed underpinned by academic rigour, and were strategic necessities for organisations making a strategic contribution to organisational performance. The Institute also had to represent the business case for the practices:

> We set out a long time ago to make that business case and substantiate it with hard, measurable evidence. Our task was to show how people management and development makes a difference in the real world, in real time, in real organisations—it's not mere serendipity or a set of fads and fancies.

Both these objectives indicate how the conception of the Institute remained one that still looked like a "qualifying association"[6] found in the traditional model of professionalism. However, the professional model had been fragmenting for some while under the weight of social change and altered collective values and expectations. Political ideology had created a productive medium for a different conception of the worker, the employee and the practitioner. The Director-General's third objective bears these ideas out: to establish the occupation as a source of authority to which organisational leaders and members could turn and know that personnel/human resource management practitioners could add "distinctive value" to the organisation:

> This profession is only good to the extent that it can help other managers of people to do their job better. . . . You can have the best knowledge of HR in the world, but if you can't put it to use in your organisation, you are wasting your time.[7]

This shows the increasing orientation of the occupation towards the delivery of performance and service to other organisational professionals through the application of expert knowledge in prescribed modes of behaviour.

The Institute made several adjustments between 2000 and 2007 to the qualification schemes whilst the Director-General was still in post.[8] The earlier schemes tended to be aimed at practitioners in more junior positions in organisations, but the new schemes were aimed at practitioners with aspirations to becoming part of their organisation's management cadre.[9] The schemes of 2000 and 2005 built on this and were explicitly set at postgraduate level. They were, according to the Director of Membership and Education, "at a significantly higher standard than before".[10]

The new qualification schemes marked a turn to emphasise knowledge, which the practitioner demonstrates through the competent behaviour underpinned by an expert application of knowledge. This, in turn, set in train the building of a practitioner who could deliver business benefits as a strategic contributor to organisational performance. In this role, there was much more overt orientation towards 'human resource management' rather than traditional 'personnel management'.

After 2003, on the attainment of this qualification, a member was able to submit their evidence of Continuing Professional Development (CPD) for admission to chartered membership. Here, the Institute retained a role as a "qualifying organisation" being responsible for both the production of practitioners and the regulation of membership of the "profession" and the professional body.[11]

The practitioner 'professional' was to be a "Thinking Performer" who was:

> an HR professional who applies a critically thoughtful approach to their job so as to make a contribution to the survival, profitability, vision and strategic goals.[12]

The "Thinking Performer" displayed competencies of Business Orientation, Application Capability, Knowledge, Understanding and Persuasion and Presentation Skills.[13]

The scheme supported an aspirational vision for the practitioner's role. The practitioner should aspire to become a "business partner".[14] This role borrowed extensively from an influential conception of the role of HR practitioners originating in the US.[15] Business partners were "knowledgeable and competent managers in their own right".[16]

The Thinking Performer competencies underpinned the Institute's *Leadership and Management* standards of 2005 in which there was a delineated set of practices as means to ends that were meaningful to the organisation and its managers, and which could be performed by someone with status and influence within their organisation. This orientation steered the practitioner away from practice mired in the people-oriented role through which employing organisations and the public had seen the practitioner for most of the twentieth century.[17] In contrast, this role was explicitly integral to and integrated with the business and its management and far away from the understanding of the public, line managers and employees which became the justification for the revision to the standards.[18]

This was a conception of the practitioner that some commentators on personnel management[19] had always seen with the practices. But few practitioners held roles with organisational seniority and concern for strategic issues, who were also able to make a strategic contribution to the organisation. In reality, the importance of sound practices for the management and development of employees had tended to be overlooked, becoming swamped in administrative detail.

The schemes of 2000 and 2005 placed the focus upon the aspirational role of the business partner[20] and continued the turn towards the practitioner as a manager rather than a "specialist professional" which had begun with schemes of the early 1990s. This is how the practitioner would demonstrate their utility, worth and the value of their contribution to the organisation through the practices. There was the desired association between organisational performance outcomes and the presence of human resource management practices, and this had been a focus for much of the HR research from the 1990s—to look for the HRM-Performance link.[21] Such an association would lay to rest once and for all any notions that the function and the practices were unimportant and irrelevant. There was much at stake in this research.

In 2004, the Institute's Director of Membership and Education asserted that enhanced enactment of practices by a qualified practitioner contributed to "successful performance"[22] and became the way in which organisations could manage the human factor of production and the employment relationship. The practitioner ensured sensible enactment of HR policies and practices. By structuring the qualifications post-Royal Charter in this way, the Institute retained an association with the traditional practitioner role as "the man in the middle"[23] and the production of good managers, a matter which had been of concern in the dealings with the Privy Council Office.[24] The aspirational role remained the business partner,[25] which by 2007 the Institute defined in this way:

> The "business partner" role represents a model to which CIPD professionals should aspire. In the future, roles will not exist for people who are not able to add value to the business objectives of the organisations for which they work.[26]

This appears like a threat to the rank and file practitioner implying a further diminution in the status of a role which had often been perceived to be of low status.[27] There was little acknowledgement of two of the other roles of Employee Champion or Administrative Experts which appear in the Ulrich model.[28] These were throwbacks to the past and not part of the march towards status. The professional qualifying schemes post-Charter supported the practitioner as "Thinking Performer", business partner and expert.

The Royal Charter had achieved many things for the Institute, as the Director-General[29] acknowledged, but it had not completed the "social" or occupational closure that commentators thought they had observed in the early years after the award of the Royal Charter.[30] This was because although the qualifications and full membership of the Institute in its capacity as a "qualifying association" were desirable, neither were mandatory for practitioners to hold a position in the field. There were no state requirements for the Institute to regulate the practitioner. The Institute, however, retained the appearances of the "qualifying association",[31] whose model the Institute had assiduously cultivated because it had been important to winning the Royal Charter. The "professional project",[32] such as it had been, was one of both continuity with the traditional professional model and change towards the Institute's agenda; this state was present after the Charter but was to grow stronger in influence after the Director-General stepped down.

## A New Leader and the Institute Turns Towards the Market

After the retirement in 2007 of the Director-General who had been instrumental in winning the Royal Charter for the Institute, the Institute employed a Chief Executive,[33] who had worked for a major international organisation in the food and drink sector. Human resource management was the terminology being increasingly used, and the new Chief Executive described human resource management as an "applied business discipline".[34]

Instead of relying on the Royal Charter as a badge of professionalism to maintain its project of legitimacy, as her predecessor had conceived it, the Institute's new Chief Executive began to strengthen links with a different set of actors who would lend legitimacy to the Institute's endeavours and remake the practitioner as the complete expert and specialist in human resource management.

In the Annual Report for the first year of her tenure, the Chief Executive spoke of the role of the Institute as a body that would:

> support organisations in delivering sustained organisational performance through HR.

The Institute would provide:

> HR professionals with the tools, skills and thought leadership[35] to do this in their own organisations.[36]

The Institute would support organisations through HR practitioners rather than support members in their organisations and in their careers. The body of knowledge appeared to be withdrawing from "theory" and becoming a set of "tools" and "skills". The notion of "thought leadership" suggests planting a stake in the ground of innovation and development for organisations.

### Organisation and Building Bridges

Not long after taking up her position, the new Chief Executive headed the Institute's acquisition of a consultancy firm, the Bridge Partnership.[37] The Institute made the announcement in *People Management* in 2009 and referred to the need for the Institute to acquire "capability". In contrast with the position in 1994 when the Institute combined with the

Institute of Training and Development, there was little sense of "capability" through the strength and quality of the Institute's membership. Instead, the acquisition appeared to indicate that there was not the capability inside the Institute to undertake the next stage of inscribing the professional standards and qualifications; this had to be acquired from elsewhere. The audience for this was not ordinary members of the Institute, but the most senior members of the HR occupation, people who did have power and influence in organisations.

This tactic of building "capability" uses language increasingly used in connection with the strategic decisions of many organisations, and also represents a subtle shift in the focus of the Institute away from the regular members and towards a member and organisational elite.

### Backlash

The Institute announced the acquisition of the Bridge Partnership to the members in an article in *People Management*[38] which coincidently happened to announce a major review of the occupation and the practices; this was the *Next Generation HR Project* which the Bridge Partnership had already begun.

A former senior Institute employee, writing in a subsequent article for *People Management*,[39] expressed his surprise at the acquisition of Bridge. Claiming to speak on behalf of "long-standing members", whose views would, he claimed, "have ranged from bafflement to confusion and some genuine concern", the former Institute employee articulates two problems: first, problems of integration were likely because of the Institute's lack of experience in these matters. Here, the former employee chose not to acknowledge the events around the "creation" of the IPD in 1994.[40] Second, and more damning for a membership organisation, he made the point that the Institute had no mandate from the membership. The Institute who had so attentively courted the membership in the lead up to the award of the Royal Charter had not, on this occasion, consulted the membership.

In a rebuttal,[41] the new Chief Executive justified the acquisition on the grounds that the *Next Generation* HR[42] project being undertaken by the Bridge Partnership was:

> the largest and most penetrating market research [. . .] ever undertaken into the needs of the HR profession.

She strongly denied his inference about "aggressively growing a consultancy business", "compromising independence", and assured her readership that any surplus funds would "be ploughed back into funding services for members and keeping membership fees low". The Chief

Executive's concluding remarks in this reply again illustrate the shift away from the regular member who would never attain senior positions, and towards the organisational elite. She said:

> In all we've done, we'll be judged on the success we have in meeting the needs of senior HR professionals.

In the exchange, the Chief Executive said that the Institute had recognised that there was a section of the membership, namely senior practitioners, who were "under-served" by the Institute and this would be rectified. The Institute was concerned that it did not serve senior members properly[43] but the scale of the activities to address this indicates the scale of the shift. To achieve greater profile among senior practitioners, the Institute turned its attention once again to the qualifications, the body of knowledge and the second anchor of the traditional professional model.

## Knowledge, an Anchor of the Traditional Professional Model—Next Generation HR and the HR Profession Map

To further and maintain any legitimacy gained by the Royal Charter, the focus of the Institute now turned to *build* links with, and a reputation among, senior practitioners and this began with the *Next Generation HR Project* which had begun under the direction of the *Bridge Partnership*. *Next Generation HR* was an important project which delineated the next phase of professional standards and practice development.[44]

The director of the *Bridge Partnership*, who were undertaking the work, was a frequent speaker from the Conference platforms, such as the Annual Conference and Exhibition for 2009, in Manchester and in practitioner journals.[45] He often reiterated warnings of the dire prospects for the HR function because senior managers were not asking the right questions about:

> how HR needs to evolve in the light of the seismic challenges organisations face particularly following the global financial crisis.[46]

The prospects, he claimed, remained gloomy without *Next Generation HR* which presented:

> a dynamic picture of how the people function is evolving—and of how its most accomplished practitioners distinctively contribute to their organisations.[47]

The *Next Generation HR* research project which began in 2009 examined the "changing nature of HR and some of the best and emergent practice".[48] It was, as one senior informant claimed, a project to find out from senior practitioners: "What good HR looks like"[49] (Institute interviewee). *Next Generation HR* was also future-focused as the researchers were looking for "debate" as to what those developments in HR might be "over the next five to ten years". This was a debate over the "implications [. . .] *for business* and for the development of the Next Generation of HR leaders".[50]

The methods the research employed included interviews and focus groups with respondents from within and external to the occupation, across organisational hierarchies in both the UK public and private sectors. The first output from the research resulted in questions and statements which indicated a further change to the priorities and focus for the Institute. In particular, the output questioned whether the HR function had "asked itself enough questions in light of the seismic shocks to our global economy", whether the function was "equipped to become a truly *insight-driven* function". There was further urgency around building new "HR partnerships to deliver this agenda" and "the need for courage, pioneering leadership and a new language".[51] The second report issued in 2011 called for HR to be "insight-driven". The language and sentiment of both these reports are fixed in the HR Profession Map.[52]

The second anchor of the traditional professional model—*knowledge* —is linked to the *organisation* of the occupation. It is connected to how the profession regulates and admits its members and guards the knowledge domain by encapsulating it within qualifications by which aspirant practitioners are judged. As noted earlier, the knowledge base and the qualification schemes were important to the Privy Council to demonstrate the Institute's *professional* credentials and thereby its worthiness to receive a Royal Charter. In this post-Charter phase when the Institute was settling into a project of a different order, the qualification schemes began to exhibit the requirements for the aspirant practitioner to have expertise in practice as well as expert knowledge. This was achieved through the *Next Generation HR project* and the resulting *HR Profession Map*[53] which became a set of professional standards.

## The HR Profession Map

The principles set out in the *Next Generation HR Project* formed the basis of the next phase of the Institute's qualification programme which was underpinned by the *HR Profession Map*. It marked a further shift of focus for the practitioner whose practice and impact came from knowledge *and* behavioural competencies, which were designed to deliver impact and the aims of the *Next Generation HR project*. This was to become the second anchor of the traditional professional model. *Knowledge* is linked to the *organisation* of the occupation because it connects how the profession regulates and admits its members and guards the knowledge domain by encapsulating it within qualifications by which aspirant practitioners are judged. The knowledge base and the qualification schemes were important to the Privy Council to demonstrate the Institute's *professional* credentials and thereby its worthiness to receive a Royal Charter. In this post-Charter phase when the Institute was settling into a project of a different order, the qualification schemes began to exhibit the requirements for the aspirant practitioner to have expertise in practice as well as expert knowledge. As indicated previously, this was achieved through the *Next Generation HR project* and the resulting *HR Profession Map* as a set of professional standards.

The Institute had reviewed its education schemes, qualifications and professional standards on a number of occasions since the first qualification frameworks were introduced in 1955. A major overhaul occurred in 1979/1980[54] and again around the time of the Charter in 2000, with some adjustments taking place between 2002 and 2008. By this time, the practices found under human resource management had settled, and the qualifications began to display signs of a different focus for the practitioner: a set of business-oriented competencies and a renewed focus upon general business knowledge. The new competencies and focus underpinned the traditional skills and the 'tools of the trade' acquired through programmed knowledge of practices within task areas of HRM, such as performance management, learning and development, employee relations and remuneration.

This apparent foresight and adaptability on the part of the Institute might suggest that the occupation's members were well placed to succeed in the organisations employing them, especially with the Charter as a sign of legitimacy and recognition. The opposite, however, appears to have been the case as some commentators[55] continued to rail against the purposelessness and futility of the personnel/human resource management practices. The *Next Generation HR project* had been an attempt to address these concerns as the Institute and senior practitioners in large organisations contributed to the project.[56]

The HR Profession Map was an attempt to delineate the areas of practice within the field of human resource management *and* to set standards of behaviour. It also described the seniority of different practitioners based upon the level of contribution they were making inside their organisations. The Map was represented and accessible on the CIPD website in an interactive fashion and was also downloadable in Portable Document Format (pdf). It became the foundation for the education and qualification scheme which the higher education sector offered if the Institute had approved that Institute's provision to practitioners and aspiring practitioners.

When a computer mouse or other pointing device hovers over any of the areas of the HR Profession Map, the segment expands to reveal a description. As an example, the core of the HR Profession Map, *Strategy*

*Insights and Solutions/Leading HR*, expands to reveal text that reinforces several key points about the new Professional Standards to the user: for example, that they understand that the ten professional areas are universal areas of practice "regardless of role, location or stage of career". Further information explains that a "successful" practitioner:

> develops actionable insights and solutions prioritised and tailored around a deep understanding of business, contextual and organisational understanding.[57]

The text continues in similar mode reminding the practitioner that the "profession" is "an applied business discipline" providing "sustainable organisational performance" to the organisation, through "situational HR solutions that stick".

The four *Bands* on the HR Profession Map represent "professional competence that defines the contribution" any practitioner makes in a particular role. The contribution may be made in respect of relationships, the focus of the activities, how and where the practitioner spends their time and how they are measured by their employer. In this way, it is clear to the practitioner where they fit in within the membership hierarchy and the hierarchy within their employing organisations.

The *HR Profession Map* also prescribes what the practitioner must do to demonstrate impact sufficiently to be operating at Band Two, which is the Band at which someone could apply to become a chartered member.

Using the activity *Developing Actionable Insight a*s an illustration, for a practitioner member to apply to upgrade to chartered member, they would need to demonstrate, through CPD, that they had used "insight" to identify "opportunities, priorities and potential risks", developed "shared insights" with others, and:

> raise(d) risks . . . that may affect the long-term reputation of the organisation.

The *HR Profession Map* marks a particular shift away from the practitioner using knowledge in their work to a set of competencies based on "organisational insight", whose "ingredients" include the indeterminate competencies of "business savvy, organisational savvy, and contextual savvy". However, it is notable that the Map frequently draws upon the terms "profession" and "professional" to legitimise its claims as to what constitutes expertise and competence in personnel/human resource management.

The overall impression arising from the *HR Profession Map*, upon which so much capital, effort and financial, rests is a strategy to promote a message that all practitioners should strive for *HR Leadership* roles, without acknowledgement of the reality that none but a few would be able to attain this during a working life. The focus was assuredly upon the creation of the practitioner as a businessperson and organisational professional.

The *HR Profession Map* drove the Institute's educational programmes and professional standards from 2010 and became part of the Code of Professional Conduct to which I will come shortly. It also presented an opportunity for stretching the CIPD 'brand', for that was what it had become beyond Britain—it was potentially exportable, itself becoming a marketable commodity.

## Organisation and Expectations Abroad

At one time, one of the most influential functions at the Institute was the Membership and Education Department. This function was responsible for defining the qualification, curriculum and professional standards which had demonstrated the close link between the members' level of education *and* the traditional professional model.[58] After 2008, however, under the Chief Executive's purview, the Membership and Education Department became the *Marketing* and Membership Department. According to the Director of Marketing and Membership, the name change was not deliberate but a co-incidence of staffing and concern for the integration of the Marketing and Membership departments.[59] The Institute was functioning as a conventional organisation in a market system, with a brand and an offering which could be exported in furtherance of organisational goals.

### The Global Reach and the HR Profession 'Mappa Mundi'[60]

The new HR Profession map arising from the *Next Generation HR* project was a flagship offering and enshrined what was contemporary thinking about professional practice and HR work. HR practice and HR work were gaining universality, with assumptions about the applicability of practice in all contexts. The HR Profession Map attracted that universality and there was some ambition to extend its reach further than the boundaries of Britain.

The Institute has always had links with countries overseas and also with organisations representing professional associations worldwide, such as the European Personnel Management Association (EAPM) and the World Federation of Personnel Management Associations (WFPMA).[61]

At the 2010 Annual Conference and Exhibition in Manchester there appeared to be an increase in overseas delegates (participant-as-researcher observer). A special area had been set aside for them for "meeting and greeting" hosted by CIPD staff from Headquarters. The increased presence of overseas visitors was due to the cancellation of the EAPM conference in the spring of 2010, when air travel had been significantly disrupted by the ash cloud from the Icelandic volcano, Eyjafjallajökull. That may have been a contributory factor; however, the Marketing and Membership Director when discussing the Institute's expatriate membership and the need to service practitioners working in international businesses said that it was important for any organisation to have a:

> more global perspective, so developing an international perspective is a kind of "must have" for us.

The Marketing and Membership Director said that recent surveys indicated that there was a sizeable group of members who had some international responsibility whether they were based in the UK or overseas. This was why it was important for the Institute to be presented with an "international perspective". She added that it was a " 'no brainer' really . . . so the question is what we want to do beyond these shores".[62]

She spoke of looking for opportunities in the Gulf, and areas of South East Asia, which she attributed directly to the acquisition of the *Bridge Partnership* which was based in Australia. Unprompted, she continued:

> there's quite a bit of activity but from a membership perspective, I think what ideally we'd like to do is establish our standards as a global benchmark.

The Marketing and Membership Director acknowledged that a number of countries had their own professional bodies,[63] against whom the Institute would not want to go "head to head", adding:

> so, it is about, how can we work in collaboration with them, given that probably in a lot of instances CIPD has got more resources and also things to offer than perhaps they have locally.

As an interpreter of these statements, it is important to acknowledge that the utterances are the opinions of the speaker. The Marketing and Membership Director may have become swept up in the possibilities in this particular interview; it appears that the Institute was certainly planning to see how the CIPD offering might be exported and was particularly interested in opening up new markets, particularly for the *HR Profession Map*. This suggests a tendency for the Institute to behave less as a member and "qualifying association",[64] and more like a commercial enterprise.

When asked for a view of how the *HR Profession Map* (or the HR Profession *Mappa Mundi*, the centre of the Institute's universe) would 'travel', and whether the underpinning knowledge requirements, apart from law, would be similar, the Marketing and Membership Director said that the HR Profession Map had been tested:

> with people who did have international roles and some people who were overseas, and we think that broadly it works, but we do accept that there is probably going to need a bit of localisation as we kind of work with specific countries, so I would say that probably 80–85% of it is translatable.

The Marketing and Membership Director did acknowledge that the cost of membership for overseas membership, particularly in developing countries, would be an issue, but in any event, it was potentially going to be an issue in the UK too. She spoke of the "proposition" for members in the UK:

> How do we charge for it, how do we bring people in, and how do we keep them in membership once they're in membership?

When asked about the potential for a meeting of minds with overseas professional bodies concerning common standards for practitioners, the Membership and Marketing Director added:

> I think there is potentially an appetite for that . . . there are a lot of standards around the world, and . . . probably people who would like their standard to be the standard . . . just like we would like our standards to be [the standard].

The Membership and Marketing Director indicated the Institute's awareness of the tendency of many students not to remain members and rise through the membership hierarchy.[65] She pondered:

> What will be attractive to them and encourage them to retain their membership once they've completed the qualifications and sort of add value back to them?

In this way, the interview was full of marketing language—offering ("how do we price it"), proposition, "choice" and segmentation:

> it's about how do we offer choice [. . .] we've had one size fits all, you pay the fees, you get the same services as everybody else and you know that's kind of it, but we've got 135,000 members and they don't all have the same set of needs.

The *HR Profession Map* and the contributory research from *Next Generation HR* project are illustrative of the changing focus of the Institute, away from the regular members as aspirant professionals. It illustrates how the Institute remained a quasi-"qualifying association",[66] however, whilst simultaneously taking account of its potentially growing market-place, and of the need to rely upon other significant agents to confer legitimacy to the practices and to itself, beyond what might have been achieved by the Royal Charter. This story concerns both continuity and change.

## The Third Anchor of Professionalism—Values

The traditional professional model had the veneer of selflessness, of altruism and of public service.[67] The consumers of the professional's offering expect conduct of the highest standard, integrity and probity. These are the logics and principles underpinning professionalism. This is one of the reasons why professions have a regulatory role so that not only can the members of a profession produce their own future members of the required standard and control the knowledge and practice, they can also regulate and discipline.[68] Therefore, there is a license to practice and a code of practice or disciplinary code.

The Institute's Code of Professional Conduct appeared to have become much more prominent following the award of the Royal Charter, and in particular from 2003 when members could apply to upgrade to become individually chartered through evidencing their continuing professional development (CPD). The requirement for a code of professional conduct is in keeping with the expectations for the Privy Council of a traditional profession, as shown in the correspondence between the Institute and the Privy Council Office.[69]

The conjunction between the member, chartered status, professional standards, conduct and the traditional professional model is clear; the Annual Report for 2003–04 shows this:

> Chartered status is much more than just a badge. It is a signal to others of the independently verified skills and experiences that its holders have accumulated, the rigorous Professional Standards they meet, and of the commitment of each of these members to continuing professional development and a code of professional conduct.[70]

Although the creation of a Code of Conduct had been part of the strategy to meet the requirements for a Royal Charter,[71] its revisions in the post-Charter period retained an association with both the expectations under the Charter, and therefore the traditional professional model but linked it more firmly with the changing professional standards and qualifications, in other words, both organisation and knowledge. In the autumn of 2008 the new Chief Executive undertook a tour of the CIPD branches to introduce herself and set out the developments for the Institute and in particular the expectations for the *Next Generation HR Project*. It was in Manchester, on 16 September 2008, at the Branch Meeting of the Institute where the Chief Executive signalled the closure of the "professional project"[72] as those who had conceived it originally might have desired. In outlining the Institute's plans, the Chief Executive expressed her doubts about the Code of Professional Conduct that had been part of the Royal Charter award. It was, she said, "too grey", that is to say, neither black nor white and open to too much interpretation.[73] There never was any legal requirement for the members to adhere to the Code because there was no occupational closure by law, de jure, no license to practice.[74] Furthermore, any 'disbarred' members would still be able to continue to hold their jobs at their organisation's discretion, and so enforcement was and remains difficult. It needed revision according to the CEO. The lightweight and "grey" effect of the Code was a manifestation of the practitioner's precarious status and power due to the 'ambiguity' in the role.[75] The Institute had sought to eliminate such ambiguity by adhering to the surface edges of the traditional professional model through the pursuit of the Royal Charter, but the nature and site of the practices meant that this was not achieved.

The standards of professional conduct in the revised Code of Conduct for 2008 focused on the Institute's reputation, had an imperative for members to improve their, and others' performance by continuous professional development (CPD). In terms of their role within any context, the focus for the practitioner was on the business, not the worker, except where the law gave the worker rights.[76]

The public interest was served by a reminder that this is linked to the "pursuit of its objects" found in the Charter and Byelaws which includes the wording:

> The promotion of the art and science of the management and development of people for public benefit.[77]

This is also an echo from the original draft petition for the Royal Charter.[78]

### Regulatory and Disciplinary Matters— The Code of Conduct

Through its post-Charter iterations, the Code has reflected the standards of behaviour found in the qualification schemes, and particularly in the *HR Profession Map*. The revised Code of Professional conduct and disciplinary procedures that were in effect (CIPD 2008c) outlined the process and a range of penalties. The ultimate sanction was the call for the member to resign from the Institute. There were disciplinary processes to judge cases brought under the Code and related disciplinary procedures, but the crux of the issue remains that there are limitations due to the nature and site of the practices, and the degree of autonomy that practitioners really have.

Once the Chief Executive had announced the review of the Code of Professional Conduct in September 2008, the Institute, through its website and *People Management*, attempted to reach the community participants through a CIPD group on the social media site *LinkedIn*. An Institute employee asked the permission of the group manager to post an announcement about member consultation on the Code so that she could reach group participants, as representative of the membership.

The tenor of the community discussion appeared to centre on the support that the Institute appeared *not* to offer for those who, having acted ethically at work or in accordance with the Code of Conduct, found themselves in conflict with their employers. This is a perennial problem for the practitioner, deriving from the tension between the practices and the site of practice. On the community discussion, there was also concern about what sanctions would be applied, to which the CIPD insider responded:

> A panel of HR professionals will hear complaints where there is a case, and if breaches of the Code are proven, levy sanctions—including expulsion from the CIPD where they feel this is appropriate.
> (CIPD LinkedIn group discussion—accessed
> 2 August 2011)

This LinkedIn exchange both highlights the nature of the practitioner and member as a professional and yet illustrates the extent to which the Institute still attempts to regulate the occupation and its practitioners. The question remains, however, as to the extent to which the Code is for the protection of the public, or to protect the reputation and legitimacy of the Institute itself and present an appropriate image to interested parties such as the Privy Council.

Although the Institute's codes of professional conduct represent adherence to the anchor of *values* as would be seen in the traditional professional model, this anchor is ephemeral but has succeeded in enfolding the other anchors of organisation and values with it.

### Public Policy

Public policy work addresses the public good ethos of traditional professionalism indicated through the *values* anchor. Much of the public policy work that the Institute effected resulted in communication and publications for general consumption and to those in power, the government.

The Institute always had an interest in public policy, particularly where public policy met organisations, employees, management and the employee relationship. The Director-General as early as 2001 had argued the need for the Institute to be active in the public arena, through having:

> an influence on governments and to do that we need, not only to adopt a high profile but to be as substantial a representative body as possible.[79]

In addition to enhancing professional standards as a way of maintaining legitimacy, from the Chief Executive's appointment in 2008, the Institute placed an even greater focus upon involvement in the public policy arena. The Institute stepped up its forays into the public policy arena, activity which, in the guise of a public good, could also increase legitimacy and the status of the Institute itself within a marketplace for the purveyors of qualifications and expertise.[80]

From 2008 onwards, the Institute's publication activity from 2008 increased through a range of regular publications which were then promoted to a wider audience by press release. The Institute also employed a team of policy advisers whose role was to seek access to ministers and politicians.[81] This move is a further signal that the Institute was moving further away from the rank and file membership and towards a more societal elite, because therein lay legitimacy maintained.

In 2008, the Institute published *Public Policy Agenda*[82] which posited the Institute's view of topics that straddled the boundary between organisational practice and public policy. Whilst outside the period of this project, it is important to establish that work in this arena continues and is spoken of as "engaging with ministers and other policymakers".[83]

Senior policy advisers and the Institute's Chief Economist (who later became Director of Policy) began to appear frequently before Parliamentary Select Committees, and, as the Annual Report for 2008–09 declared:

> secured tremendous profile for the CIPD as the authoritative voice on the labour market, implications of the recession both in the media and the corridors of power.[84]

This Annual Report recounts how the Institute appeared as a witness to House of Commons Committees on "pay and reward, labour market and diversity issues", and provided evidence to the Fair Access to the Professions Inquiry.[85] The Annual Report for 2008–09 also claimed that the increased work in the public policy arena had meant that members of the public policy team were often found on flagship television and radio programmes.[86]

## The Closure of the Institute's Professional Project

When measured against the attributes found in the traditional professional model, as far as the Institute had organised its affairs accordingly, there had been a "professional project".[87] Key Institute figures had appeared realistic as to the prospects for and desirability of professionalisation as measured by full occupational or "social closure". This would be the outcome of a traditional "professional project".[88] Any lingering desires for the occupation to be 'licensed' and regulated, however, were firmly extinguished shortly after the appointment of the new Chief Executive. At the CIPD Branch meeting in Manchester on 16 September 2008, the Chief Executive addressed the audience. During a question and answer session, one audience member asked:

> Do you envisage a time when membership is a license to practice?

The answer was an emphatic but realistic "No," without further explanation.[89]

It was difficult to tell whether the statement arose because of the realistic recognition that the practitioner's site of work and nature of the practices, as part of *management*, as the original founders had hoped, would make this impossible, or whether there was an explicit desire on the Chief Executive's part to move the organisation away from the past, and the Institute's status as a quasi-"qualifying association". However, the statement finally closed the door upon occupational control through self-regulation and the license to practice.

Despite this, the Institute had undertaken a number of strategies to progress the organisation as a significant actor bedded within society; this would confer recognition and hoped-for maintained legitimacy following the award of the Royal Charter. The Royal Charter was achieved by adhering to the traditional professional model, as a quasi-"qualifying association",[90] even though that model of professionalism appeared to be fragmenting. The model is recognisable by the way in which the Institute continued to organise around the features of the traditional professional model.

At the time the Institute won the Royal Charter, however, there were distinct signs of the Institute's project being one of traditional professionalism leading to occupational closure and a project of legitimacy; the two projects co-existed. Once the Director-General had stepped down, and the Chief Executive had been appointed as successor and CEO, the Institute consolidated its project of legitimacy by utilising the strategies and anchors of the traditional professional model.

*Organisation* concerned creating explicit links with significant and influential agents, which signifies a loosening of the link between the Institute and its regular members. Occupational control is through promoting the *knowledge and practice expertise*, because of which, a different kind of practitioner emerged. This meant that the Institute exercised a form of occupational control through facilitating the professional image and orientation of the practitioner. The *values* orientation also serves as a mechanism for occupational control, but the public good is realised through the Institute's employees (not necessarily its membership) contributing to public policy.

The Institute's evolving professional project indicates some vestigial links with the model of traditional professionalism—the three anchors of the traditional professional model—*collective organisation, knowledge and values*. There is both change and continuity. Thus, *organisation* relates to changed relationships and strategies to build influence; *knowledge* becomes evidenced as expert practice; and *values* link back to the traditional professional model and occupational control of the regular members.

The *HR Profession Map* also marks the transition of the Institute to a state in which regular members, which may include students, are assumed to be able to take on *HR leadership* roles in their organisations.

These strategies although deriving from the three anchors of the traditional model of professionalism—organisation, knowledge and values—also indicate a teetering on the brink of moving from a "qualifying association" to a type of organisation whose main objective is self-perpetuation and legitimacy by meeting societal norms and expectations through influence and behaving as a conventional organisation. This was achieved by all the while retaining the support of a constituency of members through the providing of member services and most importantly the qualifications.[91]

## Notes

1. Dryburgh G (1972) "The man in the middle".
2. Bröckling U (2015) *The Entrepreneurial Self: Fabricating a New Type of Subject.*
3. Reed M I (1996) "Expert power and control in late modernity: An empirical review and theoretical synthesis".
4. Privy Council Papers, Set I-xv, 5 June 1991the Clerk to the Privy Council to an official at the Department of Employment.
5. Crabb S (2007) "Exit interview".
6. Millerson G (1964) *The Qualifying Association: A Study in Professionalization.*
7. Crabb 2007 ibid.
8. Qualification schemes were important in the traditional professional model and remained so for the Institute as both indicators and carriers of the Institute's body of knowledge.
9. Pitfield M (1979) "Practical and professional: A new look for the IPM's education programme".
10. Whittaker J (2004) "Standards deliver".
11. Millerson 1964 ibid; "two pillars of professionalization", Faulconbridge J R and Muzio D (2012) "Professions in a globalizing world: Towards a transnational sociology of the professions".
12. Whittaker 2004 ibid.
13. The behaviours were couched in the mnemonic 'BACKUP', Johns E (Ted) (2004) *Examination Report—Professional Development Scheme—Managing*

*People*; CIPD 2007 BACKUP appears in the professional standards document, CIPD (2007) *Professional Standards*.

14. Ulrich D (1997) *Human Resource Champions: The Next Agenda for Adding Value and Delivering Results*.
15. Ulrich 1997 ibid.
16. Whittaker 2004 ibid.
17. A former Chief Examiner for the Institute described the original practice of personnel management as "muck and metals" (interview).
18. The Institute may have been influenced by the focus placed by government on the perceived gap in leadership and management in the UK, and therefore the work done by the Council for Excellence in Management and Leadership (CEML) between 2000 and 2002 and a further review of the UK National Occupational Standards in Management in 2004. CEML was established in 2000 by Department of Education and Employment and the Department of Trade and Industry. It reported upon a wide range of leadership practices in high performing organisations, making a "direct link between leadership capability and sustained high performance" (Foreword, Heyward T (2002) *Leadership Development*).
19. Clarke V M (1949) *New Times, New Methods and New Men*; Barber D (1971); (1979) *The Practice of Personnel Management*.
20. Ulrich 1997 ibid.
21. This was research began firstly in the US, and which British universities, often supported by the Institute, had also attempted to replicate. For the original links, see for example Pfeffer J (1994) *Competitive Advantage Through People: Unleashing the Power of the Workforce*; (1998) *The Human Equation*; MacDuffie J P (1995) "Human resource bundles and manufacturing performance: Organizational logic and flexible production systems in the world auto industry"; for the UK, see Patterson M G, West M A, Lawthom R and Nickell S (1997) "Impact of people management practices on business performance"; Purcell J (2003) *Understanding the People and Performance Link: Unlocking the Black Box*.
22. Whittaker 2004 ibid.
23. Dryburgh 1972 ibid.
24. Privy Council Papers Set I-xxii, 29 July 1991.
25. Ulrich 19997 ibid.
26. CIPD 2007 ibid.
27. See for example, Legge K and Exley M (1975) "Authority, ambiguity and adaptation: The personnel specialists' dilemma"; Legge K (1978) *Power, Innovation and Problem Solving in Personnel Management*; (1987) "Women in personnel management: Uphill climb or downhill slide"; (1988) "Personnel management in recession and recovery: A comparative analysis of what the surveys say", and Watson T J (1976) "The professionalization process: A critical note"; (1977) *The Personnel Managers: A Study in the Sociology of Work and Employment*; (2002a) "Professions and professionalism: Should we jump off the Bandwagon, better to study where it is going?"; (2002b) "Speaking professionally: Occupational anxiety and discursive ingenuity among human resourcing specialists".
28. Ulrich 1997 ibid; the fourth role was that of Change Agent which was perhaps the ultimate senior practitioner though which could have conferred power and status within organisations.
29. Armstrong G (2000) "The smarter charter"; Crabb S (1999) "Seal of approval"; (2000) "Major league"; 2007 ibid.
30. Gilmore S and Williams S (2007) "Conceptualising the 'Personnel Professional': A critical analysis of the chartered institute of personnel and

development's professional qualification scheme", see also Gold and Bratton 2003.

31. Millerson 1964 ibid.

32. Larson M S (1977) *The Rise of Professionalism: A Sociological Analysis.*

33. On her appointment in July 2008, the change of name for the top job at the Institute from Director-General to Chief Executive appeared to further signal a move away from the Institute's past towards a future state which reflected the logic of the market, corporatism and managerialism. The change of title is interesting and represents a shift from the bureaucratised, administrative personnel function, to the upwardly mobile and corporatised senior worker. The title was common in many organisations; however, it is striking that the title appeared in a professional body, with a membership and service ethos cast in the model of the traditional profession. The Chief Executive's arrival at the Institute also coincided with the global economic crisis that began in 2007–08. In the same way, as the Director-General had needed to take a firm grasp of the Institute's organisation and finances, the Chief Executive had to make similar choices. The Institute retrenched and reviewed its core activities in order to look for cost savings.

34. An address to the Manchester branch of the CIPD, 16 September 2008, participant as observer.

35. The term 'thought leadership' is attributed to Joel Kurtzman, editor-in-chief of *Strategy and Business* magazine in 1994. It has most recently been discussed by R A Prince and B Rogers (2012 and 2013) and is used by organisations such as Oxford Economics who describe themselves as "world leader in global quantitative analysis and evidence-based thought leadership" (Oxford Economics 2012) and features in in a *Forbes* article "What is a thought leader?"

36. CIPD (2009a) *Annual Report and Accounts 2008–2009*, page 1.

37. MacLachlan R (2009) "A 'generational change' for the HR profession". This article appeared in *People Management* and as well as talking about the research into *Next Generation HR*, announced the acquisition of the Bridge Partnership.

38. The members were notified through the pages of *People Management* (2009, page 7). The Bridge Partnership and its director Lee Seers had worked with the Chief Executive when she was Chief Personnel Officer at PepsiCo. The Bridge Partnership was acquired by the CIPD. Public notification arose in October of 2009, but not before the Bridge Partnership had been engaged on the Next Generation HR Project.

39. Brown D (2009) "Letters—a bridge-building strategy?"

40. Chapter 2 discusses this event and the precursor struggles which eventually led to the creation of the IPD in 1994 from the Institute of Personnel Management (IPD) and the Institute of Training and Development (ITD).

41. Orme J (2009) "Responding to Brown' letters—a bridge-building strategy?"

42. The outcomes of the *Next Generation HR* project formed the basis of the next revision to the knowledge and professional standards.

43. This was not, however, a new concern, as a former Institute President in 1985 had been concerned with serving the needs of senior practitioners and bringing them into membership; see Crichton A (1985) "Man of the moment—John Crosby".

44. CIPD 2009a ibid; This important project resulted in the cartography of the practitioner on the *HR Profession Map* which outlined both the body of knowledge and established behavioural competencies which appear like a basket of aspirational virtues.

45. Seers L (2009a) "Beware of outdated leadership development" page 9; (2009b) "Comment: From partners to players".
46. Seers 2009a and 2009b ibid; Seers quoted in *Personnel Today* 12 February 2013. This was not the first time that dire warnings for the prospects for the occupation had occurred; see Mackay L (1987a) "Personnel: Changes disguising decline?"; (1987b) "The future—With consultants".
47. MacLachlan 2009 ibid, page 6.
48. Seers 2010 ibid, page 2.
49. The Membership and Marketing Director interviewed in August 2010.
50. Seers 2010 ibid, emphasis added.
51. CIPD (2011) *Next Generation HR: Insight Driven*, pages 22–24.
52. CIPD (2009b) *The CIPD's HR Profession Map*.
53. CIPD 2009b ibid.
54. See Pitfield 1979 ibid.
55. See Hammond K H (19 December 2007) *Why We Hate HR* and Johnson L (2008) *The Truth About the HR Department*, in particular.
56. CIPD 2009 ibid; the research appeared to take on the assumption that there was such a thing as *HR leadership*. The research also laid the foundations for the *HR Profession Map*, the next phase of the Institute's Professional Standards.
57. CIPD 2009 ibid.
58. See Privy Council Papers Set I-xv, 5 June 1991, discussed in Chapter Two.
59. The Director of Marketing and Membership about the reasoning behind the name change claimed that the name change was not deliberate but concerned the co-incidence of: "individuals and people leaving (the Institute) at that point in time" (interview, 3 August 2010).
60. The Mappa Mundi is a thirteenth century manuscript, housed at Hereford Cathedral in Britain. It depicts a geographic, natural, historic and spiritual map of the world as known and understood by scholars at that time; https://www.herefordcathedral.org/mappa-mundi (accessed 4 September 2019).
61. The Director-General was President of the WFPMA during his time in office and there have also been significant links between the Institute and the Society for Human Resource Management (SHRM) in the United States. The Director-General contributed to an SHRM volume edited by Losey M, Meisinger S R and Ulrich D in 2006, *The Future of Human Resource Management: 64 Thought Leaders Explore the Critical HR Issues of Today and Tomorrow*.
62. Membership and Marketing Director, interview 3 August 2010.
63. For a relevant account see Farndale E and Brewster C (2005) "In search of legitimacy: Personnel management associations worldwide".
64. Millerson 1964 ibid.
65. This was borne out by a student and senior practitioner in local government in interview 24 May 2010 and interview 13 May 2010 respectively.
66. Millerson 1964 ibid.
67. There are a number of examples throughout the literature, and here are two; one from the twentieth century and the other from the twenty-first. "The profession, serving the vital needs of man, considers its first ethical imperative to be altruistic service to the client", Cogan M L (1953) "Towards a definition of profession"; Craig 2006 ibid: "keep us healthy and safe every day".
68. Faulconbridge and Muzio 2012 ibid called this the "two pillars of professionalization, the regulation of the production of producers and the regulation of the production by producers".

69. Privy Council Papers Set II-xi, 17 February 1998, a letter from the Clerk at the Privy Council to the Institute's solicitors: "Can you say how your clients would propose to regulate disciplinary matters?"
70. CIPD Annual Report 2003–04, page 4.
71. Lawrence S (1979) "Man of the moment: Jack Coates".
72. Larson 1977 ibid.
73. I attended this meeting and heard the statement.
74. Macdonald K M (1985) "Social closure and occupational registration". Macdonald discusses social closure in two way, *de jure*, in which the professional body retains a register of licensed practitioners on behalf of the state, and *de facto*, when the occupation has organised itself in such a way as to ensure closure as a reality. This is what happened with the Institute in relation to the power of the qualification which employing organisations require in an employee in HR.
75. Ambiguity noted by scholars such as Legge and Exley 1975 ibid and Legge 1978 ibid, and the "man-in-the-middle", observed most memorably by Dryburgh 1972 ibid.
76. For example: "[4.1.4] (Members) must within their own or any client organisation and in whatever capacity they are working, seek to adopt in the most appropriate way, the most appropriate people management processes and structures to enable the organisation to best achieve its present and future objectives" (CIPD Code of Conduct 2008, page 2).
77. CIPD Code of Conduct 2008, page 1.
78. Privy Council Papers, Set II-xii, 26 August 1998, a letter from the Institute's solicitors to the previous Clerk to the Privy Council.
79. The Director-General in *HR* Magazine 2001; activity in the public policy sphere also relates to the public service ethos found in the traditional professional model, see Millerson 1964 ibid; Hickson and Thomas 1969 ibid.
80. The most notable publications were in the *Outlook* and *Impact* series. For example, the House of Commons Work and Pensions Committee (2009) used evidence from the *Labour Market Outlook series* (CIPD 2005) concerning the Institute's survey about attitudes to the employment of people with long-term sickness records (House of Commons Work and Pensions Committee 2009, page 46). The same report from the Work and Pension Committee (2009, page 46) also acknowledged that the Trades Union Congress had used the Institute's *Labour Market Outlook* (CIPD 2005) in their evidence.
81. Historically, as part of the Institute's organisation of members, one of the roles that volunteer members could perform was that of Branch Policy Adviser. The Institute had always taken part in government consultations on forthcoming legislation, and the Branch Policy Adviser's role was to collect the view and opinions of branch members to send to Headquarters. In October 2008 delegates on a Branch Policy Adviser Day at the CIPD Headquarters in London were introduced to the Policy Team from headquarters (participant-as-observer). Their roles, it was said, were to get close to Westminster. There were reservations among the delegates; one seasoned Branch Policy Adviser wondered what the point was, therefore, of the branch role.
82. CIPD (2008a) *Public Policy Agenda*.
83. CIPD (2013b) *Policy Engagement*.
84. CIPD (2009) *Annual Report and Accounts 2008–2009*, page 12.
85. Cabinet Office (2009b) *Panel on Fair Access to the Professions Announced— New Opportunities White Paper*.
86. CIPD Annual report 2008–09, page 13; for an example of this, see Chapter One.
87. Larson 1977 ibid.

88. Seears N (1979) "Can personnel managers deliver?"; Coates in Lawrence 1979 ibid, and the Director-General in Crabb 1999, 2000 and 2007 ibid; Gilmore and Williams 2007 ibid.
89. I was present at the event of 16 September 2008 and heard this statement.
90. Millerson 1964 ibid.
91. This was the "professional project" noted by Gilmore and Williams 2007 ibid, who concluded that the Institute had been "rather successful" in closing the occupation off—it is extremely difficult to gain a position within the HR field in Britain without having the qualification or studying for the qualification; once the qualification is achieved, organisations are not particularly interested in whether the qualified employee rises through the Institute's member hierarchy, that is, provides evidence of continuing professional development to achieve Chartered status. The onus for achieving this overt stamp of professionalism is the individual practitioner. See Macdonald 1985 ibid.

## Bibliography

Armstrong G (2000) "The smarter charter", *People Management* 6(14): 54.

Barber D (1971); (1979) *The Practice of Personnel Management*, London: Institute of Personnel Management.

Bröckling U (2015) *The Entrepreneurial Self: Fabricating a New Type of Subject*, London: Sage Publications.

Brown D (2009) "Letters—a bridge-building strategy?" *Personnel Management* 15(23): 16, 5 November.

Cabinet Office (2009) *New Opportunities White Paper*, www.hmg.gov.uk/media/9102/NewOpportunities.pdf, accessed 14 January 2009.

CIPD (2007) *Professional Standards*, www.cipd.co.uk/NR/rdonlyres/3BF07636-4E9A-4BDB-8916-95CC94F72EC9/0/profstands.pdf.

CIPD (2009a) *Annual Report and Accounts 2008–2009*, London: CIPD.

CIPD (2009b) *The CIPD's HR Profession Map*, www.cipd.co.uk/hr-profession-map/default.htm, accessed 28 October 2009.

CIPD (2011) *Next Generation HR: Insight Driven*, CIPD, available at http://www.cipd.co.uk/binaries/Insight%20driven%20next%20gen.pdf

CIPD (2013) *Policy Engagement*. http://www.cipd.co.uk/publicpolicy/policy-engagement/default.aspx, webpage 29 June 2013.

CIPD Annual Report (2003–4) www.cipd.co.uk/about/who-we-are/annual-report.

Clarke V M (1949) *New Times, New Methods and New Men*, London: George Allen and Unwin Ltd.

Cogan M L (1953) "Towards a definition of profession", *Harvard Educational Review* 23: 33–50, Winter.

Crabb S (1999) "Seal of approval", *People Management* 5(16): 42, 19 August.

Crabb S (2000) "Major league", *People Management* 6(5): 52, 2 March.

Crabb S (2007) "Exit interview", *People Management* 13(9): 24–28, 3 May.

Craig J (ed) (2006) *Production Values, Futures for Professionalism*, London: Demos.

Crichton A (1985) "Man of the moment—John Crosby", *Personnel Management*: 28, October.

Dryburgh G (1972) "The man in the middle", *Personnel Management* 4(5): 3, May.

Farndale E and Brewster C (2005) "In search of legitimacy: Personnel management associations worldwide", *Human Resource Management Journal* 15(3): 33–48.

Faulconbridge J R and Muzio D (2012) "Professions in a globalizing world: Towards a transnational sociology of the professions", *International Sociology* 27(1): 136–152.

Gilmore S and Williams S (2007) "Conceptualising the 'Personnel Professional': A critical analysis of the chartered institute of personnel and development's professional qualification scheme", *Personnel Review* 36(3): 398–414.

Hammond K H (2007) "Why we hate HR", *FastCompany*, 19 December, www.fastcompany.com/magazine/97/open_hr.htl#, accessed 7 October 2009.

Hickson D J and Thomas M W (1969) "Professionalization in Britain: A preliminary measurement", *Sociology* 3: 37–53.

Heyward, T 2002 in K James and J Burgoyne (eds) *Leadership Development*, London: The Council for Excellent in Management and Leadership, CEML

Johns E (Ted) (2004) *Examination Report—Professional Development Scheme—Managing People*, CIPD, www.cipd.co.uk/NR/rdonlyres/F88DCBCF-26BA-4302-BA8D-EE9D4456B025/0/pqsmanpeoplr.pdf, accessed 31 May 2013.

Johnson L (2008) "The truth about the HR department", *FT.com*, http://wwww.ft.com/cms/0/ec6f81e6-ce89-11dc-877a-000077b07658.html, accessed 7 October 2009.

Larson M S (1977) *The Rise of Professionalism: A Sociological Analysis*, London and Berkeley: University of California Press, pages 99–115.

Lawrence S (1979) "Man of the moment: Jack Coates", *Personnel Management* 11(10): 36–40.

Legge K (1978) *Power, Innovation and Problem-Solving in Personnel Management*, Maidenhead: McGraw Hill.

Legge K (1987) "Women in personnel management: Uphill climb or downhill slide", in A Spencer and D B L Podmore (eds) *In a Man's World: Essays on Women in Male Dominated Professions*, London: Tavistock Publications.

Legge K (1988) "Personnel management in recession and recovery: A comparative analysis of what the surveys say", *Personnel Review* 17(2).

Legge K and Exley M (1975) "Authority, ambiguity and adaptation: The personnel specialists' dilemma", *Industrial Relations Journal* 6(3): 51–65.

Losey M, Meisinger S R and Ulrich D (2006) (eds) *The Future of Human Resource Management: 64 Thought Leaders Explore the Critical HR Issues of Today and Tomorrow*, Society for Human Resource Management, Alexandria, VA: John Wiley and Sons, Inc.

Macdonald K M (1985) "Social closure and occupational registration", *Sociology* 19(4): 541–556.

MacDuffie J P (1995) "Human resource bundles and manufacturing performance: Organizational logic and flexible production systems in the world auto industry", *Industrial and Labor Relations Review* 48(2): 197–221.

Mackay L (1987a) "Personnel: Changes disguising decline?" *Personnel Review* 16(5): 3–11.

Mackay L (1987b) "The future—with consultants", *Personnel Review* 16(4): 3–9.

MacLachlan R (2009) "A 'generational change' for the HR profession", *People Management*: 6–7, 19 November.

Millerson G (1964) *The Qualifying Association: A Study in Professionalization*, London: Routledge.

Orme J (2009) "Responding to Brown' letters—a bridge-building strategy?" *Personnel Management* 15(23): 16, 5 November.

Patterson M G, West M A, Lawthom R and Nickell S (1997) "Impact of people management practices on business performance", in *Issues in People Management*, London: Institute of Personnel Management.

Pfeffer J (1994) *Competitive Advantage Through People: Unleashing the Power of the Workforce*, Boston, MA: Harvard Business School Press.

Pfeffer J (1998) *The Human Equation*, Boston, MA: Harvard Business School Press.

Pitfield M (1979) "Practical and professional: A new look for the IPM's education programme", *Personnel Management*: 42–45, December.

Purcell J (2003) *Understanding the People and Performance Link: Unlocking the Black Box*, London: CIPD.

Reed M I (1996) "Expert power and control in late modernity: An empirical review and theoretical synthesis", *Organization Studies* 17(4): 573–597.

Seears N (1979) "Can personnel managers deliver?" *Personnel Management* 11(10).

Seers L (2009a) "Beware of outdated leadership development", *People Management* 15(1): 9.

Seers L (2009b) "Comment: From partners to players", *People Management*: 8, 19 November.

Ulrich D (1997) *Human Resource Champions: The Next Agenda for Adding Value and Delivering Results*, Boston, MA: Harvard Business School Press.

Watson T J (1976) "The professionalization process: A critical note", *The Sociological Review* 24(3): 599–608.

Watson T J (1977) *The Personnel Managers: A Study in the Sociology of Work and Employment*, London: Routledge and Kegan Paul.

Watson T J (2002a) "Professions and professionalism: Should we jump off the Bandwagon, better to study where it is going?" *International Studies of Management and Organisation* 32(2): 93–105.

Watson T J (2002b) "Speaking professionally: Occupational anxiety and discursive ingenuity among human resourcing specialists", in M Dent and S Whitehead (eds) *Managing Professional Identities: Knowledge, Performativity and the "New Professional"*, London: Routledge, Chapter 6, pages 99–115.

Whittaker J (2004) "Standards deliver", *People Management*, 30 June, online, www.cipd.co.uk/pm/peoplemanagement/b/weblog/archive/2013/01/29/standardsdeliver-2004-06.aspx.

# Part 3

# The Long Shadows of Professionalism

The title of this book, *The Professionalisation of Human Resource Management*, does assume that HR practitioners have become "professionals", but the title also begs the question of what that means to the Institute and to the HR practitioner in the twentieth century. Over the last few chapters, I have accounted for the Institute's pursuit of a Royal Charter by reference to the "professional project"[1] and the traditional model of the professions. In this concluding chapter, therefore, I want to bring several threads together by reviewing the milestones of the interactions between the actors within and between the institutions of the Royal Charter and the Institute, and other actors whose involvement and interaction are evidence. I want to answer the questions as to whether there was a "professional project" and what happened to it. This discussion inevitably leads to an assessment of the current state of the traditional model of professionalism, its substance and symbolism. Over the years with shifting sands relating to workplace and workforce development, the fragmenting traditional professional model and the vagaries of organisational life within both the Institute (and the Privy Council Office), this last chapter offers some thoughts about the past and emerging role of the Institute.

## Note

1. Gold J and Bratton J (2003) "The dynamics of professionalization: Whither the HRM profession?"; Gilmore S and Williams S (2003) *Constructing the HR Professional: A Critical Analysis of the Chartered Institute of Personnel and Development's "Professional Project"*; (2007) "Conceptualising the 'Personnel Professional': A critical analysis of the chartered institute of personnel and development's professional qualification scheme".

# 5   An Incomplete Professionalisation and New Professionalism

The story of the Institute and its encounter with the Privy Council says something about the evolving nature of several institutions—the Institute, the Royal Charter and the nature of professionalism today. Therefore, I also want to summarise what happened to the traditional professions against which a "professional project" is measured, to the Institute's "professional project", its role as a "qualifying association", and the extent to which it controls and constructs the practitioner.

## Traditional Professionalism Unchained

Professionalism[1] as an end state of a "professional project" has cast a "long shadow"[2] over the discussion of work and occupations because professionalism has acquired a specific meaning. The attainment of "professionalism" means having legitimate control over the supply of work, through professional power over the members through "associational control" and being able to protect the consumers of its services through a "sustaining ideology", without interference from the state. These conditions are relevant when it comes to examining the professionalising tendencies of the Institute but also the seeds of its inchoate "professional project".

In this way, the occupation is in a position to protect the consumers of its services without interference from the state, through a sustaining ideology. These conditions are relevant when it comes to examining the professionalising tendencies of the Institute but also the seeds of its inchoate "professional project".

Professionalism has evolved into notions of occupational closure and the financial and status benefits that are assumed to accrue. Occupational closure is a situation in which a body of knowledge and set of practices are sealed off from other occupations, and the practitioners, through the offices of an occupational association, have a market for a kind of labour. Furthermore, the occupation has secured pragmatic, moral and cognitive legitimacy within the eyes of a public and its consumers.[3]

Underpinning the traditional professional model is a theoretical domain of knowledge derived from scientific principles, tested to rigorous standards and applied in professional work.[4] The university is where 'scientific' knowledge emerges and, therefore, professions tend to create links with them, and they become the site where the producers of the work are produced, that is, where the practitioner becomes qualified and receives credentials to practice.[5]

Professional bodies guard a body of knowledge which underpins the practices of the occupational field and needs to be able to lay claim to a defined territory of work and practice built on some intellectual discipline or theory which can be tested and developed.[6] This is achieved through the codification of knowledge and the creation of the qualified practitioner through education and qualifications.

Professionals in the traditional model had the protection of a professional body, a "qualifying association",[7] whose purpose was to safeguard the body of knowledge and practice, wrap the knowledge and practice in qualifying systems, which afforded a hierarchy of membership. In this way, a wall protected the profession and the practice and knowledge from dilution of the field and from unregulated and unethical practice from the unsuitable and the charlatan. Many of these professions were organised by a professional body with a Royal Charter. In the twenty-first century, the state initiated regulatory bodies such as the health professions council. A practitioner is unable to practice if she is not on the list. These resources come to fruition as social closure and occupational closure. To those seeking admittance to the professional fold, the expectations were of received status, esteem and equal reward, and this is what prompted later professions-as-conspiracy or professions-as-stitch-up.

The traditional professional construct is imprecise but still appears dominant, carrying features that are persuasive and current in occupations seen to be professionalising. Some of these features relate to accumulation of knowledge, and training, association and public good, monopoly, autonomy, social standing and privilege, but collectively they are aspirational and underlie the idea of progress towards a state of professionalism.

Despite the long tradition in writing about the traditional professions, the quotation I have used in earlier chapters,[8] to me holds the essence of, even today, the understanding in society of the traditional professionals.[9] Professionals are educated in a field of study to a high intellectual standard, and they apply their knowledge in practice to help society in a way which is selfless. There is a rosiness about them.

The literature and commentary on the traditional professions are old. Adam Smith[10] identified a range of occupations in this model as the "liberal professions", and a range of similar occupations such as engineering and accountancy have occupied much of this commentary ever since because they have control over their own affairs, considerable status and are able to exercise a profound influence in the lives of others. The historic nature of the traditional professions reinforces the historical continuity of these occupations and yet it is necessary to be mindful of subsequent societal change, and the observation that occupations are always in flux, and:

> (n)o occupation which is characterized by professionalism as a form of control is static and unchanging.[11]

Nowadays, and just as much as in the past, when the public discusses the professions, they are usually thinking about the traditional professional model exemplified by the law, accountancy and medicine and other occupations whose professional bodies regulate their training, socialisation and access to the profession. The professions were essential to the common weal, to social harmony, protecting the public from harm. These are the "archetypal" professions, which some commentators have seen as elitist.[12] There is still, however, an unspoken reverence due to the perceived success of these occupations, the rewards attributed and prestige in society, and successive UK governments were happy to look to the professions for confirmation that social mobility was achievable, to the extent that belonging to a profession became a desirable aspiration for individuals.[13]

Only those scholars and commentators interested in the field would notice that there are occupations, some old, some new, that appear to be working towards becoming a profession. These are occupations with a goal in mind, and a "professional project". The HR function is one such occupation,[14] and this is the focus for this book.

## A Rocky Path—The Institute's Journey Towards a Kind of Professionalism

There is an association between traditional professionalism and the award of a Royal Charter, and the Privy Council Papers show this.[15] Although there is a suggestion that the forerunners of personnel and human resource management practitioners were keen to be regarded as professionals, they were also keen to be regarded as part of management.[16]

At the time the Institute was applying for a Royal Charter, the literature had led to common understandings of what traditional professionalism was, amounting to *collective organisation, knowledge* and *values* (Appendix II), and the story of the Institute's search for a Royal Charter and its putative professionalisation shows how the Institute met those challenges of *collective organisation, knowledge and values*.

For most of the twentieth century, the Institute and the practitioners had built an occupation which had become embedded and essential in organisations to a greater or lesser degree. There had been agency;

however, the socio-political and historical context in which the Institute operated had provided opportunity to claim and consolidate practice. The consolidation of practice needed constant work, however, and there was always the threat from other occupational groups and the longstanding view that the function was under-valued.

In this section, I want to examine the ways in which the Institute carried through the organisational work[17] required to look like a traditional 'profession' in relation to the dimensions of traditional professionalism —*collective organisation, knowledge* and *values*. Addressing these dimensions not only illustrates the organisational work undertaken by the Institute to achieve a form of professional status through the Royal Charter, but also shows the different constructions placed upon the process by the Institute which suggests both compliance with the demands of the Privy Council and the traditional model, and yet at the same time a different set of intentions and interests.

A professional body has a significant role in the creation, regulation, stability and maintenance of the profession as an institution.[18] A professional body needs to build a collective organisation of practitioners who are also members of sufficient standing within a field which is distinct and significant, and one of the reasons the early members of the Institute had decided to associate was to ensure that their pursuit of professionalism would not be hindered by disparate practices.[19] This is professionalism which comes about through the actions of an occupational collective, which works to create a field of practice it can claim for itself and regulate both the qualification into the profession and the behaviour of the qualified professionals. The Privy Council had those expectations,[20] and, therefore, the Institute conducted its affairs in ways that mirrored the organisation of professional associations. First, the Institute increased its membership numbers; second, the Institute communicated with members; and third, the Institute developed a code of professional conduct. These three elements are integral to the application for a Royal Charter and therefore appear as key contributors to the "professional project" as ways of exercising occupational control.

This is the Institute's "professional project" building upon the analysis of the traditional professional model accumulating around *collective organisation, knowledge and values*.

### Collective Organisation

The way in which the Institute's membership grew and how the Institute organised the membership over the twentieth century are essential elements in demonstrating a coherent and significant organisation that could claim to represent an occupation. From a base of a few hundred in the early twentieth century, membership numbers gradually rose and at the time the Institute began its search for a Royal Charter in

1968, membership numbers had been growing.[21] Despite what was a steady increase in membership, the Institute's membership numbers did not always increase in consecutive years during the late 1970s.[22] In 1994, however, membership numbers increased considerably when the Institute of Training and Development and the Institute of Personnel Management combined to form the Institute of Personnel and Development (IPD).

A further significant feature of the traditional professional model is the idea of a hierarchy of membership[23] in which the grades of membership reflect both the seniority of the practitioner and the level of the profession's qualifications achieved. Privy Council sources suggest that the Institute had the ambition of attaining 100,000 members by 2000.[24]

To claim to represent a good proportion of practitioners in the field,[25] the Institute undertook various strategies to mobilise members (and increase the numbers eligible to vote). Prior to the successful petition to the Privy Council for a Royal Charter in 2000, student members who had undertaken part of the qualification were licentiates of the Institute. On their attainment of the qualification, the member could 'upgrade' to become a graduate member; however, graduate membership conferred few rights to contribute to the development of the Institute's constitution. There were several occasions when the Institute tried to convert licentiate and graduate members to full members of the Institute, entitled to vote to alter the constitutional arrangements.[26] The Director-General also recognised that to meet the conditions for a Royal Charter it was important that graduate members converted to full membership.[27] When the Royal Charter was in prospect, the Director-General said that the Institute would seek to become a professional body that could confer chartered status on individual qualified members. Once again, there were calls in the member journal *People Management* for qualified members to upgrade to full membership so that they could take part in the vote and receive the benefits of being chartered.[28] The conversion of these inert and recalcitrant members would not only represent an increase in subscription income but would also substantiate the Institute's claim to being able to represent the "major proportion of the practitioners of a distinct profession".

In order to satisfy the Privy Council that the Institute was responsible for a complete domain of practice, the Institute, outside the main activity towards the Royal Charter and in a period which appeared quiet in relation to the pursuit of the Royal Charter, normalised the idea that the domain of training and development should be a part of the Institute's domain rather than separate. Therefore, chief among the Institute's activities was the "creation" of the Institute of Personnel and Development (IPD) by the combination of the Institute of Training and Development (ITD) with the Institute (IPM).[29] The contribution of this event towards the attainment of the Royal Charter should not be underestimated nor least because the new Institute's membership numbers were instantly boosted.

However, sources show that this was an idea that had been in the making some while and far earlier than 1994 when the Institute of Personnel and Development came into being.[30] There was much at stake for the Institute in relation to the combination of the two institutes and the two domains of practice. There was a real fear of the dilution of practices and practices which had found their ways into the purview of other occupations. At the time of the combination, there was a genuine concern that a rival management organisation, the Institute of Management (formerly British Institute of Management, now the Chartered Management Institute) would be able to claim the same domain. There would be:

> two bodies purporting to speak on behalf of personnel management professionals and putting forward to government and other views and statements of policy on the most important competitive aspect of work, the human resources of an organisation. This can surely be in no one's interest, least of all that of the personnel professional.[31]

This is *collective organisation* and the act follows the literature of the traditional professions which noted jurisdictional rivalry and conflict as part of the race to achieve professionalism.

Further strategies to achieve sufficient collective organisation included increasing the membership through creating or capitalising upon conditions whereby the certification of practitioners was considered desirable by employing organisations and by aspiring practitioners.

It was essential that the Institute was able to present evidence to the Privy Council that the application for the Royal Charter was the will of the collective membership and the Institute mobilised and persuaded the members of the need for the "professional project", using the inbuilt mechanisms for member control. There were a series of "upgrading" initiatives announced through the member journal *People Management*.[32] The reasons for this are entirely connected to the need to persuade the Privy Council Office that members were organised, well represented and supportive of the application for a Royal Charter.

### Knowledge

A profession in the traditional professional model has to have a body of knowledge that the occupation can claim for its own.[33] The Privy Council had identified the qualifications as less than expected for a professional body. From 1955, entry into full membership of the Institute was supposed to be through examination alone but by 1968, the Institute's examination leading to qualification could still be undertaken after only one year of study by correspondence course.[34]

Even more problematically, despite the assertion that entry into corporate membership from 1955 was through examination, one of the problems for the Institute at the beginning of the Royal Charter application was that many member practitioners, including senior members, had become members through experience, bypassing the examination system entirely.[35] Therefore, to address this educational and knowledge deficit, the Institute set about the reworking of the syllabus and qualification system to demonstrate that it was of the appropriate degree level standard required by the Privy Council.

The practices for managing the problem of the human factor at work had developed through the exigencies of war and scientific developments had come to be used in the workplace.[36] The execution of personnel management practices is a practical endeavour, and such practice could be learned by observation on the job. The awakening of practitioners to a set of "scientific" theories, grounded in empirical research, gathered momentum over the twentieth century and became central to the Institute's "professional project". The practices had to be converted into:

> a systematically learnable body of knowledge [. . .] capable of being translated into qualifications and learning routes, and which was capable of being evidenced by research.[37]

The Institute has supported and commissioned academic research of this type by creating ties with universities, other commercial organisations, and government departments with a remit for the conduct of economic affairs or labour relations. The output from research within universities has then featured in the Institute's own qualifications as knowledge which could then be put into practice at the workplace by practitioners as the standard. The period between 1992 and 2008 appears to have been particularly active in this regard.

In the traditional professional model, there is a strong connection between the body of knowledge, the education of the practitioners and the requirements for practitioners to undertake Continuing Professional Development (CPD). In the Institute's case, this is a further example of a characteristic emblematic of the traditional professional model blending with other characteristics as the Institute made a connection between CPD, education and the Code of Professional Conduct as a mechanism of occupational control. A member could demonstrate their CPD by attaining the Institute's qualification through part-time study whilst obtaining experience in work or by gaining the qualification first then demonstrating the application of the knowledge gained afterwards. A commitment to CPD was implicit in the various iterations of the Code of Conduct, the development of which is explained next.

*Values*

A key feature of traditional professionalism is autonomy, and this is measured by the profession's ability to regulate itself and its members, without external interference, and to practice without hindrance as the experts in a field. The autonomy of practice and regulation tends to be found in codes of conduct and associated disciplinary procedures.[38] Codes of conduct and associated disciplinary procedures concern the ability of the profession to regulate itself in two related ways. Not only does the profession determine who can be admitted to the profession, but it also regulates the behaviour and sets the standards of competence required for practitioners. Additionally, the codes set out penalties the profession could apply to those who had failed in the profession's ethical, competence or service orientations (see Appendix II). The Privy Council required the Institute to adhere to this principle. The Privy Council Office sought assurances about member discipline raised as late as 1998 as the Charter application was approaching its final phase.[39] Therefore, the development of the Institute's Codes of Conduct for members was important in the Institute's claim to be taken seriously as a professional body representing an occupation with worthy credentials to receive a Royal Charter.

The ideology of public service and altruism was integral to the traditional professional model. For the Institute, however, the idea of the practitioners doing good and the practices being a social benefit appear to have always featured as part of the remit of the practices.[40] However, many of the concerns of the practitioner regarding the well-being of the worker had been supplanted by workplace legislation, reducing the practitioner to an interpreter of rules as observed earlier. Serving a public good could only be recognised by proclamations about the purpose of the practices. However, when the Privy Council Office asked about the discipline and control of the membership, the Institute devised a Code of Conduct to satisfy the Privy Council's expectations.[41]

The first code was introduced in 1979 and was linked to the Institute's internal debate on *professionalism* and *professionalisation* and what that meant.[42] Professionalisation could impede the practitioner from performing their roles and heighten the "man in the middle-ness" observed by Dryburgh in 1972. Institute insiders were fully aware of the employed status and contextual nature of the practitioner, and so the Code itself was to be a set of "guiding principles" with:

> no statutory obligations imposed on members, no disciplinary proceedings against those in breach of the code and certainly no withdrawal of membership for non-compliance.[43]

This implies that the Institute was not in favour of pursuing a "professional project" like those found in the traditional professional model, and which later commentators appeared to see.

The Code was introduced in the early 1980s; however, it was little used and not seen as a regulatory instrument even beyond the Royal Charter.[44] But the Code was an essential component of a successful application for a Royal Charter and the Director-General recognised the difference in construction between that placed upon the Code by the Privy Council Office as one of discipline and the Institute's view as one of *guidance* on conduct rather than *instructions* on conduct that might result in disciplinary action for breaches.

The Institute itself is powerless to enforce either continuing membership or movement through the membership hierarchy, because the personnel/human resource management occupation was, and is, not closed and regulated (as the traditional professional model suggests) and could only rely upon the persuasiveness of the power of exchange—"upgrading" and progressing throughout the Institute's membership hierarchy, in exchange for post-nominal letters, voting rights and the increased services, which latterly have hinged around greater access to material on the Institute's website. Furthermore, the Institute has found it difficult to prevent lapsed but previously qualified, practitioners from using the designatory letters.[45]

Given these difficulties, it is interesting that the Director-General maintained that the issue of the Institute's Code was neither "a hugely significant issue", nor "a controversial one" (interview, 20 February 2010). His view of the Code as a set of "guiding principles" appears at odds with the statement from the Privy Council Office in which the Code of Conduct was about regulating discipline and having the ability to stop a member from practising, which indicates the Privy Council's expectation of the Institute professionalising along the traditional model. In contrast, the Institute's approach to the Code appears to be about providing guidance to the practitioner in their work as professionals in organisations.

## The Fragmenting Professional Model and Change

The late twentieth and early twenty-first centuries have seen an infraction of the boundaries of the occupations in the traditional professional model and profound changes which alter the way the traditional professionals work and the site where the work is done. This is not new. There have been three observed trends indicating that the traditional professional model was changing. These are first, "the increasing professionalisation of work"; second, the increase in occupations "found in the professional category"; and third, "the increasing bureaucratization of work in general".[46]

Analysis of social commentaries indicates that these changes began in post-war Britain upon the establishment of the welfare state, thus suggesting that this type of professionalism is still a historic and situated construct. This change is due to the social and regulatory changes wrought in western economies[47] which have opened new markets for new types of consumers. The occupational control of the traditional professions exercised upon the regular practitioner had been strong but is weakened,[48] because those practitioners find themselves open to competition from other potential rival occupations claiming similar jurisdictions, with increasing constraints on their autonomy and scrutiny of the practice of their specialised knowledge and skill due to trust failing on the part of their consumers. Therefore, as several authors have observed in relation to medicine and the law,[49] both context and lived experience have changed in two ways: first, in terms of the relationship between the profession and the state; and second, in the relationship between the profession and their users or consumers.

Occupational elites have arisen within a hierarchy of the profession which causes a separation between them and the regular member professionals and so a medical elite pronounces upon their occupational domain, making guidelines and rules for regular practitioners who will become interpreters of the rules and practice. The autonomy of lawyers is frayed as increasingly working in Managed Professional Businesses (MPB), the member lawyer will be kept outside the enclosure of ownership and autonomy. It seems that the traditional professions have become corporatised, so that:

> The manager has become professionalised; the professional has become managerialised.[50]

The traditional professions had developed a shape and look particularly over the twentieth century but since the traditional professional model became a topic for discussion and analysis, the social and industrial world changed considerably and inevitably. The twentieth century witnessed a growth in the managerial classes, their power and the dominance of managerial thinking and practice. This phenomenon occurs most markedly in the UK public sector, and in the large managed professional businesses.[51] Occupations arising from new branches of knowledge and locations for the practice of expert work impose an alternate way of thinking about what work was done, where it was done and who performed the work.

The changed site and bureaucratisation of work undermines the autonomy of the professions because bureaucracy and professional work have different ideologies and characteristics. Organisations expect obedience to structures and rules that are outside the efforts professionals expend upon socialisation and orientation to work.[52] Even those professionals in the traditional professional model are becoming "remade" inside their employing organisations rather than relying upon the collegiality of a professional association where they enjoyed more autonomy. In this way, managerialism and professionalism have become odd bedfellows, and the earlier writers on the traditional professions would not recognise current aspects of managing such as scrutiny, audit and performativity.

Understanding the change that has taken place has led to later analyses of the traditional professions based on expertise and knowledge and their associated power, and so it is important to recognise new regulatory and occupational contexts and an evolving professional model in the various contexts in which they occur.[53]

Despite the fissures in the traditional model, the public still looks for key markers in the professions: education to a high degree, a professional practice which they could trust, honesty and integrity, selfless service. The ethos of doing no harm meant that the traditional professions were regulated—there was a list of accredited practitioners to trust.

Despite the many recent changes occurring to those professions in the traditional model, the characteristics found in earlier studies of the traditional professions of the traditional professional construct appear to persist. The understanding of what constitutes a profession is institutionalised to *collective organisation, knowledge* and *values,* and the Privy Council Papers (see Appendix I) show the extent to which the Privy Council Office expected to see the traditional professional model as late as 1991.[54] These characteristics have been relied upon by occupations attempting to legitimate "claims for recognition and privilege"[55] as is found in a "professional project".

Scholars and commentators have seen different forms of professionalism occurring and new occupations with their own professionalisations occurring, and observers place the occupation of the personnel/human resource practitioners among such occupations despite the Institute's claim to longevity.[56] New and emerging occupations need to establish themselves and establish their right to exist; they need to establish legitimacy.

## The Organised, Managed, Knowledgeable and Entrepreneurial

In addition to the reconstituted professionals are those occupations in organisations who are "organisational or managerial" professions such as managers and administrators, the "entrepreneurial professions" and knowledge workers.[57] Some of these occupations have organised under the collective association of a supra-occupational organisation "in order to gain status and enable successful job mobility".[58]

These occupations build their professionalism and legitimacy on claims of expertise. Expertise privileges the practitioner who possesses managerial and entrepreneurial skills which include not only technical expertise but also a claimed ability to enhance the business in which they are located. This type of professionalism paves the way for three effects: first, the questioning of expertise that is asked for; second, the notion of professional success relates to the ability of the professional to contribute to the financial outcomes of the business, and not to the intangible outcomes such as fairness, altruism and "even-handedness".[59] Third, 'the piper calls the tune', and the employer who pays the wage will curtail autonomy if it is not in the interests of the organisation. Professionalism built on the legitimacy of expertise requires both power and control over resources and the application of expertise. Consequently, there is a likelihood of both intra-organisational and inter-occupational conflict over the resource of expertise, as these rivals seek to monopolise and legitimise their versions of knowledge and practice.[60]

The organisational professional with expert power is able to play to uncertainty, creating dependency based on fear, uncertainty and doubt. Experts tend to seize control of organisational and managerial processes and are able to engage in "occupational upgrading".[61]

Professionalism in modern contexts is a discursive device for control, identity and legitimacy. *Professionalism* requires resources such as language, often as rhetoric, vocabularies and discourse to sustain it. Rather than being solely an intrinsic orientation to work, "we are all expected to be professional, to perform professionally".[62] Consequently, the requirement for this type of professionalism is something imposed externally by employers and is seen in artefacts such as codes of behaviour, competency frameworks and HR documents such as the person specification. Professionalism in this way becomes a disciplinary mechanism,[63] a mechanism of external control.

*Professionalism* as external control is also a disciplinary measure used by employers and by occupational associations, and it works to create self-discipline and requires "self-work". Professionalism used in this way requires "effective mechanisms of occupational socialization and identity formation and maintenance" through professional associations creating qualification systems, requiring continuing professional development. This arises because of a vestigial and symbolic link with the training and education expected in the traditional professional model[64]; it is also a source of external legitimacy.

Occupations that have not recognised the potential of a "professional project" may also employ *professionalism* as a discursive device within a struggle for occupational control, occupational change, recognition and legitimacy.[65] In this context *professionalism* means a professional orientation to work. In this, practitioners are creating identities which will contribute to "professional projects".[66]

Despite the changes apparent in the traditional model, the retention of *professionalism* as an ideal[67] **and** the emergence of 'new' categorisations of professional occupations, the associated professional discourse has become a mechanism for helping and promoting social and occupational change or "occupational upgrading".[68] *Professionalism* then is a "discourse" of ideas and values capable of creating "governable" identity.[69]

It has become a normalised, normative and rhetorical term, which, even when imposed from above, enables legitimacy and which practitioners assimilate in the expectation of higher status and rewards both as individual practitioners and as a collective.[70] It relates to display and image-making, especially when linked to the acquisition of qualifications and adherence to external requirements. This is the presentation of a professional image as an ideology because it conveys the "interests of a group" and is part of the solution to the legitimacy and the right to exist"[71]; it establishes legitimacy because it is still associated with the traditional professional model.

## Concluding Remarks

Before offering a verdict on the Institute's professional project and the professionalisation of HR, it is important to make these observations; that in the trajectory of human affairs, there is always a tendency for misunderstanding, of mistake and not a conspiracy. Throughout the documents, there are several occasions when both the Privy Council Office and the Institute only saw in the communications what they expected to see. The confusion over the meaning of the Institute's library in the sense of the public service ethos in this instance appears to underscore the difficulties in substantiating claims to professionalism under the traditional professional model, as different elements of the professional model take on different meanings depending upon the party who is interpreting it.

Most significantly it is important to acknowledge the role of the prevailing tides of social and political affairs over which few actors have any control. Yet, the skilful role of human agents in the pursuit of objectives is also relevant in the tale of the professionalisation of HR, even as they are caught between the Scylla and Charybdis of the Privy Council Office and societal events. This is shown in many public announcements. The Director-General spoke on many occasions to different audiences about what he knew his audience would want to hear addressing both the Privy Council and the members.[72]

By the time the Royal Charter had been achieved in 2000, the Institute appears to have met the expectations of the Privy Council. This was a project that began in 1968 very much as a "professional project". It was a project whose trajectory was neither linear nor smooth, and which occasionally experienced and withstood threats from outside the field, such as the historic separation of training, the growing claims for professionalisation from managers, intervention in the field from the government concerning the review of occupational standards and the influence from the European Union.

Between 1968 and 2000 when the Royal Charter was granted, the traditional professional model appears to have been fragmenting, and as the Institute grew closer to the Royal Charter, the Privy Council acknowledged this. The statements from the Director-General to the Privy Council indicate that the Institute did not want to operate as a regulator of the practices and practitioners,[73] and this indicates that the Institute's professional project was moving away from the "professional project" as originally conceived.

In the Institute's story, however, there are points of congruence with a "professional project" in the matters of organisation, the knowledge base and the espoused values of the *professional* practitioner. However, a "professional project" in the traditional model needed the key element of sanction by the state to self-regulate, and the state would include both qualifications into the profession, and closure through regulating admittance and disbarring. Even with the Royal Charter, this important aspect remained unfulfilled for full professionalisation in line with the traditional model. However, adhering to the features inherent in the model of professionalism that appeared to be valued by the Privy Council and winning the Royal Charter was a means to the end of achieving a level of recognition that would engender legitimacy among a certain group of consumers. The Royal Charter has secured less in the way of *professional* status as suggested by a *professional project* but was the trigger for individuals to claim *professionalism*, a badge with the word 'profession' and 'competent' embossed upon it. This suggests that the Institute's path was twin-tracked, demonstrating both the aspects of the traditional professional model and an orientation towards becoming a facilitator of the means by which the individual practitioner could seek professionalism through identity. In this way, the Institute could engender legitimacy for itself by claiming to be able to speak on behalf of practitioners in the field. Any benefit accruing to the Institute and the practitioner following the dealings with the Privy Council Office and internal responses appears short-lived as further work and effort had to be expended to promote and maintain the veneer of legitimacy.

The Institute's "professional project" was a search for recognition and legitimacy and once the Royal Charter was won, the Institute had to work hard, and still does, to retain the legitimacy to speak for the practitioners, have authority and mastery over a coherent domain of practice and maintain the search for legitimacy and occupational control.

After a long time and a great deal of effort and persistence set against a changing socio-political backdrop, the Institute received the Royal Charter in 2000. To achieve this, both parties, including the institutions of the state, had to accept some form of change, although it appeared grudging and slow. The Institute's motivations for pursuing the Royal Charter since 1968 had been contested, and organisational pursuits and strategies had appeared to have contributed to achieving the goal.

There were attempts to organise and mobilise the membership in the run-up to the award of individual chartership and attempts by the Institute to adapt the knowledge base so that it would appear relevant to the changing needs of organisations under the human resource management discourses. Following the award of the Royal Charter and the power to award individual chartered status to members, the Institute had to negotiate two paths. The first was to capitalise on the award of the Royal Charter to further the Institute's legitimacy. Second, the Institute had to maintain its claim to be a protector of a body of knowledge which is reflected in the shaping and socialisation of the practitioner[74] through the qualification schemes in which routines were defined and prescribed. Third, the Institute had to satisfy the Privy Council expectations for traditional professionalism, the third anchor, *values*, and it did this by putting considerable work into the Code of Conduct and its output for general consumption and public policy work; these are links to the public good ethos of traditional professionalism.

The Institute received a Royal Charter in 2000, and in 2003 individual members could become chartered members by showing commitment to Continuing Professional Development (CPD). CPD proved the attainment of a level of career seniority in which members could create an impact in their employing organisations. The attainment of the Royal Charter had been an ambition of the Institute's Director-General, but the ambition was less to do with professionalisation in the model of classical professionalism[75] and more to do with legitimacy and status and, as the Director-General said, "respectability" for the Institute and the members.

However, in any case, the Royal Charter did not of itself complete a professionalisation in the manner which the traditional professional model suggested. There was no social or occupational closure, no "license to practice".[76] When the Royal Charter was achieved in 2000, the "professional project" was explicitly one of legitimacy with an attendant focus upon the practitioner as a self-making professional.

Over the period of the Institute's search for a Royal Charter the model of traditional professionalism to which a "professional project" referred, had begun to fragment and several other conceptions of professionalism emerged focusing upon expertise.[77] These came about because of changing institutional factors, changing collective values and ideas, global perspectives and belief in the power of the market and corporations to deliver market-based solutions. The new conceptions of the professional required the practitioner to be expert and to behave in ways in which the traditional professional behaved. This meant evoking feelings of confidence and eliciting trust in the recipients of the practitioner's expertise.

Trust is "a fluid concept which undergoes redefining at different times"[78] and late capitalism is one such time. So, the question of who is trusted and on what basis is a central feature in defining professionalism. The traditional professions engendered trust in the recipients of their services; the public knew or assumed that there was expertise underpinned by professional codes of conduct and values of service. In recent years, the public, however, has found the professional wanting in many respects and this has resulted in a challenge to competence, a lack of trust and increased regulation for the sake of public protection. The state delegated the role of keeping the list to the professional body and therefore trusted the professional body to regulate membership and the body of knowledge and practice. This is occupational closure or social closure.[79]

Following the award of the Royal Charter in 2000, and the amendment to the Institute Byelaws, the Institute acquired the right to confer the title of *"chartered member"* upon individual members from 2003. There could have been a sense that all was accomplished if the Royal Charter was indeed the apogee of recognition of *professionalism*. However, instead of being able to reap the reward of thirty years of endeavour, there was further work to do to maintain any legitimacy and status which the award of the Royal Charter might have brought to the Institute, the practices and the practitioner. The Royal Charter could not, and did not, complete the professionalisation that some commentators would have expected: professionalism in line with the traditional professional model on the Institute and the practitioners. There were several reasons for this. One reason is that socio-political and cultural pressures which had begun at a glacial pace in the twentieth century began to accelerate towards the end of this period and into the twenty-first century. These pressures had wrought notable change to those elite professions what had been such a fascination for commentators and the public. Many other occupations have evolved; all seek to elevate the status of the practitioners and the practices. Some of these occupations have achieved social or occupational closure, as would have been seen in Larson's "professional project". This is achieved by supra-occupational bodies retaining lists of qualified practitioners and the state requiring regulation and reaccreditation. Many of the professional bodies for these occupations have Royal Charters.

Whatever the Institute's motivation for seeking the Royal Charter, its acquisition could never achieve professionalism in the traditional professional model. Therefore, on the one hand, the key actor responsible for maintaining the momentum for the Royal Charter had been realistic in his ambitions, and on the other, the classical model of professionalism had been fragmenting over many years and was no longer the force it was.

In discussing the attainment of the Royal Charter, it is equally important to recognise that a different kind of professionalism is emerging that is far-reaching in most occupations and the HR practitioner is an illustration of this. The Institute's project to maintain the legitimacy won through the Royal Charter continued but under a new conception of the practitioner, as an organisational expert, and what constitutes professional practice, all the while maintaining the links with the traditional professional model in terms of *knowledge* and *values*. It is a story of both change and continuity, and that is what has characterised this particular "occupational upgrading".[80] Being professional becomes more than knowledge and skill, the expertise, it is the mode in which expertise is enacted—the practitioner draws upon a basket of virtues, and both self-regulates and is regulated. This mode appears regularly in other modern occupations, the remnants of the traditional professions and as the current way of regulating all workers.

Before discussing the meaning of the Royal Charter and the events around its pursuit and acquisition for the HR profession, the Institute and professionalism, it is worth commenting upon the ephemera which underlie what appear to be major effects of organisation as it bumps against socio-political events and elite agency.

Ideas about professionalism, and societal hierarchy cling on to a past structure which had long outlived its usefulness and relevance. Pursuits, preoccupations and interests in one quarter do not carry the same level of urgency, meaning and momentum—agents and actors come and go. This is manifest in the messiness of the dealings between the Privy Council Office and the various leaders of the Institute. None of the institute's desires found common ground with the various senior officials at the Privy Council. They came and went, and all that remained were files which were not necessarily in a coherent fashion. They only tell part of the story. In a digital world, where pronouncements are cheap and erasable, how can anyone know what really happened?

The story of the Institute's relationship with the Privy Council covers a significant period of time and takes in many aspects of societal change which is shown in the changed context for the traditional professions. And still, the image of the professional and what that means has cast a "long shadow"[81] and has persisted, infiltrating significant aspects of work and social life.

The traditional professions have a logic of professionalism still, although they exist in an occupational space which is corporatised, functioning on bureaucratic principles, with autonomy increasingly constrained, and having to earn the trust of their consumers. Their allegiance, though, is still with their professional practice and the professional body which guards and maintains it. In contrast, the increasing number of modern occupations claiming professionalism does so because of their status striving within the constraints of the market, which is their underpinning logic.

What role does this leave for the professional body? The professional body for present-day personnel practitioners, the subject of this book, began in 1913 and since then appears to have developed in the mode of the traditional professional model—the professional body acquired knowledge and developed practices which could be executed in a range of circumstances. To belong to a professional body was an attractive proposition, and the Institute acquired members seeking to belong and accrue their qualifications and some esteem. The Institute curated a body of knowledge and to do this to this day, it developed a Code of Conduct and thus showed how it could regulate its members in policy at least. Finally, after over thirty years of trying, the Institute received a Royal Charter, which certainly at the time the Institute had first applied to the Privy Council was a marker of a professional body in the traditional model.

In 2000 with the award of the Royal Charter, some thought this the apogee of the Institute's progress. The search for the Royal Charter and its association with traditional professionalism had been a source of dissent and tension among some luminaries within the field. Those who associated the Royal Charter with the traditional professional model were fearful of what it would mean for the regular member practitioner, and most significantly that it might curtail the ability of the practitioner to deal effectively with the worker. In other words, it would remove them symbolically and psychologically from the role which they should be doing on behalf of the worker and the organisation—occupying that unique position between the organisation's management and the worker. There was to be too much seeking after status and practitioners would forget their roots.

There were other problems, too. The knowledge was borrowed from other disciplines and created into practices to suit the nature of the practitioner. Over time, the practices were elaborated, often rebadged, carved up and reassembled in ways which reflected the contemporary discourses of society, and the striving for status of the practitioner. The practices, however, were vulnerable to being claimed by other corporate professions—if this was expert knowledge, then there were other corporate professionals keen to take it. The practitioner still did not escape the "man-in-the middle-ness" of which Mr Dryburgh had complained in 1972; there was a perceived professional chip on the shoulder which had always dogged the practitioner from the earliest days through to the days of the personnel practitioner in the 1970s and even noticed by the Director-General in the 1990s as he sought to achieve the Royal Charter. There is much that can be researched and written concerning the historical gendered tradition in the practices, but this stems from the notion of the middle-class women as welfare supervisors ministering to women and children in the workplace.[82]

The Institute's professional project was set against the socio-economic and political context which included the struggle for women to advance in the workplace. A further struggle for the Institute was the array of new occupations arising which could also claim the territory of knowledge and practice—here, it is important to think of the inter-professional wariness that practitioners have had for accountants and ICT practitioners, both of whom were capable and desirous of wresting resources and control of investment or data projects which had employees as their focus, from the hands of a function which appeared weak within the organisation.

What role does that leave for practice? How do practices evolve? For traditional professions it is through science; for professions like HR it is through repackaged and rebranded practice, rhetoric to maintain it. So, this is the role for the Institute—a hub around which practitioners and other interested parties coalesce, and in which attempts are made to control through credentialism and identity.

Finally, it is important to consider what the story of the professionalisation of HR through the pursuit and acquisition of the Royal Charter reveals about the process in the Institute's case at the Privy Council. The institutional work performed by a range of Clerks and Deputy Clerks concerned maintaining the status quo, maintaining the integrity of the Royal Charter even in the face of expanding social, political and technological thinking.

### Holding Back the Tide—The Process at the Privy Council

The role of the Privy Council Office in the processes for awarding Royal Charters was to maintain the integrity and status of the Royal Charter as an institution. When I contacted the Privy Council Office about their dealings with the Institute, my contact was at pains to say that it was difficult to generalise about each award of a Royal Charter, and that there was not one single procedure. By examining the Institute's experience, however, it is possible to see some key anchors of a process. On the initial approach, mediated by an existing Charter holder, the Institution of Production Engineers,[83] the Privy Council offered initial (although incomplete, as it turned out) advice on how the professional body matched up to the institutionalised understandings. The key actors from the respective bodies engaged in a series of dialogue and exchanges. The Privy Council engaged with various advisers who were likely to know the standing and reputation of the petitioning body. In the Institute's case, this resulted in more work to do in order to meet the expectations. When the Institute's petition was nearing closure, the Privy Council placed a notice of the application in the *London Gazette*. Successful applications received the Royal Charter with the rights, privileges and obligations written in.

Underlying this process both at the beginning and throughout the time the Institute was seeking a Royal Charter was the Privy Council Office's view that professional bodies seeking a Royal Charter were a profession in the traditional model. Standards and expectations right until 1991 were firmly situated within the institutionalised view of professions which had been dominant throughout the twentieth century.[84] These requirements included a body of knowledge which the requirement for qualifications of degree level demonstrated. There was a clear public good, public service ethos and enough mass of members undertaking practices which are sufficiently unique and bounded. This view remained until 1991 when the clearest signal came when the Privy Council sought their relevant advisers' views of the petitioning body. These requirements are entirely in keeping with what the literature of the twentieth century had suggested.[85] The most significant expectation which only became a requirement towards the end of the process was that of closure, the twin pillars of professionalisation.[86]

In the case of the Institute, the award of the Royal Charter was to the Institute as a body; however, some three years later, the Institute was given the right to confer chartered status on individual members, subject to them meeting certain requirements for being qualified within the credentialing system which the Privy Council expected and which the Institute had sought to make suitable and of the expected level as a body of knowledge. The time lag between the award of the Royal Charter to the Institute and the date when individual members could be chartered appeared as an embarrassment, an event to be explained. The Director-General, commenting upon the event in an interview with *People Management*, said that it had been a two-stage process and the British Institute of Management had been observing the Institute's progress and had gone to professional and individual chartered member status at the same time.

Until the 1990s, late on in the Institute's application, the actors at the Privy Council Office appeared to look with disdain on the Institute and personnel management as a suite of practices connected with the dirty business of commerce and industry, maintaining a Victorian view of the superiority of the traditional professions over emerging occupations. The Privy Council Office appeared reluctant participants in the Institute's endeavours and dismissive of their approaches. Furthermore, they continued to throw obstacles in the Institute's path each time the Institute responded to the inquiries. Issues included standards of qualifications, the admittance of members on the basis of organisational seniority and experience, the notion of disciplining members through a disciplinary code of conduct and the public access to the library. None of these questions appears to have been set out as specific requirements at the outset.

One of the obstacles which the Institute encountered was their practice to admit senior practitioners without the qualification. The Privy Council were so firmly wedded to the view of the traditional professional model that it took advice from a government department to point out that in the field of national vocational education, there had been a shift of practice to the accreditation of prior learning (APL) or accreditation of prior experiential learning (APEL), and that the Institute for once was in the correct lane of the road. This lack of knowledge and social intelligence shows the entrenched nature of some elite institutions who appeared to cling to the past, rather than making progress, and were attempting to hold back the tide against the wash of a society attempting to move forward. The entire episode between 1968 and 2000 had been characterised by one actor lagging social trends, adhering firmly to the logic of professionalism, appearing elite and dismissive of occupations which were based in commerce and organisation. There was a view that the Institute was parvenu, despite the Institute's practices and organisation stemming from 1913; it was, they thought unlikely to last. Throughout the exchanges between the Institute and the Privy Council, there do appear scenes of supplication between an elite who appear out of touch and a petitioner.

### A Verdict on the Institute's "Professional Project" and the Professionalisation of HR

The search for professionalism through the Royal Charter was by no means a clear-cut goal as the engagement developed between the Institute and the Privy Council. Furthermore, there has long been debate over whether personnel management and HR was ever a profession. In the early part of the period, it appears that internal debate was unfolding within the Institute about the merits of professionalisation[87] and in 2010, the retired Director-General in an interview had admitted: "It isn't self-evident that personnel/HR people are a coherent profession."[88] These commentators were concerned with both the prospects for and desirability of professionalisation in line with the traditional professional model.

Nevertheless, the conditions for professionalism concern professional power in relation to the market for work, the work itself and in relation to the state shown in the organisational and organising effort[89] which the Institute put into acquiring a Royal Charter and what happened beyond. In drawing a line from the Institute to the three conditions that have to be present,[90] it is tempting to conclude that the Institute has been able to professionalise to a significant extent along a professionalising continuum. Closer inspection, however, would reveal an uncompleted road. Numbers of members do not mean that the Institute has *any* power either over the supply of services or the regulation of the services. The notion of 'services' is slippery, being embodied in what the practitioner does.

The Institute's professional project became explicit through progress towards and the attainment of the Royal Charter in 2000, but this had always been an aim of the original welfare workers.[91] The Institute is an occupational association that *mimics* the accoutrements of the professional associations found in the "model of classical professionalism"[92] and a "professional project". A "professional project" highlights the strategy that an occupation has to achieve "professionalism" and which "organizes the production of producers and the transaction of services for a market" and concerns "jurisdictional expansion".[93] The barriers to entry to the occupational territory are deliberately exclusionary, and this is relevant when considering how the conditions appeared that seemed to enable a market for specialised labour to arise.

The Institute's professional project, modelled in the frame of the traditional model of professionalism, had the appearance of being extant at the organisation's foundation in 1913, and since 1968 and the first application to the Privy Council for a Royal Charter, had the appearance of being distinctly viable[94] until realism and the context for practice altered. Although the Institute began as a member organisation, as an organisation subject to many influences, it has strayed from the path of being a membership organisation which served the needs of members, their practice and their development. From 2008 onwards, and the arrival of the Chief Executive on the retirement of the Director-General, the Institute has acted as an entity seeking to maintain its own legitimacy and relevance—its reason for being. This appears especially the case after 2008 when the Institute faced itself towards the market with an increasing publications portfolio and public policy agenda. As recently as 2012, the Institute's website explicitly talks about "influencing policy in UK government, at the highest levels".[95]

The interview which the Director-General gave in 1999 before the Institute received the Royal Charter[96] concluded with the admission that the Royal Charter would not:

> catapult (practitioners) into the boardroom, or into the inner circle of public policy. We are getting there already through the value of our members' contributions to organisational effectiveness and the good of society.

The interview is redolent with the language of *professionalism* in the traditional model as rhetoric for the purpose of persuading the membership rather than *professionalisation* or *professionalism* in the traditional professional model. The language is significant in that it indicates the importance of the Royal Charter's association with *professionalism*, but whilst avoiding the words 'human resource management', situates the practices and the practitioner in a modern organisational context.

### HR Professionalism for the Future

The Institute accomplished everything the Privy Council Office required of it to receive the Royal Charter, everything that would be expected of a traditional profession. By the time the Institute received the Royal Charter, the Institute had developed and extended a body of knowledge, laid claim to and maintained a territory of work, and continually guarded it against infraction from other organisational professions. It had developed a hierarchy of membership and a system of qualifications with a code of conduct within the professional standards. Individual members could become individually chartered.

To some extent, the Institute's project was aided by circumstances. During the 1970s and 1980s when the Institute was in pursuit of a Royal Charter, the socio-political environment facilitated the conditions whereby the practitioner and the practices appeared to become essential for the regulation and good conduct of employee relations. Thus, the skilled personnel management practitioner became involved in industrial relations and the interpretation of legislation, an activity which continued into the 1990s and beyond.

The *professional* personnel/human resources practitioner's practice, therefore, is not always guided by esoteric knowledge and skilled hands but by the top-down imposition of regulations by the state.[97] During the 1980s and 1990s, human resource management discourses were emerging and being taken up by many organisations, and practices were becoming more elaborate, again requiring interpretation of often programmed solutions purchased from other experts such as consultants. The emphasis was on "special competence", the expertise of the organisational professional. This is recognised in the research project undertaken in 1986 for the Institute:

> The role of the personnel practitioner as the "in-between" person seems to have gone. Personnel specialists appear to be managers first and personnel people second. [. . .] There is, after all, the problem for personnel practitioners in showing that they do give value for money and that they do have a special competence to offer.[98]

But practitioners retained an aura of insecurity about them concerning their value and the value of the practices. This stems from the "man-in-the-middleness",[99] the tensions and ambiguities which have haunted the occupation since its early formation. The practitioner has been able to rely on the professional body for up to date knowledge and credentials[100] and a host of other member services. Yet they lack the professionalism of the traditional professions, the freedom to act, and the capacity to seek high reward and status.

Human resource management professionals are mainly found in organisations where other organisational elites prescribe the quality and quantity of their work and remuneration. To achieve chartered membership, a member needs to be qualified through accredited programmes of study or in some circumstances with a practitioner of sufficient standing and experience in their own organisations, through a route where experience and seniority counted. They are organisational professionals, and their practices will remain subject to power and jurisdictional struggles; their path to power and career development depends on how the organisation values them, such valuing often given by the very systems of performance measurement that the human resource practices demand. Career development is also dependent on the self-work and mode of operation of the practitioner.

The professional standards contain not only the body of knowledge—borrowed, accumulated, curated and developed—but a set of competencies beyond skill. Indeed, the modes of operation are more akin to virtues—curiosity, the courage to challenge, being a role model—these are aspirational attributes which challenge the most resourceful of humans.

Professionalism in the traditional sense is unobtainable, and so practitioners and the Institute put their faith in discursive professionalism for control and constructing meaning and identity for different audiences.[101] The attainment of professionalism through professionalisation is an identity project,[102] and it is more useful to ask what practitioners do to turn themselves into professionals.

Thus, the case of the Institute and the professionalisation of HR show a move towards a different type of professionalism, away from the traditional model and more explicitly and realistically towards one in which practitioners are required to work towards *professionalism* by assuming behaviours and a professional orientation to the work in ways that are mediated by guidelines and exhortations from a self-styled professional body or "qualifying association".[103]

When presented from the Institute's perspective, the story shows how the Institute, by negotiating with the Privy Council and complying with the requirements, created the conditions for itself by which the Royal Charter could be awarded. But the Privy Council were so wedded to the embodiment of professionalism in its purest form that the officials did not notice that social trends and occupations had moved on. There is a sense at the end of the story that the Privy Council were beaten by this and the dogged determination of a shifting array of actors inside the Institute, most successfully by the Director-General.

The title of this monograph *The Professionalisation of HR* has taken in a number of themes; the changing shape of the traditional professional model, on which professionalising occupations still model themselves, the significance of the very British institution of the Royal Charter and its closeness to the traditional model of professionalism and exposed some of the threads which have made the award of the Royal Charter significant in the professionalisation of HR.

There are two intended meanings to the phrase "long shadows" at the start of this part of the book. Both are equally apt; long shadows usually denote the close of a day, and indeed there was an ending to the Institute's professional project and the search for a Royal Charter. There was also an ending implied in the changing construct of the traditional professions. The phrase, however, can also be applied to something powerful and dominant, which continues to have effects long after it seems necessary. This is also pertinent as the characteristics of the traditional professional model—*collective organisation, knowledge and values*—are still sought after, assumed and seen in many occupations even now.

## Notes

1. Birkett W P and Evans E (2005) "Theorising professionalisation: A model for organising and understanding histories of the professionalising activities of occupational associations of accountants", page 104.
2. Hodgson D (2008) "The new professionals: Professionalisation and the struggle for occupational control in the field of project management", page 232.
3. Suchman M (1995) "Managing legitimacy: Strategic and institutional approaches".
4. Cogan M L (1953) "Towards a definition of profession", page 49, Barber B (1963) "Some problems in the sociology of the professions".
5. Larson M S (1977) *The Rise of Professionalism: A Sociological Analysis*, page 17.
6. Cogan 1953 ibid, page 49; Brundage J A (1994) "The rise of the professional Jurist in the thirteenth century".
7. Millerson G (1964) *The Qualifying Association: A Study in Professionalization*.
8. Cogan 1953 ibid.
9. The view exemplified here has persisted, and later authors have suggested the same or similar characteristics, see Dent M and Whitehead S (eds) (2002) *Managing Professional Identities: Knowledge, Performativity and the "New Professional"*; Hodgson 2008 ibid; Adler P S, Kwon S-K and Heckscher C (2008) "Professional work: The emergence of collaborative community"; Craig J (ed) (2006) *Production Values, Futures for Professionalism*.
10. Smith A (2005; 1776) *An Inquiry into the Nature and Causes of the Wealth of Nations*.
11. Johnson T J (1972) *Professions and Power*, page 59.
12. Johnson 1972 ibid; Larson 1977 ibid, page 49; Evetts J (2003) "The sociological analysis of professionalism: Occupational change in the modern world".
13. Cabinet Office (2009a) *New Opportunities White Paper*.
14. Other examples include management consultancy (Alvesson M and Johansson A W (2002) "Professionalism and politics in management consultancy work"; Kipping M (2011) "Hollow from the start? Image professionalism in management consulting"; Hodgson 2008 ibid; Muzio D, Hodgson D, Faulconbridge J, Beaverstock J and Hall S (2011) "Towards corporate professionalization: The case of project management, management consultancy and executive search"; project management, or personnel/human resource management (Gold and Bratton 2003 ibid; Gilmore and Williams 2003, 2007 ibid). In Britain, the state's understanding of which occupations constitute a profession is wide. From the 2009 Cabinet Office *New Opportunities White Paper*, it becomes clear that to state actors many occupational fields are professions—a crowded field indeed! The *New Opportunities White Paper* drew a distinction in the language between "high" and "lower" professions, and, of course, "high-status professions", and appeared to accept that the construct of the profession is not fixed. This was something Etzioni had also commented upon, see Etzioni A (ed) (1969) *The Semi Professions and Their Organization; Teachers, Nurses, Social Workers*.
15. Privy Council Papers Set I-xv, 5 June 1991 ibid.

16. Niven M (1967) *Personnel Management 1913–1963: The Growth of Personnel Management and the Development of the Institute.*

17. This is institutional work, a tool from new-institutional theory. New institutional theory is a toolbox and some of the tools are useful for illuminating and explaining. The theory has evolved through theoretical development and empirical application to a range of contexts. In new-institutional theory is the notion of institutional logics and underlying this book is the notion that the Institute's organisation work is achieved by the prevailing institutional logics. In the later period, the Institute has competing institutional logics between managerialism allied to capitalism and neo-liberalism and professionalism, and this influenced the institutional work done, and the mode and timing of that institutional work. Institutional logics also form a bridge between the institution(s) and the institutional work and thus provide an explanation for that work. Tools of new institutional theory provide a set of vocabularies "to explain organizational phenomena", but although these tools are useful to shed light on a situation, they should always remain secondary to the narrative; this is why I have only discussed it at this point. Alford R R and Friedland R (1985) *Powers of Theory: Capitalism, the State, and Democracy*; Friedland R and Alford RR (1991) "Bringing society back in: Symbols, practise, and institutional contradictions'; Thornton P H and Ocasio W (1999) "Institutional logics and the historical contingency of power in organizations: Executive succession in the higher education publishing industry, 1958–1990", page 804 said that institutional logics were "the socially constructed, historical patterns of material practices, assumptions, values, beliefs and rules by which individuals produce and reproduce their material subsistence, organize time and space, and provide meaning to their social reality". Lawrence T B and Suddaby R (2006) "Institutions and institutional work"; Institutional work is a concept in New Institutional theory, and the schema established by Lawrence and Suddaby (2006 ibid, page 215); types include mimicry, definition, theorisation, policing, valorising, constructing networks and routinising. Analysis of organisation and actor agency is at the heart of the story of the professionalisation of HR, as it is in any examples of professionalisations. See also, Powell W W and DiMaggio P J (eds), *The New Institutionalism in Organizational Analysis*; Palmer D, Biggart N and Dick B (2008) "Is the new institutionalism a theory?", page 770; Jepperson R L (1991) "Institutions, institutional effects and institutionalism"; Scott W R (2001) *Institutions and Organizations*, page 48.

18. Leicht K T (2005) "Professions" page 604; Scott W R (2008a) "Lords of the dance: Professionals as institutional agents", page 227); Morris P W G, Crawford L, Hodgson D, Shepherd M M and Thomas J (2006) "Exploring the role of formal bodies of knowledge in defining a profession: The case of project management", page 712; DiMaggio P J and Powell W W (1983) "The iron cage revisited: Institutional isomorphism and collective rationality in organizational fields"; Greenwood, R, Suddaby R and Hinings C R (2002) "Theorizing change: The role of professional associations in the transformation of institutionalized fields".

19. Niven 1967 ibid.

20. Privy Council Papers Set I-xv, 5 June 1991.

21. Niven (1967) ibid reports that there were less than 6000 members in 1963 but by 1976, there were more than 18,500 in 1976 (see Marks W (1978) *Politics and Personnel Management: An Outline History, 1960–1976*, page 183).

22. Tyson S and Fell A (1986) "The crisis in personnel management".

23. Hickson D J and M W Thomas (1969) "Professionalization in Britain: A preliminary measurement", page 42 and Appendix II.
24. Privy Council Papers Set II-vii, a file note at the Privy Council, undated but after 14 November 1996.
25. Privy Council Papers Set I-xv, 5 June 1991, a letter from the Deputy Clerk to the Privy Council to an adviser from the Department of Employment. The significance of a membership hierarchy is that only the grades of member, fellow and companion are permitted to vote at the Annual General Meetings, or an Extraordinary General Meeting (EGM) and therefore have a say in the Institute's development which included approval to apply for the Royal Charter.
26. See Williams C (1999) "Corporate ascent" pages 1–2. The graduate needed to show, through their continuing professional development (CPD) that they had an "appropriate level of management experience". The headline figures that the Institute tends to quote in its publications are inclusive of all member grades, including student and affiliate members. Thus the headline figure obscures a problem that the Institute has long had and that concerns the conversion of non-corporate members (students and affiliates) to full membership. Following 1994 and the "creation" of a new Institute, the IPD, from the IPM and ITD, Privy Council Office Papers Set II-vii, after 14 November 1996, reveal that of the 79,000 members in 1996, some 31,000 were not full members.
27. Privy Council Papers Set II-vii, 14 November 1996 shows the importance of the conversion of the Institute's graduate members to full membership in 1996 that "about 40%" of members had a first degree. The file note also states that the Director-General had said: "If all existing Graduates upgraded as soon as they became eligible to do so, the proportion of corporate members with a degree would soon be comfortably above 80%."
28. Crabb S (1999) "Seal of approval", page 42, Privy Council Papers Set III-i, 21 November 2002; Crawshaw N (2002) "Another level"; Crofts P (2003) "Upgrade campaign is on", other later campaigns see Crofts P (2004a) "Benefits of upgrading"; 2004b "Stepping up a level"; (2005) "A good time to upgrade"; Williams C (2003) "How to . . . be a chartered CIPD member". When considering the reluctance of many recently qualified members or members with sufficient experience to climb the Institute's membership hierarchy, one oral source (interviewed on 13 May 2010) suggested a reason which was that although the Institute's qualification had secured the graduate member their first recognisable organisational role in personnel/human resource management, the employing organisation did not insist upon their employee (the Institute's member) developing further in the Institute's knowledge and professional mode, and climbing the Institute's grade hierarchy. This in itself illustrates the contradictions inherent within the idea of the personnel/human resource management practitioner as a *professional*, and the reality of being an organisational member, where recognition and status within the organisation rather than the profession are more significant.
29. The Institute attempted to mobilise the members of both the IPM and the ITD in 1993, and in the December 1993 issue of *Personnel Management*, there was a four-page spread entitled *The Case for Combination*. In the article various senior practitioners from both Institutes wrote articles in support of the proposal to combine. It was the last issue which a long-standing editor edited. At the end of the article, she saw that there was a real sense that both government and businesses ignored both institutes, not least because of their earlier failure to agree. She wrote:

"The last attempt to merge the two institutes failed largely through apathy. This time it really matters. Government and chief executives say, "A plague on both your houses" and ignore us because we can't get our act together. This time let's make it happen. A new combined institute is the only logical way forward for the professional. VOTE for the IPD!""

This contribution is interesting as far as a 'merger', both as a term and an idea, was in general circulation, and whether deliberately or accidentally, the outgoing editor released the proposed name of the new institute, the Institute of Personnel and Development, the IPD.

30. Privy Council Papers Set I, I-iii, 6 February 1977; a letter from the Institute's Assistant Director, Training, Organisation and Manpower Planning to the Companies Administration Division at the Department of Trade (carbon copy received at Privy Council). The letter concerns the potential effect of an amalgamation with the Institution of Training Officers Ltd. It illustrates the Institute's zeal to enclose the domain of training and personnel management completely and shows that the intention was far earlier than the date the enclosure was finally accomplished in 1994 which Daniels K (2012) ibid discusses. It also indicates the Institute's awareness of a number of potential problems, in particular, the sensitivities around perceptions of the Institute's purposeful strategy of aggrandisement.

31. Cowan in Personnel Management 1993 ibid page 29.

32. See Williams 1999 ibid; 2003 ibid. Such announcements were designed to be persuasive so that members could "have [their] say in the institute's future and the Royal Charter".

33. Cogan 1953 ibid, page 49; Carr-Saunders A M and Wilson P A (1933) *The Professions*; Parsons T (1939) "The professions and social structure"; Greenwood E (1957) "Attributes of a profession"; 1966 ibid; Hickson and Thomas 1969 ibid.

34. Niven 1967 ibid, page 121. Further, there were certain exemptions for holders of particular qualifications, on which the Clerk at the Privy Council commented in a file note, (Privy Council Papers Set I-ii, 1 February 1968). Further criticisms at the Privy Council were that the Institute's students could spread out their examination "sitting", and although the syllabus covered a number of topics, "none of this involved study in depth". The Privy Council observations led to the development of what is a system of qualifications that was not only linked to membership but was also concerned with meeting Privy Council requirements.

35. Although personnel managers in larger organisations were more likely to hold a relevant qualification, such as a BA Business Administration, the Institute's professional qualification, or a Diploma in Management Studies, observed that the Institute's membership had been based upon experiential learning, rather than formal academic qualifications. The focus upon experiential learning was due to lack of suitable educational provision and assumed that the practices could form a concrete body of knowledge. There were a high number of the Institute's students without higher education qualifications, but with the Institute's qualification instead. They suggest that this might be due to the perception among students that the Institute's qualification was important both for career development and organisational status *and* membership of a cadre of professional elites. See Timperley S R and Osbaldeston M D (1975) "The professionalization process: A study of an aspiring occupational organization", page 618 and Ridgeway C (1982) "The role of the secretary in personnel management", page 18.

36. Jacques R (1996) *Manufacturing the Employee: Management Knowledge from the 19th to the 21st Centuries*; Kaufman B E (2008) *Managing the*

*Human Factor: The Early Years of Human Resource Management in American Industry.*

37. The Director-General, interview 20 February 2010.
38. Hickson and Thomas 1969 ibid, page 38; Burrage et al. 1990 ibid, page 205.
39. Privy Council Papers Set II-xi, 17 February 1998, a letter from the Clerk to the Privy Council to the Institute's solicitors concerning the outcome of a consultation with their advisers. This is the Privy Council's expectation if the Institute was a *qualifying association* (Millerson 1964 ibid) and expressions of public good continue to be enshrined in the Charter documents themselves.
40. See Chapter 1; Proud 1916; Clarke 1949.
41. Privy Council Papers Set II-xi, 17 February 1998 ibid; on introducing a revised Code of Conduct in 2012, a recent President of the Institute claimed that the Institute had "always had a code of conduct" (see Wright V (2012) "View from the CIPD: Accountable to all). This is, however, not the case, as consideration of the first Code of Conduct appears not to have occurred until 1979.
42. See Lawrence S (1979) "Man of the moment: Jack Coates", page 40. According to the then outgoing Institute President although the new Conservative government promised "new freedoms for businesses", she was concerned about the ability of the occupation to "deliver" and stated that this would be "a tall order taxing the highest professional skills" Seears N (1979) "Can personnel managers deliver?".
43. Lawrence 1979 ibid, page 40.
44. The Director-General (interview 20 February 2010) viewed the code as a way of:

    "trying to articulate . . . what standards of behaviour our members would be expected to work to rather than as being a disciplinary code under which they could be sanctioned and punished, although they could and very infrequently were".

    The Director-General gave examples, often humorous, of the few disciplinary hearings, there were annually and the sanctions that could be meted out:

    "We had one guy in Scotland in one of the local authorities, he fiddled expenses . . . and was dismissed by his employer and the Branch brought a complaint under the professional code of conduct . . . so that went through and he was demoted from corporate membership and required to have a mentor for two or three years, or something—and there were several cases like that—they usually involve dishonesty."
45. A CIPD employee who was responsible for the branch network complained about non-members presenting business cards with designatory letters that were not valid, or whose membership had lapsed (participant as an observer, Branch Policy Advisers' Day in Central London, October 2008).
46. Pavalko R M (1971) *The Sociology of Occupations and Professions*, page 188.
47. Greenwood et al. 2002 ibid, page 60.
48. Dent M (2008) "Medicine, nursing and changing professional jurisdictions in the UK; Flood J (2008) "Partnership and professionalism in global law firms: Resurgent professionalism?".
49. For example, Dent 2008 ibid; Flood 2008 ibid.
50. Dent 2008 ibid, page 116; Cooper D J, Hinings C R, Greenwood R and Brown J L (1996) "Sedimentation and transformation in organizational change: The case of Canadian law firms"; Muzio D and Ackroyd S (2008) "Change in the legal profession: Professional agency and the legal labour

process", page 50; Dent and Whitehead 2002 ibid, page 6. In examining the fate of the established professions as they respond to these challenges, Dent 2008 ibid; Flood 2008 ibid and Muzio and Ackroyd 2008 ibid note the establishment of occupational elites.

51. In the context of the public sector, several scholars have named this phenomenon as New Public Management (see Ferlie E, Ashburner L, Fitzgerald L and Pettigrew A (1996) *The New Public Management in Action*; Evetts J (2009) "New professionalism and new public management: Changes, continuities and consequences"; Noordegraaf M (2011) "Remaking professionals? How associations and professional education connect professionalism and organizations", but the phenomenon privileging other management occupations exists; this has been the nemesis of the personnel and human resource management function over the years. The public-sector organisation, where many professionals of the traditional type work, has succumbed to the blandishments of the market and the entrepreneurial mode (Ferlie et al 1996 ibid). Managerialism within New Public Management restricts the professionals' traditional autonomy and "service delivery" as they "must be monitored and managed", and "professional services must be rationed, and professional behaviour must be evaluated" (See. Noordegraaf 2011 ibid, page 468). In the UK public sector, a managerial cadre for the coordination of organisational tasks rather than public administrators and public servants coordinate activities of the public sector.

52. Pavalko 1971 ibid. Pavalko also added that this type of fragmentation creates the conditions for inter-organisational conflict (page 188).

53. Lewis R and Maude A (1953) *The English Middle Classes*; Wilensky H I (1964) "The professionalization of everyone?"; Suddaby R and Viale T (2011) "Professionals and field-level change: Institutional work and the professional project", observed that the processes of professionalisation "generate new types of actors or legitimate formerly marginalised actors into dominant roles"; see also Baron J N, Dobbin F R, Devereaux Jennings P (1986) "War and Peace: The Evolution of Modern Personnel Administration in US Industry", concerning the field of personnel and human resource management in the United States (Baron et al 1986 ibid). Some commentators have seen different forms of professionalism emerging and occupations with their own professionalisations.

54. This follows the literature, mainly from the twentieth century. Carr-Saunders and Wilson 1933 ibid; Parsons 1939 ibid; Greenwood 1957; (1966) "The elements of professionalization"; Wilensky 1964 ibid; Hickson and Thomas 1969 ibid. The Privy Council Officers associated the Royal Charter with the traditional model of professionalism and assumed that the Institute's aspirations were the same. The papers also show how the Royal Charter was linked to this model of professionalism coalescing around the characteristics of *collective organisation, knowledge and values* (Appendix II). Of note is the letter from the Clerk to the Privy Council to one of the advisers at the Department of Employment in 1991, some twenty-three years after the Institute first approached the Privy Council (Privy Council Papers Set I-xv, 5 June 1991 a letter from the Clerk to the Privy Council to an adviser at the Department of Employment).

55. These are made explicit in the earlier quotations from Cogan 1953 ibid, page 49 and Barber 1963 ibid, page 672 and include knowledge, education, codes of ethics; they are also referent characteristics and values, explaining why the professions appear to have institutional characteristics (see Scott 2008 ibid; Dacin M T, Goodstein J and Scott W R (2002) "Institutional theory

and institutional change"; Bloor D and Dawson P (1994) "Understanding professional culture in organizational context", page 282).

56. Gilmore and Williams 2003, 2007 ibid; Gold and Bratton 2003 ibid. Understanding the change that has taken place has led to later analyses of the traditional professions based on expertise and knowledge and their associated power. This has facilitated the recognition of evolving professionalism recognising new regulatory and occupational contexts. This strengthens the importance of locating the study of occupations and professions in their proper contexts. Suddaby and Viale (2011 ibid, page 431) observed that the processes of professionalisation "generate new types of actors or legitimate formerly marginalised actors into dominant roles" as indicated by Baron et al 1986 ibid. Baron et al (1986) concerning the field of personnel and human resource management in the United States.

57. Lewis and Maude 1953 ibid and Wilensky 1964 ibid already foreshadowed the growth of organisational and managerial professions. See also Reed M and Anthony P (1992) "Professionalizing management and managing professionalization: British management in the 1980s"; Swailes S (2003) "Professionalism: Evolution and measurement", page 131.

58. Swailes 2003 ibid, page 131.

59. Sciulli D (2010) *Structural and Institutional Invariance in Professions and Professionalism*, page 17.

60. Reed M I (1996) *Expert Power and Control in Late Modernity: An Empirical Review and Theoretical Synthesis*, page 586; Reed echoes Wilensky 1964 ibid page 146, who observed "power struggles and status strivings" in professionalisation. Hanlon G (1998) "Professionalism as enterprise: Service class politics and the redefinition of professionalism"; Fincham R (2012) "Expert labour as a differentiated category: Power, knowledge and organisation", page 209; 212 classified occupations based upon their degree of expertise which helps to understand the phenomenon of emerging modern occupations, differentiating between different types of expert work. These are the traditional elite occupations, professional services which include elite occupations in professional service firms, business services which are "high-status" occupations, but not necessarily organised (these include IT and management consultancy), the quasi-professions who mirror elite professions but who are "not necessarily on a professional trajectory" among which HRM, project management and public relations appear (Fincham 2012 ibid, page 209), and finally the knowledge workers, described as "a category of knowledge-intensive work defined by analytic problem solving". Management consultancy is an example of "corporate professionalism" see Kipping et al 2006 ibid, and Muzio et al 2011 ibid in their comparative work on management consulting, project management and executive search found that these occupations have a knowledge base with a practical orientation. Not all groups engaged in such a struggle will succeed in their professionalisations or "occupational upgrading". In Britain, project management and management consulting are two examples that have not succeeded in professionalising. On the other hand, accountancy, psychology, nursing, teaching and podiatry are examples of those occupations that have professionalised, by dint of governmental regulatory requirements which are devolved to a range of professional or occupational associations, such as the Healthcare Professions Council.

61. Fincham 2012 ibid; Reed 1996, ibid, page 579; Muzio D and Kirkpatrick I (2011) "Introduction: Professions and organizations—a conceptual framework", page 392, who asserted that occupational control of organisational

and managerial processes "does represent a professional project" and furthermore does privilege management and add weight to their status and "occupational upgrading" (Sciulli 2010 ibid).

62. Dent and Whitehead 2002 ibid page 1.
63. Evetts 2011 ibid, page 408; Kipping 2011 ibid, page 533.
64. Aldridge M and Evetts J (2003) "Rethinking the concept of professionalism: The case of journalism", page 556.
65. Fournier V (1999) "The appeal to 'professionalism' as a disciplinary mechanism"; Aldridge and Evetts 2003 ibid. Occupational groups, whether professionals or emerging professions use discursive devices drawn from views of their own experiences and relationships with key stakeholders. In Wai-Fong and Clegg's study of nursing in Britain, the implementation of practices and the language of *professionalism* were extant in the search for occupational closure by nursing in Britain, illustrating the power of both the language and ideas of *professionalism*; Wai-Fong C and Clegg S (1990) "Professional closure: The case of British nursing".
66. Lok J (2010) "Institutional logics as identity projects"; Muzio and Kirkpatrick 2011 ibid, page 400, Kipping 2011 ibid, page 544 called "professionalism" a "linguistic construct" which mimicked the traditional professions and gave as an example the case of management consultancy, in which *professionalism* was used as a mark of excellence, and then as a discursive device to control practitioner behaviour. Kipping concluded that the empty "linguistic construct" had to be bolstered by increased bureaucratic controls.
67. Muzio et al 2011 ibid; Muzio and Kirkpatrick 2011 ibid; Evetts 2011 ibid. Although by 1990 Larson (1977 ibid, page 49) had retreated from that position in which a "professional project" concerned the acquisition of a closed market and monopoly, the idea of a "professional project" as part of "occupational upgrading" (see Sciulli 2010 ibid) remains powerful as it carries the meanings of power, prestige and closure observed in the "archetypal" professions (see Larson 1977 ibid).
68. Evetts 2003 ibid; Sciulli 2010 ibid.
69. Anderson-Gough F, Grey C and Robson K (1998) "Work hard, play hard: An analysis of organizational cliché in two accountancy practices"; Fournier 1999 ibid.
70. Evetts 2011 ibid, page 408.
71. Preece D A and Nicol B N (1980) "Personnel management, power and the certification process"; *professionalism* as a rhetorical device resolves the "tension which it embodies in the disjunction between the part (the interest of an occupation group) and the whole (the society in which that occupation is carried out on).
72. Privy Council Papers Set II-vii, anonymous file note, after 14 November 1996. "(The Director-General) said that the membership had voted, in the context of the merger that the IPD should aim to obtain a Charter. The Institute was a unique body whose important contribution to the economy should be recognised. Personnel aspects were increasingly central to the success or failure of organisations, and recognition of the IPD by means of a Charter would help bring home the importance of the discipline. In other words, it was not seen just a matter of status for members of the Institute." This is an example of the actors speaking to different audiences, the Director-General speaking to different audiences—status is of interest to members—for example in other pronouncements and in the interview of 2010, but to the Privy Council issues of status were not good, but attention to a public good was important.
73. Privy Council Papers Set II-vii, after 14 November 1996, ibid.

74. Bucher R and Stelling J G (1977) *Becoming Professional*; Shuval J T and Gilbert L (1978) "Attempts at professionalization of pharmacy: An Israel case study"; Aldridge and Evetts 2003 ibid, page 556.
75. See Millerson 1964 ibid; Hickson and Thomas 1969 ibid.
76. Social closure, occupational closure, "de jure" closure: see Larson 1977 ibid; Abbott A (1988) *The System of Professions*; Macdonald K M (1985) "Social closure and occupational registration".
77. Reed 1996 ibid; Hanlon 1998 ibid; Swailes 2003 ibid.
78. Hanlon 1998 ibid, page 59.
79. Social closure, occupational closure, "de jure" closure: see Larson 1977; Abbott 1988 ibid; Macdonald 1985 ibid.
80. Sciulli 2010 ibid, page 5.
81. Hodgson 2008 ibid, page 232.
82. As I work with practitioners seeking accreditation, I often look around the classroom and see an abundance of females and some, but very few males, aspiring to become practitioners. It is difficult to know for certain whether the structural gendered membership of the profession has contributed to the inability of the Institute to get further and sooner with its professional project, and to say anything else would be unhelpful, albeit interesting, speculation.
83. Privy Council Papers Set I-i, 15 January 1968 a letter between the Institution of Production Engineers and the Privy Council.
84. This is literature exemplified by Carr-Saunders and Wilson 1933 ibid; Cogan 1953 ibid; Greenwood 1957, 1966 ibid; Parsons 1939 ibid; Millerson 1964 ibid; Hickson and Thomas 1969 ibid; Wilensky 1964 ibid.
85. Privy Council Papers Set I-xv, 5 June 1991, a letter from the Deputy Clerk to the Privy Council to an official at the Department of Employment which explains the circumstances under which charters are given.
86. Faulconbridge J R and Muzio D (2008) "Organizational professionalism in globalizing law firms".
87. This is indicated by two key Institute insiders (Seears 1979 and Coates in Lawrence 1979 ibid, page 40), and reflected by Preece and Nicol 1980, and Coke S (1983) "Putting professionalism in its place"; Coates in Lawrence 1979 ibid, page 40; Seears 1979; later at the time of the combination of the ITD and IPM another practitioner who contributed to the article in *Personnel Management* 1993 did say that the IPM had been concerned with professionalisation.
88. Director-General interview 20 February 2010.
89. This is *institutional work*, from the body of tools in New-Institutional theory; see note 19.
90. Birkett and Evans 2005 ibid, page 105.
91. Niven 1967 ibid.
92. Hodgson 2008 ibid, page 232.
93. Birkett and Evans 2005 ibid; Larson 1977 ibid; De Vries et al 2009.
94. Bringing the Institute's story into the late twentieth and early twenty-first century, it is less clear that the award of the Royal Charter brought the professional project to successful conclusion. The notion was impossible due to the nature of the practices, and the site of the practices, but more significantly, the model of traditional professionalism had already begun to lose its shape and meaning and had evolved into something else.
95. CIPD (2012) *About Us—for the Profession*.
96. Crabb 1999 ibid, page 42.
97. This is reminiscent of Dent's (2008 ibid, page 116) view of the changed requirements for medical practice, as the traditional professional model changed; see Dent 2008 ibid.

98. Mackay L and Torrington D (1986) *The Changing Nature of Personnel Management,* page 161–162.
99. See Dryburgh 1972 ibid. The Director-General in interview with me in February 2010 when explaining the Charter and some of the things he had accomplished said: "The Institute had a sense that [. . .] the profession was regarded as a bit of a non-profession, at least it wasn't a proper profession in the sense that accountancy was."
100. The ability of the profession to both circumscribe the knowledge and produce the practitioner through programmes of qualifications has distinct links with the traditional model and has been observed with the prospects for the professionalisation of the personnel/human resource practitioner (Lengnick-Hall M L and Aguinis H (2012) "What is the value of human resource certification? A multi-level framework for research", pages 246–257). Thus, the "power of expertise" (Reed 1996 ibid, page 586) can be discerned in the "professional project". The power strategy of the independent liberal professions, the traditional professional, is "monopolization", that of the entrepreneurial professional, "marketization" and, importantly for this study, the power strategy of the organisational professionals is "credentialism" (Reed 1996 ibid, page 586).
101. Preece and Nicol 1980 ibid, page 32 noted intra-occupational conflict in relation to personnel management in the early 1980s arising between those who sought to develop "exclusiveness" as a power strategy, and those who said expertise was a source of power. *Professionalism* is, therefore, an important idea in relation to the Institute's "professional project" and connects to the internal debate in the Institute concerning the wisdom of professionalising in the traditional mode. See also Watson T J (2002b) "Speaking professionally: Occupational anxiety and discursive ingenuity among human resourcing specialists".
102. Reed C (2018) "Professionalizing corporate professions: Professionalization as identity project".
103. CIPD (2013a) "CIPD—Championing better work and working lives—CIPD", and (2013b) "About us"; Millerson 1964 ibid.

## Bibliography

Abbott A (1988) *The System of Professions,* Chicago: University of Chicago Press.
Adler P S, Kwon S-K and Heckscher C (2008) "Professional work: The emergence of collaborative community", *Organization Science* 19(2): 359–376.
Aldridge M and Evetts J (2003) "Rethinking the concept of professionalism: The case of journalism", *British Journal of Sociology* 54(4): 547–564.
Alford R R and Friedland R (1985) *Powers of Theory: Capitalism, the State, and Democracy,* Cambridge: Cambridge University Press.
Alvesson M and Johansson A W (2002) "Professionalism and politics in management consultancy work", in T Clark and R Fincham (eds) *Critical Consulting: New Perspectives on the Management Advice Industry,* Oxford: Blackwell.
Anderson-Gough F, Grey C and Robson K (1998) "Work hard, play hard: An analysis of organizational cliché in two accountancy practices", *Organization* 5(4): 562–592.
Andrews T M and Waerness K (2011) "Deprofessionalization of a female occupation: Challenges for the sociology of professions", *Current Sociology* 59(1): 42–58.

Barber B (1963) "Some problems in the sociology of the professions", *Daedalus Journal of the American Academy of Arts and Sciences* 92(4): 669–688.

Baron J N, Dobbin F R and Devereaux Jennings P (1986) "War and peace: The evolution of modern personnel administration in US industry", *The American Journal of Sociology* 92(2): 350–383.

Birkett W P and Evans E (2005) "Theorising professionalisation: A model for organising and understanding histories of the professionalising activities of occupational associations of accountants", *Accounting History* 10(1): 99–127.

Bloor D and Dawson P (1994) "Understanding professional culture in organizational context", *Organization Studies* 15(2): 275–295.

Brundage J A (1994) "The rise of the professional Jurist in the thirteenth century", *Syracuse Journal of Law and Commerce* 20: 185, Spring.

Bucher R and Stelling J G (1977) *Becoming Professional*, London: Sage Publications.

Burrage M, Jarausch K and Siegrist H (1990) "An actor-based framework for the study of the professions", in M Burrage and R Torstendahl (eds) *Professions in Theory and History: Rethinking the Study of the Professions*, London: Sage Publications.

Cabinet Office (2009) *New Opportunities White Paper*, www.hmg.gov.uk/media/9102/NewOpportunities.pdf, accessed 14 January 2009.

Carr-Saunders A M and Wilson P A (1933) *The Professions*, Oxford: Clarendon Press.

CIPD (2012) *About Us—for the Profession*, www.cipd.co.uk/cipd-hr-profession/about-us/for-profession.aspx, accessed 3 September 2012.

CIPD (2013a) *CIPD—Championing Better Work and Working Lives—CIPD*, web page portal, www.cipd.co.uk, accessed 10 May 2013.

CIPD (2013b) *About Us*, www.cipd.co.uk/cipd-hr-profession/about-us/, accessed 21 July 2013.

Cogan M L (1953) "Towards a definition of profession", *Harvard Educational Review* 23: 33–50, Winter.

Coke S (1983) "Putting professionalism in its place", *Personnel Management*: 44–45.

Constable J and McCormick R (1987) *The Making of British Managers: A Report for the BIM and CBI into Management Training, Education and Development*, London: British Institute of Management.

Cooper D J, Hinings C R, Greenwood R and Brown J L (1996) "Sedimentation and transformation in organizational change: The case of Canadian law firms", *Organization Studies* 17(4): 623–647.

Crabb S (1999) "Seal of approval", *People Management* 5(16): 42, 19 August.

Craig J (ed) (2006) *Production Values, Futures for Professionalism*, London: Demos.

Crawshaw N (2002) "Another level", *People Management* 8(21): 81.

Dacin M T, Goodstein J and Scott W R (2002) "Institutional theory and institutional change", *The Academy of Management Journal* 45(1): 43–56.

Daniels K (2012) *A History of the CIPD and HR*, CIPD, www.cipd.co.uk/hr-resources/factsheets/history-hr-cipd.aspx, accessed May 2012.

Dent M (2008) "Medicine, nursing and changing professional jurisdictions in the UK", in D Muzio, S Ackroyd and J-F Chanlat (eds) *Redirections in the Study of Expert Labour-Established Professions and New Expert Occupations*, Basingstoke: Palgrave Macmillan.

Dent M and Whitehead S (eds) (2002) *Managing Professional Identities: Knowledge, Performativity and the "New Professional"*, London: Routledge.

De Vries R, Dingwall R and Orfali K (2009) "The moral organization of the professions", *Current Sociology* 57: 555–580.

DiMaggio P J and Powell W W (1983) "The iron cage revisited: Institutional isomorphism and collective rationality in organizational fields", *American Sociological Review* 48: 147–160.

Etzioni A (ed) (1969) *The Semi-Professions and Their Organization: Teachers, Nurses, Social Workers*, New York: Free Press.

Evetts J (2003) "The sociological analysis of professionalism: Occupational change in the modern world", *International Sociology* 18(2): 395–415.

Evetts J (2009) "New professionalism and new public management: Changes, continuities and consequences", *Comparative Sociology* 8: 247–266.

Evetts J (2011) "A new professionalism? Challenges and opportunities", *Current Sociology* 59(4): 406–427.

Faulconbridge J R and Muzio D (2008) "Organizational professionalism in globalizing law firms", *Work, Employment and Society* 22(1): 7–25.

Ferlie E, Ashburner L, Fitzgerald L and Pettigrew A (1996) *The New Public Management in Action*, Oxford: Oxford University Press.

Fincham R (2012) "Expert labour as a differentiated category: Power, knowledge and organisation", *New Technology, Work and Employment* 27(3): 208–223.

Flood J (2008) "Partnership and professionalism in global law firms: Resurgent professionalism?" in D Muzio, S Ackroyd and J-F Chanlat (eds) *Redirections in the Study of Expert Labour-Established Professions and New Expert Occupations*, Basingstoke: Palgrave Macmillan.

Fournier V (1999) "The appeal to 'professionalism' as a disciplinary mechanism", *The Sociological Review* 47(2): 280–307.

Friedland R and Alford R R (1991) "Bringing society back in: Symbols, practise, and institutional contradictions", in W W Powell and P J DiMaggio (eds) *The New Institutionalism in Organizational Analysis*, Chicago, IL: University of Chicago Press.

Gilmore S and Williams S (2003) *Constructing the HR Professional: A Critical Analysis of the Chartered Institute of Personnel and Development's "Professional Project"*, www.mngt.waikato.ac.nz/ejrot/cmsconference/2003/proceedings/hrmphenomena/Gilmore.pdf, accessed 7 January 2009.

Gilmore S and Williams S (2007) "Conceptualising the 'Personnel Professional': A critical analysis of the chartered institute of personnel and development's professional qualification scheme", *Personnel Review* 36(3): 398–414.

Gold J and Bratton J (2003) *The Dynamics of Professionalization: Whither the HRM Profession?* Paper delivered at the Third Critical Management Studies Conference, Stream 8, Human Resource Management Phenomena—HRM and beyond.

Greenwood E (1957) "Attributes of a profession", *Social Work* 2: 445–450.

Greenwood E (1966) "The elements of professionalization", in H M Vollmer and D L Mills (eds) *Professionalization*, Englewood Cliffs, NJ: Prentice Hall, pages 9–19.

Greenwood, R, Suddaby R and Hinings C R (2002) "Theorizing change: The role of professional associations in the transformation of institutionalized fields", *Academy of Management Journal* 45(1): 58–80.

Hammond K H (2005) "Why we hate HR", *FastCompany*, 1 August, www.fastcompany.com/magazine/97/open_hr.htl#, accessed 7 October 2009.

Handy C (1987) *The Making of Managers: A Report on Management Education, Training and Development in the USA, West Germany, France, Japan and the UK*, London: National Economic Development Office.

Hanlon G (1998) "Professionalism as enterprise: Service class politics and the redefinition of professionalism", *Sociology* 32(1): 43–64.

Hargadon A B and Douglas Y (2001) "When innovation meet institutions: Edison and the design of the electric light", *Administrative Science Quarterly* 46(3): 476–501.

Heracleous L and Barrett M (2001) "Organizational change as discourse: Communicative actions and deep structures in the context of information technology implementation", *Academy of Management Journal* 44(4): 755–778.

Hickson D J and Thomas M W (1969) "Professionalization in Britain: A preliminary measurement", *Sociology* 3: 37–53.

Hinings C R and Greenwood R (2002) "Disconnects and consequences in organization theory?" *Administrative Science Quarterly* 47(3): 411–421.

Hodgson D (2008) "The new professionals: Professionalisation and the struggle for occupational control in the field of project management", in D Muzio, S Ackroyd and J-F Chanlat (eds) *Redirections in the Study of Expert Labour-Established Professions and New Expert Occupations*, Basingstoke: Palgrave Macmillan.

Hoffman A J (1999) "Institutional evolution and change: Environmentalism and the US chemical industry", *Academy of Management Journal* 42: 351–371.

Investors in People—UK Commission for Employment and Skills *Investment in People—Background*, www.investorsinpeople.co.uk/About/Pages/default.aspx, accessed 28 June 2013.

Jacques R (1996) *Manufacturing the Employee: Management Knowledge from the 19th to the 21st Centuries*, London and Thousand Oaks, CA: Sage Publications.

Jennings P D and Zandbergen P A (1995) "Ecologically sustainable organizations: An institutional approach", *Academy of Management Review* 20: 1015–1052.

Jepperson R L (1991) "Institutions, institutional effects and institutionalism", in W W Powell and P J DiMaggio (eds) *The New Institutionalism in Organizational Analysis*, Chicago: University of Chicago Press, pages 1143–1163.

Johnson L (2008) "The truth about the HR department", *FT.com*, http://wwww.ft.com/cms/0/ec6f81e6-ce89-11dc-877a-000077b07658.html, accessed 7 October 2009.

Johnson T J (1972) *Professions and Power*, London and Basingstoke: Macmillan Press Ltd.

Kaufman B E (2008) *Managing the Human Factor: The Early Years of Human Resource Management in American Industry*, Ithaca and London: ILR an Imprint of Cornell University Press.

Kenny T P (1972) "Professional examinations for British training staff", *Training and Development Journal*: 40–43, February.

Khaire M and Wadhwani R D (2010) "Changing landscapes: The construction of meaning and value in a new market category—modern Indian art", *Academy of Management Journal* 53(6): 1281–1304.

King D S (1993) "The conservatives and training policy 1979–1992: From a tripartite to a neoliberal regime", *Political Studies* XLI: 214–235.

Kipping M (2011) "Hollow from the start? Image professionalism in management consulting", *Current Sociology* 59(4): 530–550.

Kraatz M S and Block E S (2008) "Organizational implications of institutional pluralism", in R Greenwood, C Oliver, R Suddaby and K Sahlin-Anderson (eds) *Handbook of Organizational Institutionalism*, Thousand Oaks, CA: Sage Publications, pages 243–276.

Larson M S (1977) *The Rise of Professionalism: A Sociological Analysis*, London and Berkeley: University of California Press.

Lawrence S (1979) "Man of the moment: Jack Coates", *Personnel Management* 11(10): 36–40.

Lawrence T B, Hardy C and Phillips N (2004) "Institutional effects of interorganizational collaboration: The emergence of proto-institutions", *Academy of Management Journal* 45(1): 281–290.

Lawrence T B and Suddaby R (2006) "Institutions and institutional work", in S R Clegg, C Hardy and W R Nord (eds) *The Sage Handbook of Organization Studies*, 2nd edition, London: Sage Publications, pages 215–254.

Legge K (1987) "Women in personnel management: Uphill climb or downhill slide", in A Spencer and D B L Podmore (eds) *In a Man's World: Essays on Women in Male-Dominated Professions*, London: Tavistock Publications.

Legge K (1988) "Personnel management in recession and recovery: A comparative analysis of what the surveys say", *Personnel Review* 17(2).

Legge K (1995) *Human Resource Management: Rhetorics and Realities*, London: Palgrave Macmillan.

Lengnick-Hall M L and Aguinis H (2012) "What is the value of human resource certification? A multi-level framework for research", *Human Resource Management Review* 22(4): 246–257.

Leicht K T (2005) "Professions", in G Ritzer (ed) *Encyclopaedia of Social Theory*, Thousand Oaks, CA: Sage Publications.

Lewis R and Maude A (1953) *The English Middle Classes*, Great Britain: Penguin Books.

Lok J (2010) "Institutional logics as identity projects", *Academy of Management Journal* 53(6): 1305–1335.

Mackay L and Torrington D (1986) *The Changing Nature of Personnel Management*, London: Institute of Personnel Management.

Maguire S, Hardy C and Lawrence T B (2004) "Institutional entrepreneurship in emerging fields: HIV/AIDS treatment advocacy in Canada", *Academy of Management Journal* 47: 657–679.

Marks W (1978) *Politics and Personnel Management: An Outline History, 1960–1976*, London: Institute of Personnel Management.

Millerson G (1964) *The Qualifying Association: A Study in Professionalization*, London: Routledge.

Monopolies Commission (1970) *A Report on the General Effect on the Public Interest of Certain Restrictive Practices so Far as They Prevail in Relation to the Supply of Professional Services*, London: Her Majesty's Stationery Office, www.competition-commission.gov.uk/rep_pub/reports/1970_1975/fulltext/059c01.pdf, accessed 13 January 2009.

Morris P W G, Crawford L, Hodgson D, Shepherd M M and Thomas J (2006) "Exploring the role of formal bodies of knowledge in defining a profession: The case of project management", *International Journal of Project Management* 24: 710–721.

Muzio D and Ackroyd S (2008) "Change in the legal profession: Professional agency and the legal labour process", in D Muzio, S Ackroyd and J-F Chanlat (eds) *Redirections in the Study of Expert Labour-Established Professions and New Expert Occupations*, Basingstoke: Palgrave Macmillan.

Muzio D, Hodgson D, Faulconbridge J, Beaverstock J and Hall S (2011) "Towards corporate professionalization: The case of project management, management consultancy and executive search", *Current Sociology* 59(4): 443–464.

Muzio D and Kirkpatrick I (2011) "Introduction: Professions and organizations—a conceptual framework", *Current Sociology* 59(4): 389–405.

Niven M (1967) *Personnel Management 1913–1963: The Growth of Personnel Management and the Development of the Institute*, London: Institute of Personnel Management.

Noordegraaf M (2011) "Remaking professionals? How associations and professional education connect professionalism and organizations", *Current Sociology* 59(4): 465–488.

Palmer D, Biggart N and Dick B (2008) "Is the new institutionalism a theory?" in R Greenwood, C Oliver, R Suddaby and K Sahlin-Anderson (eds) *Organizational Institutionalism*, London: Sage Publications, Chapter 32, pages 769–782.

Parsons T (1939) "The professions and social structure", *Social Forces*: 457–467, May.

Pavalko R M (1971) *The Sociology of Occupations and Professions*, Itasca, IL: F E Peacock Publishers Inc.

Personnel Management (1993) "The case for combination", *Personnel Management* 25(12): 26–32.

Powell W W and DiMaggio P J (1991) (eds) *The New Institutionalism in Organizational Analysis*, Chicago, IL: University of Chicago Press.

Preece D A and Nicol B N (1980) "Personnel management, power and the certification process", *Personnel Review* 9(4): 27–32.

Reed C (2018) "Professionalizing corporate professions: Professionalization as identity project", *Management Learning* 49(2): 222–238.

Reed M and Anthony P (1992) "Professionalizing management and managing professionalization: British management in the 1980s", *Journal of Management Studies* 29(5): 591–613.

Reed M I (1996) "Expert power and control in late modernity: An empirical review and theoretical synthesis", *Organization Studies* 17(4): 573–597.

Ridgeway C (1982) "The role of the secretary in personnel management", *Leadership and Organization Development Journal* 3(2): 17–20.

Sahlin-Andersson K (1996) "Imitating success: The construction of organizational fields", in B Czarniaswka and G Sevon (eds) *Translating Organizational Change*, Berlin: Walter de Gruyter and Co, pages 13–48.

Sciulli D (2010) *Structural and Institutional Invariance in Professions and Professionalism*, Oslo, Norway: Senter for profesjonssudier.

Scott W R (2001) *Institutions and Organizations*, Thousand Oaks, CA: Sage Publications.

Scott W R (2008a) "Lords of the dance: Professionals as institutional agents", *Organisational Studies* 29(2): 219–238.

Scott W R (2008b) *Institutions and Organisations: Ideas and interests*, Thousand Oak, CA: Sage Publications.

Seears N (1979) "Can personnel managers deliver?" *Personnel Management* 11(10).

Selznick P (1949) *TVA and the Grass Roots: A Study in the Sociology of Formal Organization*, Berkeley and Los Angeles, CA: University of California Press.

Shuval J T and Gilbert L (1978) "Attempts at professionalization of pharmacy: An Israel case study", *Social Science and Medicine*: 19–25.

Suchman M (1995) "Managing legitimacy: Strategic and institutional approaches", *Academy of Management Review* 20: 571–611.

Suddaby R and Viale T (2011) "Professionals and field-level change: Institutional work and the professional project", *Current Sociology* 59(4): 423–442.

Swailes S (2003) "Professionalism: Evolution and measurement", *Service Industries Journal* 23(2): 130–149.

Thornton P H and Ocasio W (1999) "Institutional logics and the historical contingency of power in organizations: Executive succession in the higher education publishing industry, 1958–1990", *American Journal of Sociology* 105(3): 801–843.

Timperley S R and Osbaldeston M D (1975) "The professionalization process: A study of an aspiring occupational organization", *The Sociological Review* 23(3): 607–627.

Tyson S and Fell A (1986) "The crisis in personnel management", in S Tyson and A Fell (eds) *Evaluating the Personnel Function*, London: Hutchinson Education, Chapter 8.

Wai-Fong C and Clegg S (1990) "Professional closure: The case of British nursing", *Theory and Society* 19(2): 135–172.

Watson T J (2002) "Speaking professionally: Occupational anxiety and discursive ingenuity among human resourcing specialists", in M Dent and S Whitehead (eds) *Managing Professional Identities: Knowledge, Performativity and the "New Professional"*, London: Routledge, Chapter 6, pages 99–115.

Wilensky H I (1964) "The professionalization of everyone?" *American Journal of Sociology* 70(2): 137–158.

Williams A P O (2010) *The History of UK Business and Management Education*, Bingley: Emerald Group Publishing.

Williams C (1999) "Corporate ascent", *People Management* 5(8): 1–2.

Williams C (2003) "How to . . . be a chartered CIPD member", *People Management* 9(20): 52–53, 8 October.

Wright V (2012) *View from the CIPD: Accountable to All*, http://blog.peoplemanagement.co.uk/2012/04/view-from-the-cipd-accountable-to-all/#more-983, accessed 25 April 2012.

# Author Biography

**Ruth Elizabeth Slater** is a chartered member of the Chartered Institute of Personnel and Development (CIPD) and holds a PhD from the Department of Organisation, Work and Technology, Lancaster University. Additionally, she holds two master's degrees: in Strategic Human Resource Management and in HR and Knowledge Management. She is a seasoned HR professional and has worked in several organisations within HRM prior to working in higher education.

Ruth is Course Leader on the full-time MSc in HRM and HRD at the University of Central Lancashire. This is a programme accredited with the CIPD, the professional body for HR and HRD practitioners. She also supervises both undergraduate and postgraduate dissertations and work-based projects, and doctoral candidates.

Ruth researches management and work practices, and organisational history. She is a member of the Institute for Research into Organisations, Work and Employment (iROWE) at the University of Central Lancashire. She has undertaken historical research to set the formation and development of the former Institute of Personnel Management (IPM) into a broader context. Ruth is interested in helping practitioner-researchers use participatory and collaborative methods of research in their own organisations.

# Bibliography

Abbott A (1988) *The System of Professions*, Chicago, IL: University of Chicago Press.

Abel-Smith B and Stevens R (1967) *Lawyers and the Courts: A Sociological Study of the English Legal System 1750–1965*, London: Heinemann.

Adler P S, Kwon S-K and Heckscher C (2008) "Professional work: The emergence of collaborative community", *Organization Science* 19(2): 359–376.

Aldridge M and Evetts J (2003) "Rethinking the concept of professionalism: The case of journalism", *British Journal of Sociology* 54(4): 547–564.

Alford R R and Friedland R (1985) *Powers of Theory: Capitalism, the State, and Democracy*, Cambridge: Cambridge University Press.

Alvesson M and Johansson A W (2002) "Professionalism and politics in management consultancy work", in T Clark and R Fincham (eds) *Critical Consulting: New Perspectives on the Management Advice Industry*, Oxford: Blackwell.

Alvesson M and Kärreman D (2000) "Taking the linguistic turn in organisational research: Challenges, responses, consequences", *Journal of Applied Behavioural Science* 36: 136–158.

Anderson A M (1922) *Women in the Factory: An Administrative Adventure 1893–1921*, London: John Murray.

Anderson-Gough F, Grey C and Robson K (1998) "Work hard, play hard: An analysis of organizational cliché in two accountancy practices", *Organization* 5(4): 562–592.

Andrews T M and Waerness K (2011) "Deprofessionalization of a female occupation: Challenges for the sociology of professions", *Current Sociology* 59(1): 42–58.

Anthony P and Crichton A (1969) *Industrial Relations and the Personnel Specialists*, London: BT Batsford Limited.

Armstrong G (1994) "Comment: A sound foundation for the IPD", *Personnel Management* 26(7): 20.

Armstrong G (2000) "The smarter charter", *People Management* 6(14): 54.

Armstrong M (1977) *A Handbook of Personnel Management Practice*, London and Sterling, VA: Kogan Page.

Armstrong M (2009) *Armstrong's Handbook of Human Resource Practice*, 11th edition, London and Sterling: Kogan Page.

Armstrong P (1985) "Changing management control strategies: The role of competition between accountancy and other organisational professions", *Accounting, Organizations and Society* 10(2): 129–148.

Armstrong P (1986) "Management control strategies and inter-professional competition: The cases of accountancy and personnel management", in D Knights and H Willmott (eds) *Managing the Labour Process*, Aldershot: Gower.

Bailey M (2011) "Policy, professionalism, professionality and the development of HR practitioners in the UK", *Journal of European Industrial Training* 3(5): 487–501.

Barber B (1963) "Some problems in the sociology of the professions", *Daedalus*: 669–688.

Barber D (1971) *The Practice of Personnel Management*, London: Institute of Personnel Management.

Barber D (1979) *The Practice of Personnel Management*, London: Institute of Personnel Management.

Barley S R and Tolbert P S (1997) "Institutionalization and structuration: Studying the link between action and institution", *Organisation Studies* 18(1): 93–117.

Baron J N, Dobbin F R and Devereaux Jennings P (1986) "War and peace: The evolution of modern personnel administration in US industry", *The American Journal of Sociology* 92(2): 350–383.

Beer M and Spector B (1985) "Corporate wide transformations in human resource management", in R E Walton and P R Lawrence (eds) *Human Resource Management, Trends and Challenges*, Boston: Harvard Business School Press.

Beer M, Spector B, Lawrence P R, Mills D Q and Walton R E (1984) *Managing Human Assets*, New York: Free Press.

Birkett W P and Evans E (2005) "Theorising professionalisation: A model for organising and understanding histories of the professionalising activities of occupational associations of accountants", *Accounting History* 10(1): 99–127.

Blackford K M H and Newcomb A (1915) *The Job, the Man, the Boss*, Garden City, NY: Doubleday, Page and Company.

Bloor D and Dawson P (1994) "Understanding professional culture in organizational context", *Organization Studies* 15(2): 275–295.

Brewster C and Hegewisch A (eds) (2017) *Policy and Practice in European Human Resource Management: The Price Waterhouse Cranfield Survey*, London: Taylor & Francis.

Bröckling U (2015) *The Entrepreneurial Self: Fabricating a New Type of Subject*, London: Sage Publications.

Brooks W R (1986) *Pettyfoggers and Vipers of the Commonwealth: The "Lower Branch" of the Legal Profession in Early Modern England*, Cambridge: Cambridge University Press.

Brown D (2009) "Letters—a bridge-building strategy?" *Personnel Management* 15(23): 16, 5 November.

Brundage J A (1994) "The rise of the professional Jurist in the thirteenth century", *Syracuse Journal of Law and Commerce* 20: 185, Spring.

Bucher R and Stelling J G (1977) *Becoming Professional*, London: Sage Publications.

Burrage M (1990) "Introduction: The professions in sociology and history", in M Burrage and R Torstendahl (eds) *Professions in Theory and History: Rethinking the Study of the Professions*, London: Sage Publications.

Burrage M, Jarausch K and Siegrist H (1990) "An Actor-based framework for the study of the professions", in M Burrage and R Torstendahl (eds) *Professions in Theory and History: Rethinking the Study of the Professions*, London: Sage Publications.

Burrage M and Torstendahl R (eds) (1990) *Professions in Theory and History*, London: Sage Publications.

Cabinet Office (2009a) *New Opportunities White Paper*, www.hmg.gov.uk/media/9102/NewOpportunities.pdf, accessed 14 January 2009.

Cabinet Office (2009b) *Panel on Fair Access to the Professions Announced— New Opportunities White Paper*, www.cabinetoffice.gov.uk/newsroom/news_releases/2009/090113_nopanel.aspx, accessed 14 January 2009.

Cadbury E (1912) *Industrial Organization*, London and New York: Longmans Green and Co.

Carr-Saunders A M and Wilson P A (1933) *The Professions*, Oxford: Clarendon Press.

Chartered Institute of Personnel and Development (2003) *Annual Report 2002–2003*.

CIPD (2007) *Professional Standards*, www.cipd.co.uk/NR/rdonlyres/3BF07636-4E9A-4BDB-8916-95CC94F72EC9/0/profstands.pdf.

CIPD (2008a) *CIPD Appoints Current Chief Economist John Philpott to Head Up New Public Policy Department*, CIPD Press Office, HTTP://www.cipd.co.uk/pressoffice/_articles/021208Johnphilpottsappointment.htm, accessed 17 March 2009.

CIPD (2008b) *Code of Professional Conduct and Disciplinary Procedures*, London: CIPD, February.

CIPD (2009a) *Annual Report and Accounts 2008–2009*, London: CIPD.

CIPD (2009b) *The CIPD's HR Profession Map*, www.cipd.co.uk/hr-profession-map/default.htm, accessed 28 October 2009.

CIPD (2012) *About Us—for the Profession*, www.cipd.co.uk/cipd-hr-profession/about-us/for-profession.aspx, accessed 3 September 2012.

CIPD (2013a) *CIPD—Championing Better Work and Working Lives—CIPD*, web page portal, www.cipd.co.uk, accessed 10 May 2013.

CIPD (2013b) *About Us*, www.cipd.co.uk/cipd-hr-profession/about-us/, accessed 21 July 2013.

CIPD Annual Report (2003–4) www.cipd.co.uk/about/who-we-are/annual-report.

CIPD Press Office (2003) *CIPD Members Vote "Yes" to Individual Chartered Status*, Press release 5 June, www.cipd.co.uk/pressoffice/_articles/05062003083008.htm?IsSrchRes=1, accessed 24 November 2010.

Clarke D (2010a) *CIPD—Tale of a Fake Fatcat*, http://donaldclarkplanb.blogspot.com/2010/06/cipd-tale-of-fake-fatcat.html, accessed 9 June 2019.

Clarke D (2010b) *CIPD Accused of Incompetence in Telegraph*, http://donaldclarkplanb.blogspot.com/2010/07/cipd-accused-of-incompetence-in.html, accessed 27 July 2010.

Clarke D (2010c) *CIPDs Jackie Orme Issues Grovelling Apology & Pulls Report Monday*, 26 July, http://donaldclarkplanb.blogspot.com/2010/07/cipds-jackie-orme-issues-grovelling.html, accessed 27 July 2010.

Clarke V M (1949) *New Times, New Methods and New Men*, London: George Allen and Unwin Ltd.

Cogan M L (1953) "Towards a definition of profession", *Harvard Educational Review* 23: 33–50, Winter.

Coke S (1983) "Putting professionalism in its place", *Personnel Management*: 44–45, February.

Constable J and McCormick R (1987) *The Making of British Managers: A Report for the BIM and CBI into Management Training, Education and Development*, London: British Institute of Management.

Cooper D J, Hinings C R, Greenwood R and Brown J L (1996) "Sedimentation and transformation in organizational change: The case of Canadian law firms", *Organization Studies* 17(4): 623–647.

Cooper D J and Robson K (2006) "Accounting, professions and regulation: Locating the sites of professionalization", *Accounting, Organizations and Society* 31: 415–444.

Crabb S (1999) "Seal of approval", *People Management* 5(16): 42, 19 August.

Crabb S (2000) "Major league", *People Management* 6(5): 52, 2 March.

Crabb S (2007) "Exit interview", *People Management* 13(9): 24–28, 3 May.

Craig J (ed) (2006) *Production Values, Futures for Professionalism*, London: Demos.

Crawshaw N (2002) "Another level", *People Management* 8(21): 81.

Crichton A (1985) "Man of the moment—John Crosby", *Personnel Management*: 28, October.

Crofts P (2003) "Upgrade campaign is on", *People Management* 9(13): 62, 25 June.

Crofts P (2004a) "Benefits of upgrading", *People Management* 10(8): 60, 22 April.

Crofts P (2004b) "Stepping up a level", *People Management* 10(2): 60, 29 January.

Crofts P (2005) "A good time to upgrade", *People Management* 11(12): 53, 16 June.

Crompton R (1987) "Gender, status and professionalism", *Sociology* 21(3): 413–428.

Czarniawska B (2008) "How to misuse institutions and get away with it: Some reflections on institutional theory(ies)", in R Greenwood, C Oliver, R Suddaby and K Sahlin-Anderson (eds) *Organizational Institutionalism*, London: Sage Publications, Chapter 32, pages 769–782.

Daniels K (2012) *A History of the CIPD and HR*, CIPD, www.cipd.co.uk/hr-resources/factsheets/history-hr-cipd.aspx, accessed May 2012.

Davis G F, Dieckman K A and Tinsley C H (1994) "The decline and fall of the conglomerate firm in the 1980s: The deinstitutionalisation of an organizational form", *American Sociological Review* 59: 547–570.

Delbridge R and Keenoy T (2010) "Beyond managerialism?" *International Journal of Human Resource Management* 21(6): 799–817.

Dent M (2008) "Medicine, Nursing and Changing Professional Jurisdictions in the UK", in D Muzio, S Ackroyd and J-F Chanlat (eds) *Redirections in the Study of Expert Labour-Established Professions and New Expert Occupations*, Basingstoke: Palgrave Macmillan.

Dent M and Whitehead S (eds) (2002) *Managing Professional Identities: Knowledge, Performativity and the "New Professional"*, London: Routledge.

De Vries R, Dingwall R and Orfali K (2009) "The moral organization of the professions", *Current Sociology* 57: 555–580.

DiMaggio P (1988) "Interest and agency in institutional theory", in L G Zucker (ed) *Institutional Patterns and Organizations: Culture and Environment*, Cambridge, MA: Ballinger, pages 3–22.

DiMaggio P J and Powell W W (1983) "The iron cage revisited: Institutional isomorphism and collective rationality in organizational fields", *American Sociological Review* 48: 147–160.

Dingwall R (2004) "Profession and social order in a global society", *Revista Electronica de Investigacion Educativa* 6(1), http://redie.uabc.mx/vol6no1/contents-dingwall.html, accessed 4 December 2008.

Drake McFeely M (1988) *Lady Inspectors: The Campaign for a Better Workplace 1893–1921*, New York: Basil Blackwell.

Dryburgh G (1972) "The man in the middle", *Personnel Management* 4(5): 3, May.

Duman D (1983) *The English and Colonial Bars in the Nineteenth Century*, London: Croom Helm.

Etzioni A (ed) (1969) *The Semi-Professions and Their Organization: Teachers, Nurses, Social Workers*, New York: Free Press.

Evetts J (2003) "The sociological analysis of professionalism: Occupational change in the modern world", *International Sociology* 18(2): 395–415.

Evetts J (2009) "New professionalism and new public management: Changes, continuities and consequences", *Comparative Sociology* 8: 247–266.

Evetts J (2011) "A new professionalism? Challenges and opportunities", *Current Sociology* 59(4): 406–427.

Farndale E and Brewster C (2005) "In search of legitimacy: Personnel management associations worldwide", *Human Resource Management Journal* 15(3): 33–48.

Faulconbridge J R and Muzio D (2008) "Organizational professionalism in globalizing law firms", *Work, Employment and Society* 22(1): 7–25.

Faulconbridge J R and Muzio D (2012) "Professions in a globalizing world: Towards a transnational sociology of the professions", *International Sociology* 27(1): 136–152.

Ferlie E, Ashburner L, Fitzgerald L and Pettigrew A (1996) *The New Public Management in Action*, Oxford: Oxford University Press.

Fickers A (2012) "Towards a new digital historicism? Doing history in the age of abundance", *View Journal of European Television History and Culture* 1(1): 19–26.

Fincham R (2012) "Expert labour as a differentiated category: Power, knowledge and organisation", *New Technology, Work and Employment* 27(3): 208–223.

Finegold D and Soskice D (1988) "The failure of training in Britain: Analysis and prescription", *Oxford Review of Economic Policy* 4(3): 21–53.

Fligstein N (1997) "Social skill and institutional theory", *American Behavioural Scientist* 40: 397–405.

Flood J (2008) "Partnership and professionalism in global law firms: Resurgent professionalism?" in D Muzio, S Ackroyd and J-F Chanlat (eds) *Redirections in the Study of Expert Labour-Established Professions and New Expert Occupations*, Basingstoke: Palgrave Macmillan.

Fombrun C J (1983) "Strategic management: Integrating the human resource systems into strategic planning", in *Advances in Strategic Management*, Vol. 2, Greenwich, CT: JAI Press.

Fombrun C J, Tichy N and Devanna M (1984) *Strategic Human Resource Management*, New York: John Wiley and Sons.

Fournier V (1999) "The appeal to 'professionalism' as a disciplinary mechanism", *The Sociological Review* 47(2): 280–307.

Fowler A (1987) "When chief executives discover HRM", *Personnel Management*: 3, January

Friedland R and Alford R R (1991) "Bringing society back in: Symbols, practices, and institutional contradictions", in W W Powell and P J DiMaggio (eds) *The New Institutionalism in Organizational Analysis*, Chicago, IL: University of Chicago Press.

Gephart R P (1993) "The textual approach: Risk and blame in disaster sensemaking", *Academy of Management Journal* 36(6): 1465–1514.

Gilb C L (1976) *Hidden Hierarchies: The Professions and Government*, Greenwood Pub Group.

Gilmore S and Williams S (2003) *Constructing the HR Professional: A Critical Analysis of the Chartered Institute of Personnel and Development's "Professional Project"*, www.mngt.waikato.ac.nz/ejrot/cmsconference/2003/proceedings/hrmphenomena/Gilmore.pdf, accessed 7 January 2009.

Gilmore S and Williams S (2007) "Conceptualising the 'Personnel Professional': A critical analysis of the chartered institute of personnel and development's professional qualification scheme", *Personnel Review* 36(3): 398–414.

Gold J and Bratton J (2003) *The Dynamics of Professionalization: Whither the HRM Profession?* Paper delivered at the Third Critical Management Studies Conference, Stream 8, Human Resource Management Phenomena—HRM and beyond.

Goldner F H and Ritti R R (1967) "Professionalization as career immobility", *American Journal of Sociology* 72(5): 489–502.

Greenwood E (1957) "Attributes of a profession", *Social Work* 2: 445–450.

Greenwood E (1966) "The elements of professionalization", in H M Vollmer and D L Mills (eds) *Professionalization*, Englewood Cliffs, NJ: Prentice Hall, pages 9–19.

Greenwood R, Suddaby R and Hinings C R (2002) "Theorizing change: The role of professional associations in the transformation of institutionalized fields", *Academy of Management Journal* 45(1): 58–80.

Guest D (1979) "American perspectives—systematic management of human resources by R B Peterson and L Tracy Addison-Wesley—a review", *Personnel Management*: 49, December.

Hall L and Torrington D (1998) *The Human Resource Function: The Dynamics of Change and Development*, London: Financial Times Pitman Publishing.

Hammond K H (2007) "Why we hate HR", *FastCompany*, 19 December, www.fastcompany.com/magazine/97/open_hr.htl#, accessed 7 October 2009.

Handy C (1987) *The Making of Managers: A Report on Management Education, Training and Development in the USA, West Germany, France, Japan and the UK*, London: National Economic Development Office.

Hanlon G (1998) "Professionalism as enterprise: Service class politics and the redefinition of professionalism", *Sociology* 32(1): 43–64.

Hardy C and Phillips N (2002) "Discourse analysis: Investigating processes of social construction", *Qualitative Research Methods Series* 50.

Hargadon A B and Douglas Y (2001) "When innovation meet institutions: Edison and the design of the electric light", *Administrative Science Quarterly* 46(3): 476–501.

Heracleous L and Barrett M (2001) "Organizational change as discourse: Communicative actions and deep structures in the context of information technology implementation", *Academy of Management Journal* 44(4): 755–778.

Hickson D J and Thomas M W (1969) "Professionalization in Britain: A preliminary measurement", *Sociology* 3: 37–53.

Hinings C R and Greenwood R (2002) "Disconnects and consequences in Organization theory?" *Administrative Science Quarterly* 47(3): 411–421.

Hodgson D (2008) "The new professionals: Professionalisation and the struggle for occupational control in the field of project management", in D Muzio, S Ackroyd and J-F Chanlat (eds) *Redirections in the Study of Expert Labour-Established Professions and New Expert Occupations*, Basingstoke: Palgrave Macmillan.

Hoffman A J (1999) "Institutional evolution and change: Environmentalism and the US chemical industry", *Academy of Management Journal* 42: 351–371.

Holmes G (1982) *Augustan England: Professions, State and Society 1680–1730*, London: Allen and Unwin.

HR Magazine (2001) *We're Not Exclusive, Irrelevant, Time-Expired or Elitist*, www.hrmagazine.co.uk/hr/news/1013918/were-exclusive-irrelevant-expired-elitist, accessed 8 February 2013.

Institute of Personnel and Development: British Association for Commercial and Industrial Education (MSS.97/BACIE), Modern Records Centre, University of Warwick.

Investors in People—UK Commission for Employment and Skills *Investment in People—Background*, www.investorsinpeople.co.uk/About/Pages/default.aspx, accessed 28 June 2013.

Jacques R (1996) *Manufacturing the Employee: Management Knowledge from the 19th to the 21st Centuries*, London and Thousand Oaks, CA: Sage Publications.

Jennings P D and Zandbergen P A (1995) "Ecologically sustainable organizations: An institutional approach", *Academy of Management Review* 20: 1015–1052.

Jepperson R L (1991) "Institutions, institutional effects and institutionalism", in W W Powell and P J DiMaggio (eds) *The New Institutionalism in Organizational Analysis*, Chicago: University of Chicago Press, pages 1143–1163.

Johns E (Ted) (2004) *Examination Report—Professional Development Scheme—Managing People*, CIPD, www.cipd.co.uk/NR/rdonlyres/F88DCBCF-26BA-4302-BA8D-EE9D4456B025/0/pqsmanpeoplr.pdf, accessed 31 May 2013.

Johnson L (2008) "The truth about the HR department", *FT.com*, http://wwww.ft.com/cms/0/ec6f81e6-ce89-11dc-877a-000077b07658.html, accessed 7 October 2009.

Johnson T J (1972) *Professions and Power*, London and Basingstoke: Palgrave Macmillan.

Kaufman B E (2008) *Managing the Human Factor: The Early Years of Human Resource Management in American Industry*, Ithaca and London: ILR an Imprint of Cornell University Press.

Keenoy T (1990a) "HRM: A case of the wolf in sheep's clothing", *Personnel Review* 19(2): 3–9.

Keenoy T (1990b) "Human resource management: Rhetoric, reality and contradiction", *International Journal of Human Resource Management* 1(3): 363–384.

Keenoy T (1997) "Review article: HRMism and the languages of re-presentation", *Journal of Management Studies* 34(5): 825–841.

Keenoy T (1999) "HRM as hologram: A polemic", *Journal of Management Studies* 36(1): 1–23.

Keenoy T (2009) "Human resource management", in M Alvesson, T Bridgman and H Willmott (eds) *The Oxford Handbook of Critical Management Studies*, Oxford: Oxford University Press, Chapter 22, pages 454–472.

Kenny T P (1972) "Professional examinations for British training staff", *Training and Development Journal*: 40–43, February.

Khaire M and Wadhwani R D (2010) "Changing landscapes: The construction of meaning and value in a new market category—modern Indian art", *Academy of Management Journal* 53(6): 1281–1304.

King D S (1993) "The conservatives and training policy 1979–1992: From a tripartite to a neoliberal regime", *Political Studies* XLI: 214–235.

Kipping M (2011) "Hollow from the start? Image professionalism in management consulting", *Current Sociology* 59(4): 530–550.

Kraatz M S and Block E S (2008) "Organizational implications of institutional pluralism", in R Greenwood, C Oliver, R Suddaby and K Sahlin-Anderson (eds) *Handbook of Organizational Institutionalism*, Thousand Oaks, CA: Sage Publications, pages 243–276.

Langley A (2009) "Studying processes in and around organizations", in D Buchanan and A Bryman (eds) *The Sage Handbook of Organizational Research*, London: Sage Publications, Chapter 24, pages 409–429.

Larson M S (1977) *The Rise of Professionalism: A Sociological Analysis*, London and Berkeley: University of California Press.

Lawrence S (1979) "Man of the moment: Jack Coates", *Personnel Management* 11(10): 36–40.

Lawrence T B, Hardy C and Phillips N (2004) "Institutional effects of interorganizational collaboration: The emergence of proto-institutions", *Academy of Management Journal* 45(1): 281–290.

Lawrence T B and Suddaby R (2006) "Institutions and institutional work", in S R Clegg, C Hardy and W R Nord (eds) *The Sage Handbook of Organization Studies*, 2nd edition, London: Sage Publications, pages 215–254.

Legge K (1978) *Power, Innovation and Problem-Solving in Personnel Management*, Maidenhead: McGraw Hill.

Legge K (1987) "Women in personnel management: Uphill climb or downhill slide", in A Spencer and D B L Podmore (eds) *In a Man's World: Essays on Women in Male-Dominated Professions*, London: Tavistock Publications.

Legge K (1988) "Personnel management in recession and recovery: A comparative analysis of what the surveys say", *Personnel Review* 17(2).

Legge K (1995) *Human Resource Management: Rhetorics and Realities*, London: Palgrave Macmillan.

Legge K and Exley M (1975) "Authority, ambiguity and adaptation: The personnel specialists' dilemma", *Industrial Relations Journal* 6(3): 51–65.

Leicht K T (2005) "Professions", in G Ritzer (ed) *Encyclopaedia of Social Theory*, Thousand Oaks, CA: Sage Publications.

Lengnick-Hall M L and Aguinis H (2012) "What is the value of human resource certification? A multi-level framework for research", *Human Resource Management Review* 22(4): 246–257.

Lewis R and Maude A (1953) *The English Middle Classes*, Great Britain: Penguin Books.

Lilleker D G (2003) "Interviewing the political elite: Navigating a potential minefield", *Politics* 23(3): 207–214.

Loft A (1988) *Understanding Accounting in Its Social and Historical Context: The Case of Cost Accounting 1914–1975*, New York: Garland.

Lok J (2010) "Institutional logics as identity projects", *Academy of Management Journal* 53(6): 1305–1335.

Losey M, Meisinger S R and Ulrich D (eds) (2006) *The Future of Human Resource Management: 64 Thought Leaders Explore the Critical HR Issues of Today and Tomorrow*, Society for Human Resource Management, Alexandria, VA: John Wiley and Sons, Inc.

Lucas B E and Strain M M (2010) "Keeping the conversation going: The archive thrives on interviews and oral history", in A E Ramsey, W E Sharer, B L'Eplattenier and L S Mastrangelo (eds) *Working in the Archives: Practical Research Methods for Rhetoric and Composition*, Carbondale, IL: Southern Illinois University, pages 259–277.

Macdonald K M (1985) "Social closure and occupational registration", *Sociology* 19(4): 541–556.

MacDuffie J P (1995) "Human resource bundles and manufacturing performance: Organizational logic and flexible production systems in the world auto industry", *Industrial and Labor Relations Review* 48(2): 197–221.

Mackay L (1987a) "Personnel: Changes disguising decline?" *Personnel Review* 16(5): 3–11.

Mackay L (1987b) "The future—with consultants", *Personnel Review* 16(4): 3–9.

MacLachlan R (2009) "A 'generational change' for the HR profession", *People Management*: 6–7, 19 November.

Maguire S, Hardy C and Lawrence T B (2004) "Institutional entrepreneurship in emerging fields: HIV/AIDS treatment advocacy in Canada", *Academy of Management Journal* 47: 657–679.

Marchington M and Wilkinson A (2008) *Human Resource Management at Work: People Management and Development*, London: CIPD.

Marks W (1978) *Politics and Personnel Management: An Outline History, 1960–1976*, London: Institute of Personnel Management.

Marland H (1987) *Medicine and Society in Wakefield and Huddersfield 1780–1870*, Cambridge: Cambridge University Press.

Mason J (2002) *Qualitative Researching*, 2nd edition, London; Thousand Oaks, CA: Sage Publications.

Mazza C and Strandgaard Pedersen J (2015) "Good reading makes good action: Nothing so practical as a managerial panacea?" in A Örtenblad (ed) *Handbook of Research on Management Ideas and Panaceas: Adaptation and Context*, Cheltenham: Edward Elgar, Chapter 19, page 349.

Millerson G (1964) *The Qualifying Association: A Study in Professionalization*, London: Routledge.

Monopolies Commission (1970) *A Report on the General Effect on the Public Interest of Certain Restrictive Practices so Far as They Prevail in Relation* to the Supply of Professional Services, London: Her Majesty's Stationery Office, www.competition-commission.gov.uk/rep_pub/reports/1970_1975/ fulltext/059c01.pdf, accessed 13 January 2009.

Morris P W G, Crawford L, Hodgson D, Shepherd M M and Thomas J (2006) "Exploring the role of formal bodies of knowledge in defining a profession: The case of project management", *International Journal of Project Management* 24: 710–721.

Muzio D and Ackroyd S (2008) "Change in the legal profession: Professional agency and the legal labour process", in D Muzio, S Ackroyd and J-F Chanlat (eds) *Redirections in the Study of Expert Labour-Established Professions and New Expert Occupations*, Basingstoke: Palgrave Macmillan.

Muzio D, Ackroyd S and Chanlat J-F (eds) (2008) *Redirections in the Study of Expert Labour-Established Professions and New Expert Occupations*, Basingstoke: Palgrave Macmillan.

Muzio D, Hodgson D, Faulconbridge J, Beaverstock J and Hall S (2011) "Towards corporate professionalization: The case of project management, management consultancy and executive search", *Current Sociology* 59(4): 443–464.

Muzio D and Kirkpatrick I (2011) "Introduction: Professions and organizations—a conceptual framework", *Current Sociology* 59(4): 389–405.

Neal M and Morgan J (2000) "The professionalization of everyone? A comparative study of the development of the professions in the UK and Germany", *European Sociological Review* 16(1): 9–26.

Niven M (1967) *Personnel Management 1913–1963: The Growth of Personnel Management and the Development of the Institute*, London: Institute of Personnel Management.

Noordegraaf M (2011) "Remaking professionals? How associations and professional education connect professionalism and organizations", *Current Sociology* 59(4): 465–488.

O'Donnell D, McGuire D and Cross C (2006) "Critically challenging some assumptions in HRD", *International Journal of Training and Development* 10(1): 4–16.

Ogden J, Halford S and Carr L (2017) "Observing web archives: The case for an ethnographic study of web archiving", In *Proceedings of the 2017 ACM on Web Science Conference*, ACM, pages 299–308, June.

Orme J (2009) "Responding to Brown' letters—a bridge-building strategy?" *Personnel Management* 15(23): 16, 5 November.

Örtenblad A (ed) (2015) *Handbook of Research on Management Ideas and Panaceas: Adaptation and Context*, Cheltenham: Edward Elgar Publishing.

Palmer D, Biggart N and Dick B (2008) "Is the new institutionalism a theory?" in R Greenwood, C Oliver, R Suddaby and K Sahlin-Anderson (eds) *Organizational Institutionalism*, London: Sage Publications, Chapter 32, pages 769–782.

Parsons T (1939) "The professions and social structure", *Social Forces*: 457–467, May.

Patterson M G, West M A, Lawthom R and Nickell S (1997) "Impact of people management practices on business performance", in *Issues in People Management*, London: Institute of Personnel Management.

Pavalko R M (1971) *The Sociology of Occupations and Professions*, Itasca, IL: F E Peacock Publishers Inc.

Perkin H (1989) *The Rise of Professional Society*, London: Routledge and Kegan Paul.

Personnel Management (1993) "The case for combination", *Personnel Management* 25(12): 26–32.

Peterson R B and Tracy L (1979) *Systematic Management of Human Resources*, Reading, MA: Addison-Wesley Publishing Company.

Pfeffer J (1994) *Competitive Advantage Through People: Unleashing the Power of the Workforce*, Boston, MA: Harvard Business School Press.

Pfeffer J (1998) *The Human Equation*, Boston, MA: Harvard Business School Press.

Phillips M (2005) "A gentlemanly body: The (excessive) case of the institute for the motor industry", in C Gustafsson, A Rehn and D Skold (eds) *Excess and Organization: Proceedings of SCOS XXIII: Stockholm 2005*, Stockholm, Sweden: Royal Institute of Technology.

Phillips N, Lawrence T B and Hardy C (2004) "Discourse and institutions", *Academy of Management Reviews* 29(4): 635–652.

Pitfield M (1979) "Practical and professional: A new look for the IPM's education programme", *Personnel Management*: 42–45, December.

PM Editorial (2000) "Institute gets its charter", *People Management* 6(4): 13.

PM Editorial (2003a) "Status of affairs", *People Management* 9(9): 49, 1 May.

PM Editorial (2003b) "Individual status gets 'yes' vote", *People Management* 9(12): 7, 12 June.

PM Editorial (2003c) "Upgrade campaign is on", *People Management* 9(13): 62, 26 June.

PM Editorial (2003d) "Privy council backs new title", *People Management*, 24 July.

PM Editorial (2003e) "CIPD launches individual chartered membership", www.cipd.co.uk/pm/peoplemanagement/b/weblog/archieve/2013/01/29/9468a-2003-10.aspx, online only, Volume 9, 1 October.

Ponzoni E and Boersma K (2011) "Writing history for business: The development of business history between 'old' and 'new' production of knowledge", *Management and Organizational History* 6(2): 123–143.

Powell W W (1991) "Expanding the scope of institutional analysis", in W W Powell and P J DiMaggio (eds) *The New Institutionalism in Organizational Analysis*, Chicago: University of Chicago Press, pages 183–203.

Powell W W and DiMaggio P J (eds) (1991) *The New Institutionalism in Organizational Analysis*, Chicago: University of Chicago Press.

Preece D A and Nicol B N (1980) "Personnel management, power and the certification process", *Personnel Review* 9(4): 27–32.

Prest W R (1972) *The Inns of Court under Elizabeth and the Early Stuarts 1590–1640*. London: Longman.

Prest W R (1986) *The Rise of the Barristers: A Social History of the English Bar 1590–1640*, Oxford: Clarendon Press.

Proud D E (1916) *Welfare Work: Employers; Experiments for Improving Working Conditions in Factories*, London: G E Bell.

Purcell J (2003) *Understanding the People and Performance Link: Unlocking the Black Box*, London: CIPD.

The Quality Assurance Agency for Higher Education (2004) *Guidelines on the Accreditation of Prior Learning*, www.qaa.ac.uk/docs/qaa/quality-code/

accreditation-prior-learning-guidelines.pdf?sfvrsn=edadf981_12, accessed 6 November 2018.

Rao H, Morrill C and Zald M N (2000) "Power plays: How social movements and collective action create new organizational forms", *Research in Organizational Behavior* 22: 239–282.

Reader W J (1966) *Professional Men: The Rise of Professional Classes in Nineteenth-Century England*, London: Weidenfeld and Nicolson.

Reed C (2018) "Professionalizing corporate professions: Professionalization as identity project", *Management Learning* 49(2): 222–238.

Reed M and Anthony P (1992) "Professionalizing management and managing professionalization: British management in the 1980s", *Journal of Management Studies* 29(5): 591–613.

Reed M I (1996) "Expert power and control in late modernity: An empirical review and theoretical synthesis", *Organization Studies* 17(4): 573–597.

Ridgeway C (1982) "The role of the secretary in personnel management", *Leadership and Organization Development Journal* 3(2): 17–20.

Roberts J and Coutts J A (1992) "Feminization and professionalization: A review of an emerging literature on the development of accounting in the United Kingdom", *Accounting, Organizations and Society* 17(3–4): 379–395.

Sahlin-Andersson K (1996) "Imitating success: The construction of organizational fields", in B Czarniaswka and G Sevon (eds) *Translating Organizational Change*, Berlin: Walter de Gruyter and Co, pages 13–48.

Sciulli D (2010) *Structural and Institutional Invariance in Professions and Professionalism*, Oslo, Norway: Senter for profesjonssudier.

Scott W R (2001) *Institutions and Organizations*, Thousand Oaks, CA: Sage Publications.

Scott W R (2008a) "Lords of the dance: Professionals as institutional agents", *Organisational Studies* 29(2): 219–238.

Scott W R (2008b) *Institutions and Organisations: Ideas and Interests*, Thousand Oak, CA: Sage Publications.

Seears N (1979) "Can personnel managers deliver?" *Personnel Management* 11(10).

Seers L (2009a) "Beware of outdated leadership development", *People Management* 15(1): 9.

Seers L (2009b) "Comment: From partners to players", *People Management*: 8, 19 November.

Selander S (1990) "Associative strategies in the process of professionalization: Professional strategies and scientification of occupations", in M Burrage and R Torstendahl (eds) *Professions in Theory and History*, London: Sage Publications, page 139ff.

Selznick P (1949) *TVA and the Grass Roots: A Study in the Sociology of Formal Organization*, Berkeley and Los Angeles, CA: University of California Press.

Sharpe P H (1979a) "WANTED: A professional organisation for human resources managers", *Industrial and Commercial Training* 11(6): 230–232.

Sharpe P H (1979b) "IPM+ITO=IPTM progress report", *Industrial and Commercial Training* 11(9): 386–389.

Shuval J T and Gilbert L (1978) "Attempts at professionalization of pharmacy: An Israel case study", *Social Science and Medicine*: 19–25.

Siegrist S (1990) "Professionalization as a process: Patterns, progression and discontinuity", in M Burrage and R Torstendahl (eds) *Professions in Theory and History*, London: Sage Publications.

Sisson K (1990) "Introducing the human resource management journal", *Human Resource Management Journal* 1(1): 1–11.

Smith A (2005); (1776) *An Inquiry into the Nature and Causes of the Wealth of Nations*, The Electronic Classics Series, Jim Manis Ed, Penn State University, http://www2.hn.psu.edu/faculty/jmanis/adam-smith/wealth-nations.pdf, accessed 12 June 2014.

Smith A (n.d.) *An Inquiry into the Nature and Causes of the Wealth of Nations*, Raleigh, NC: Generic NL Freebook Publisher, HTTP://search.ebscohost.com/login.aspx?direct=true&db=nlebk&AN=1086046&site=ehost-live, 28 February 2019.

Suchman M (1995) "Managing legitimacy: Strategic and institutional approaches", *Academy of Management Review* 20: 571–611.

Suddaby R, Foster W M and Quinn Trank C (2010) "Rhetorical history as a source of competitive advantage", *The Globalization of Strategy Research: Advances in Strategic Management* 27: 147–173.

Suddaby R and Greenwood R (2005) "Rhetorical strategies of legitimacy", *Administrative Science Quarterly* 50: 35–67.

Suddaby R and Viale T (2011) "Professionals and field-level change: Institutional work and the professional project", *Current Sociology* 59(4): 423–442.

Swailes S (2003) "Professionalism: Evolution and measurement", *Service Industries Journal* 23(2): 130–149.

Thomason G F (1975); (1976); (1978); (1981); (1988) *A Textbook of Personnel Management*, London: Institute of Personnel Management.

Thornton P H and Ocasio W (1999) "Institutional logics and the historical contingency of power in organizations: Executive succession in the higher education publishing industry, 1958–1990", *American Journal of Sociology* 105(3): 801–843.

Timperley S R and Osbaldeston M D (1975) "The professionalization process: A study of an aspiring occupational organization", *The Sociological Review* 23(3): 607–627.

Torrington D and Hall L (1987) *Personnel Management: A New Approach*, Englewood Cliffs; London: Prentice-Hall International

Torrington D and Hall L (1998) "Letting go or holding on: The devolution of operational personnel activities", *Human Resource Management Journal* 8(1): 41–55.

Tyson S and Fell A (1986) "The crisis in personnel management", in S Tyson and A Fell (eds) *Evaluating the Personnel Function*, London: Hutchinson Education, Chapter 8.

Ulrich D (ed) (1990) *Delivering Results: A New Mandate for Human Resource Professionals*, Boston, MA: Harvard Business School Press.

Ulrich D (1997) *Human Resource Champions: The Next Agenda for Adding Value and Delivering Results*, Boston, MA: Harvard Business School Press.

Ulrich D and Brockbank W (2005) *The HR Value Proposition*, Boston, MA: Harvard Business School Press.

University Forum for Human Resource Development *About*, www.ufhrd.co.uk/wordpress/?page_id=5, accessed 25 November 2010.

Vollmer H M and Mills D L (eds) (1966) *Professionalization*, Englewood Cliffs, NJ: Prentice Hall Inc.

Wai-Fong C and Clegg S (1990) "Professional closure: The case of British nursing", *Theory and Society* 19(2): 135–172.

Walker S P (1995) "The genesis of a professional organization in Scotland: A contextual analysis", *Accounting, Organizations and Society* 20(4): 285–310.

Watson T J (1976) "The professionalization process: A critical note", *The Sociological Review* 24(3): 599–608.

Watson T J (1977) *The Personnel Managers: A Study in the Sociology of Work and Employment*, London: Routledge and Kegan Paul.

Watson T J (2002a) "Professions and professionalism: Should we jump off the Bandwagon, better to study where it is going?" *International Studies of Management and Organisation* 32(2): 93–105.

Watson T J (2002b) "Speaking professionally: Occupational anxiety and discursive ingenuity among human resourcing specialists", in M Dent and S Whitehead (eds) *Managing Professional Identities: Knowledge, Performativity and the "New Professional"*, London: Routledge, Chapter 6, pages 99–115.

Whittaker J (2004) "Standards deliver", *People Management*, 30 June, online, www.cipd.co.uk/pm/peoplemanagement/b/weblog/archive/2013/01/29/standardsdeliver-2004-06.aspx.

Wilensky H I (1964) "The professionalization of everyone?" *American Journal of Sociology* 70(2): 137–158.

Williams A P O (2010) *The History of UK Business and Management Education*, Bingley: Emerald Group Publishing.

Williams C (1999) "Corporate ascent", *People Management* 5(8): 1–2.

Williams C (2003) "How to . . . be a chartered CIPD member", *People Management* 9(20): 52–53, 8 October.

Willmott H (1986) "Organising the profession: A theoretical and historical examination of the development of the major accountancy bodies in the UK", *Accounting Organizations and Society* 11(6): 555–580.

Wright V (2012) *View from the CIPD: Accountable to All*, http://blog.peopleman agement.co.uk/2012/04/view-from-the-cipd-accountable-to-all/#more-983, accessed 25 April 2012.

Yanow D (2009) "Organizational ethnography and methodological angst: Myths and challenges in the field", *Qualitative Research in Organizations and Management: An International Journal* 4(2): 186–199.

Zucker L G (1983) "Organizations as institutions", *Research in the Sociology of Organizations* 2: 1–47.

# Appendix I Privy Council Papers

These documents were received following a Request under the UK Freedom of Information Act. Following discussion initiated by the Privy Council Office, in the spirit of genuine historical inquiry, the Privy Council Office released the documents, without the Freedom of Information Act protocols. I am indebted to those officers at the Privy Council Office. There are three clear sets of documents in the Privy Council Papers relating to the dealings with the Institute.

Documents within each Set are numbered in Roman numerals.

## 1968–1993: Set I

| Doc no | Date | Sender/Recipient, or writer |
|---|---|---|
| Set I-i | 15 Jan 1968 | A letter from the Institution of Production Engineers the Clerk of the Privy Council. Letter concerning a lunch meeting at which the President and a Director of the IPM would attend. The letter encloses "literature about IPM which will help you fill this little gap in your knowledge" |
| Set I-ii | 1 Feb 1968 | A file note written by the Clerk of the Privy Council. Based on the information given to him, the Clerk of the Privy Council thought that an application was likely to be 'premature' because "after studying their examination regulations and syllabus, the standard required could not strictly be regarded as being professional". He gives his reasons for this view. One of these reasons is significant— |
| | | "There were a number of degree and diploma courses listed in their particulars, which exempted the holders from the Institute's examinations—there was no other profession that I (the Clerk of the Privy Council) knew of where this could be done." |
| | | The Clerk cites Margaret Niven (1967: 151) which according to the Clerk indicates "that personnel management had only really started in 1955". |

| Doc no | Date | Sender/Recipient, or writer |
|--------|------|------------------------------|
| Set I-iii | 6 Feb1977 | A letter from the Institute's Assistant Director, Training, Organisation and Manpower Planning to the Companies Administration Division at the Department of Trade (carbon copy received at Privy Council). The letter concerns the potential effect of an amalgamation with the Institution of Training Officers Ltd. |
| Set I-iv | 22 Feb 1977 | An official at the DTI to the Institute's Assistant Director, Training, Organisation and Manpower Planning—a reply to the letter of 6 Feb 1977 concerning "historical continuity". |
| Set I-v | 25 Feb 1977 | A letter from the Institute's Assistant Director, Training, Organisation and Manpower Planning to the Clerk of Privy Council. The letter is seeking comments on the possible effects of an amalgamation between the IPM and the ITOL. The letter refers to the "anticipated resistance of the membership to a conventional 'takeover' ". The letter poses the idea that members of the new body would be admitted to corporate membership on the basis of examination only. |
| Set I-vi | Between 25 Feb 1977 and 10 March 1977 | A file note on which the signature is undecipherable, but it is a Privy Council official. The file note appears to be a file note prompted by the receipt of the earlier letter (Set I-iii) that acted as a reminder of the soundings already taken in 1968. The writer of the note claims not to know about the Institution of Training Officers or "to what extent the IPM has improved its standards since 1968". |
| Set I-vii | 10 March 1977 | The signature is undecipherable—it is a Privy Council official and is an internal note between officials. The file note describes the IPM as "a borderline case". |
| Set I- viii | 10 March 1977 | The letter is a carbon copy between the Clerk of the Council to the Institute's Assistant Director, Training, Organisation and Manpower Planning. The letter proposes a meeting and requests "information about examinations and entry qualifications etc for both bodies, and the level of management at which members are employed". |
| Set I-ix | 15 March 1977 | A letter from the Institute's Assistant Director, Training, Organisation and Manpower Planning to the Clerk of the Privy Council. The letter encloses the information requested and confirms a meeting set for 3 pm on 22 March 1977. |
| Set 1-x | 22 March 1977 | A file note which was written by the Clerk to the Privy Council, which outlines reflections following the meeting called to discuss the effect, if any, that the amalgamation of ITOL and IPM would have. |

There the correspondence and dealings cease until 1991.

| Doc no | Date | Sender/Recipient, or writer |
|---|---|---|
| Set I-xi | 22 Feb 1991 | A letter from the Institute Secretary to the Deputy Clerk to Privy Council in which it is clear that there had been a meeting between the Institute and the Privy Council on 21 February 1991 concerning a petition for a charter. |
| Set I-xii | 22 Feb 1991 | A file note in which a Privy Council official, probably the Deputy Clerk to the Privy Council, expresses the view that he was "generally impressed". The Institute's Secretary had been asked to undertake some "research on the status of the IPM qualification and the proportion of members admitted by examination". The writer also notes that Lee was unaware of the EU Directive on the mobility of professionals. By invoking the EC directive, it is clear that in the minds of the Privy Council, a Charter would signify a profession in the traditional professional model. |
| Set I-xiii | 1 May 1991 | A letter from the Institute's Secretary to the Deputy Clerk at the Privy Council, planning for Privy Council officials to visit IPM House, the Institute's Headquarters on 8 May 1991. |
| Set I-xiv | 1 May 1991 | A letter from the Institute's Secretary to the Deputy Clerk at the Privy Council; it follows the February letter (Set I-xi) and sets out responses to the Privy Council's concerns. The Secretary stated that there would be a vote at an Extraordinary General Meeting on 17 May 1991 to seek member support for a charter application. The Secretary's letter also states that the IPM qualification "was recognised as one of degree standard by the Burnham Further Education Committee in 1980". In 1987, the Professional Education Scheme was recognised as the PG Diploma by the CNAA -70 CAT points out of 120 required for a master's degree. The Institute's Secretary addressed the issue of direct entry—10% of applicants for membership were assessed through viva voce. |
| Set I-xv | 5 June 1991 | A letter from the Deputy Clerk to the Privy Council to an official at the Department of Employment explaining how the Institute has approached the Privy Council about a Royal Charter. The letter outlines the conditions under which Royal Charters are awarded to |

professional bodies. The writer expresses concerns about educational standards but acknowledges that since the first application in 1968, the Institute appears "to have made substantial progress and now claims that its qualification is of degree standard". The letter refers to EC Directive 48/89—the question of Chartered status had already "been identified as a basis for the inclusion of professional qualifications".

"The question of educational standards is of particular importance . . . but educational requirements below degree level for corporate members would seriously undermine the case."

The detracting factors appeared to be the Institute's emphasis upon practitioners, senior personnel managers without formal qualifications" and the recognition that personnel management was "a wide discipline with an area of overlap with other bodies, such as the BIM which also harbours charter ambitions".

The practitioner route could be closed, and it could be argued that personnel management was "at least as distinct a discipline as marketing".

The Institute of Marketing received its charter on 7 February 1989.

Following the explanation, there is a clear request from the Privy Council to the Department of Employment—how is the Institute regarded?

Other departments of state were included in the copies of the letters—the Department of Education and Science, the Cabinet Office and the Department of Trade and Industry.

The Privy Council would decide whether to invite the Institute to make a formal application "in the light of comments received".

Once past that hurdle, the PCO would also require the recommendations of the Secretaries of State.

| | | |
|--------|------|------------------------------|
| Set I-xvi | 10 July 1991 | A letter from an official from the Enterprise Initiative division (Education and Training branch) of the DTI, to the Clerk at the Privy Council Office, confirming that the DTI is making internal inquiries and promising a "substantive response" in due course. |

*(Continued)*

| Doc no | Date | Sender/Recipient, or writer |
|---|---|---|
| Set I-xvii | 9 July 1991 | A letter from an official at the Further and Higher Education Branch of the Department of Education and Science to the Clerk at the Privy Council Office. The letter asks for more information, specifically "copies of the examinations set over the past two or three years at Stages 1 and 2 and, to assess standards, examples (say, two each of student scripts adjudged to be of lower, middle and upper levels". The official uses the language 'scrape', "good" and "outstanding" |
| Set 1-xviii | 11 July 1991 | A letter from an official at the Employment Department to the Clerk at the Privy Council. The letter states that the Employment Department was not "enthusiastic" on the basis of the letter of conditions established in the Privy Council letter of 3 June 1991 (Set I-xv), particularly the conditions on distinctiveness and clear boundaries of occupational practice. The letter does suggest that the Privy Council should recognise the trend toward assessment of competence rather than knowledge through examination. This reflects the change to a National Vocational Qualification system. |
| Set I-ixx | 23 July 1991 | A letter from the Institute's Secretary to the Clerk at the Privy Council; the letter explains she is leaving to take up a post at the Chartered Institute of Management. She passes on the name of her successor. |
| Set I-xx | 30 July 1991 | A letter from the Institute to an official at the Privy Council enclosing student scripts—last two examinations (same year). (Earlier years, as requested, cannot be forwarded as they have been destroyed.) |
| Set I-xxi | 31 July 1991 | The official at the Privy Council Office sends the scripts and other information to the official at the Further and Higher Education Branch at the Department of Education and Science. |
| Set I-xxii | 29 July 1991 | Although this letter is out of place in the Privy Council bundle of papers, this letter has significant enclosures and is from the Institute Director–Membership and Education. There is a document accompanying the scripts *Submission of the Professional Education Scheme of the Institute of Personnel Management to the Privy Council*. There were 19 appendices including 24 examination scripts and 6 management reports. The document talks about the Institute's objectives: |

- "To provide an association of professional standing for its members through which the widest possible exchange of knowledge and experience can take place
- To develop a continuous evolving professional body of knowledge to assist its members to do their jobs more effectively in response to changing demands and conditions
- To develop and maintain professional standards of competence
- To encourage investigation and research in the field of personnel management and the subjects related to it
- To present a national viewpoint of personnel management and to establish and develop links with other bodies both national and international concerned with personnel"

Three mechanisms for achieving the objectives:

a "Making the continuously developing body of information and knowledge available to members and management generally through an active information service, conferences, courses, publications and by any other available means
b Providing high standards of training for the profession and entry into Corporate Membership of the Institute by means of exams conducted by the Institute and by objectively assessed experience
c Taking positive steps to encourage investigation and research in the field of personnel management and subjects related to it."

The submission focuses on the emphasis the Institute has always placed on 'professional training' since 1913.
It acknowledged the increasing professionalisation of management and the intention to take part in that.

| Set I xxiii | 20 August 1991 | A letter from the DTI responding to the Privy Council's question. There are concerns that chartered status would make the Institute "too inflexible". This echoes the view of the Department of Education and Science.
Also, although the Privy Council were concerned about the entry requirements, both the DES and DTI point out that the trend was towards more open access and competence-based APL routes. |

*(Continued)*

(Continued)

| Doc no | Date | Sender/Recipient, or writer |
|--------|------|----------------------------|
| Set 1-xxiv | 22 August 1991 | This is a letter expressing the view of the Cabinet Office for the Civil Service to the Privy Council Office. The letter says, "We, like others, have no strong views on the IPM", but the Civil Service is "keen to encourage greater professionalism within personnel management in the civil service". The Civil Service itself runs the IPM qualifications; however, it did not rate the information disseminated, calling "the quality of their published research . . . somewhat patchy". |
| Set I-xxv | 11 September 1991 | A letter from the Department of Education and Science, the Further and Higher Education branch to the Privy Council. This letter points out that much of the provision is found in the FE sector, not HE. There is overlap, and terms are vague such as "pass degree level" and "good pass degree level". He critiques the content of both examination questions and the responses seen in the scripts sent—limited analysis. |
| Set I-xxvi | 18 September 1991 | A letter from the Privy Council to the new Institute Secretary describing the position as "not altogether encouraging". The chance of a successful petition was "at best borderline". He advocates waiting for 2–3 years. |
| Set I-xxvii | 23 September 1991 | A letter from the Privy Council Office to the Institute returning the scripts. |
| Set I-xxviii | 27 September 1991 | A letter from the Institute Secretary to the Privy Council Office acknowledging receipt. |

There is a gap in the record.

| Doc no | Date | Sender/Recipient, or writer |
|--------|------|----------------------------|
| Set I-xxix | 11 August 1993 | A file note between officials at the Privy Council Office. The Institute had asked the Employment Department, the Permanent Secretary to sponsor a petition. The unknown person from the Department Secretary had been asked for advice and he, in turn, was asking the Privy Council Office. The official at the Privy Council Office was unaware of the history, but he gave what appears to be a stock answer: "If and when a Charter was referred, the fact would be gazetted and anyone who wished to express a view would be free to do so. In the first instance, however, the Institute would be well advised to get in touch with the Privy Council." |

Document metrics.

| Submission/Report | 1 |
|---|---|
| File Note | 6 |
| Letter | 22 |

Number of pages    54

| 1968 | 2 | Docs 1–2 | 1991 | 17 | Docs 11–28 |
|---|---|---|---|---|---|
| 1977 | 8 | Docs 3–10 | 1993 | 1 | Doc 29 |

The Privy Council Papers cease for two years during which time the Institute combined with the Institute of Training and Development (ITD).

## 1996–2000: Set II

| Doc no | Date | Sender/Recipient, or writer |
|---|---|---|
| Set II-i | 16 September 1996 | A letter from the Institute's solicitors to the Clerk to the Privy Council. This letter encloses an interview with the Director-General which had appeared in *People Management*. The Institute had put the matter into the hands of a solicitor who explains the earlier contact between the Institute and the Privy Council Office, but the letter clearly states that the Institute wants to pursue an application for a Royal Charter. The creation of the Institute of Personnel and Development occurred in 1994. The Institute's solicitors outline the Institute's mission: |

- "To lead in the development and promotion of good practice in the field of the management and development of people, for application both by professional members and their organisational colleagues;
- To service the professional interests of members; and
- To uphold the highest ideals in the management and development of people."

The solicitor is appealing on the grounds of the Institute's position as the only body "which services specialists in the management and development of people", its size and geographical coverage, the pre-eminence of some of its members—"Senior

(*Continued*)

| Doc no | Date | Sender/Recipient, or writer |
|--------|------|------------------------------|
| | | members of the Institute are invited to speak at international conferences and gatherings, and are able to disseminate UK best practice around the world." |
| | | The solicitor explains where members may be found, and the Institute's standards "which are at the level of a post-graduate diploma", coupled with practitioner experience, which would give corporate membership. |
| | | The letter outlines the importance given to continuing professional development, membership numbers (August 1996) 29,000 corporate (full) members. 19,000 members who are working to provide the relevant CPD, 31,000 associates and affiliates, some of whom are "working towards meeting the standards of the Institute". |
| | | One of the Institute's objectives "is to promote the management and development of people for public benefit". This is achieved by the qualification scheme, research, "development of professional policy, including the publication of guidance notes on best practice and the provision of library and information and legal advisory services". |
| | | The Institute publishes a fortnightly journal *People Management,* provides conferences and has sound financial footing. |
| Set II-ii | 3 Oct 1996 | A Letter from the Institute's solicitor to the Clerk to the Privy Council. The Privy Council had not received the first letter and its enclosures possibly due to a postal strike. |
| Set II-iii | 7 Oct 1996 | A letter from the Clerk to the Privy Council to the Institute's solicitors, apologising for not replying sooner. It looks as if there had been a letter to the Privy Council on 10 September, which was identical to the letter on 16 September, which went missing. The Clerk is happy to arrange a meeting. He says, "Such a meeting would enable me to consult advisers with a view to advising you in due course, on a personal basis, as to whether a Petition would be likely to be successful." |
| Set II-iv | No date but probably 22 or 23 Oct | A file note at the Privy Council which shows that the solicitor had telephoned on 21 October; he had not realised that the previous correspondent was no longer there. There is a reference to a meeting on 14 November. The solicitor is seeking an |

|  |  | early view as to whether there would be a likelihood of success. The writer of the file note consulted the file, contacted the solicitor on 22 October and said "that it would not be possible to give any kind of preliminary view before the meeting". |
|--|--|--|

The file note continues, "However, I said that I thought the discussion was likely to centre very much on *what the institute thought was* the public interest case for granting the Institute of Charter. Other major issues were likely to be the academic qualifications for entry to the Institute, how far the Institute covered the majority of practitioners in the field, and the extent of the Institute's contact with Government. I said I thought another issue for advisers was likely to be the extent to which personnel management continued to be regarded as a specialism as opposed to a function which was increasingly dispersed within organisations."

The italics in the previous quotation are handwritten amendments.

| Set II-v | 10 October 1996 | A letter from the Institute's solicitors to the Clerk to the Privy Council with arrangements for a meeting at 1030 on 14 November 1996. The attendees were the Director-General, the Institute Secretary, the Institute's Director of Membership and Education, the Institute's solicitors and another solicitor from a different firm. |
|--|--|--|
| Set II-vi | 18 November 1996 | A letter from the Director-General to the Clerk to the Privy Council thanking him for meeting on 14 November. There had been a slide presentation, six copies of which were now enclosed with the letter, along with information packs. "I hesitate to burden you with so much paper, so please feel free to discard any that proves surplus to requirements."<br><br>"We look forward to hearing further from you when you have been able to take your soundings and give consideration to our wish to proceed with a formal application when you judge appropriate." |
| Set II-vii | Undated but after 14 November 1996 | A file note, but there is no writer listed. Point 1 discusses the ITD/IPM issue. We learn according to the file note that "the IPM had been a long-established body from which the ITD had broken away 25 years previously". |

| Doc no | Date | Sender/Recipient, or writer |
|--------|------|------------------------------|

The ITD had a membership of about 20,000 "but had been largely unsuccessful in establishing a distinct knowledge base separate from that of the IPM and the IPM had wanted again to become an integrated Institute so as to be unquestionably pre-eminent in the field. The merger had been voted on by a majority of 4 to 1 in both Institutes, and had been a success."

The Clerk to the Privy Council had asked a question about the difference in culture and qualifications between the members of the two institutes. The file note reports, "The IPD had tended to have more senior members whereas members of the ITD saw themselves primarily as technicians. The qualifications which the ITD had introduced were quite respectable but practically based, and the Institute (which had been an early convert to the NVQ system) had not been successful in establishing a credible graduate qualification."

In 1996, the current membership was 79,000; 31,000 were not corporate members.

The objects and aims:

"(The Director-General) said that the objects of the Institute are, for the public benefit, to promote and develop the science and practice of the management and development of people (including the promotion of research and publication of the useful results of such research). More specifically, the Institute aims to advance continuously the management and development of people for the benefit of individuals, employers and the community at large, to be the professional body for those specialising in advancing this process; and to be recognised as the leading authority and influence in the field.

To this end, the Institute has as its mission to lead in the development and promotion of good practice, for application both by professional members and by their organisational colleagues; to serve the professional interests of members, and to uphold the highest ideals in the management and development of people. (The Director-General) emphasised that the Institute is thus directed both at the professionalism of its own members and also at the greater good of the UK at large. The Institute is primarily an educational charity and does not seek a regulator role or a closed shop arrangement. Much emphasis is place(d) on helping non-professionals to improve their own performance in the field, at a time when the management of organisations is undergoing a major change."

The file note also talks about governance and membership grades—graduate, licentiate, associate and affiliate (studying and non-studying). Associates—certificate holders and S/NVQ level 3. Licentiate—"signified that an individual has met the requirements of one or two fields of the Institute's professional standards. The file note adds: "(for example, Training and Development specialists may prefer to remain Licentiates rather than gain a wider qualification.) Three fields (Core management, core Personnel and Development, and Generalist/specialist personnel and development) of the professional standards needed to be completed for an individual to become a graduate."

File note outlines education route, and the assessment of competence against national standards, so it is possible to gain a qualification and a relevant NVQ.

"Setting Standards for the Profession"

"(The Director-General) said that many organisations use the IPD's standards as a basis on which to review their own standards and the number of personnel meeting the IPD's Graduate level qualification is credit-rated by the Open university validation service at 85 points, which comfortably exceed first degree level and can be used to count towards the points needed for a master's degree. This enables IPD-qualified members to complete a master's degree in 12 months."

CPD was mentioned as a route to securing a higher grade of membership.

There is an account of the way in which the Institute disseminates "best practice". The file note continues "Within the UK there is close contact with Government Departments at senior levels including the OPS and involvement with the learned journals. The IPD has also for example sponsored fellows at the LSE."

| Doc no | Date | Sender/Recipient, or writer |
|--------|------|------------------------------|
| | | There was an emphasis on research—£300K allocated and close links with the ESSRC. "It is the Institute's practice to include topics of current national interest in their conference agenda." "Public profile" "The Institute is frequently consulted by the Government, the European Commission and other bodies on issues concerning people and employment; and IPD representatives sit on Government-appointed national and local bodies such as the Employment Occupational Standards Council and the Management Charter Initiative. The Institute also makes nominations to many public bodies such as Industrial Tribunals, the Equal Opportunities Commission, and the Higher Education Funding Council." Finance—£10m in reserves. Target membership of 100,000 by 2000. "About 40% of people currently enrolling have a relevant degree; and if all existing Graduates upgraded as soon as they became eligible to do so the proportion of corporate members with a degree would soon be comfortably above 80%." "Reasons for Charter application" (The Director-General) said that the membership had voted, in the context of the merger, that the IPD should aim to obtain a Charter. The Institute was a unique body whose important contribution to the economy should be recognised. Personnel aspects were increasingly central to the success or failure of organisations, and recognition of the IPD by means of a charter would help bring home the importance of the discipline. In other words, it was not seen just a matter of status for members of the Institute." At the end of the meeting, it was clear that the Clerk to the Privy Council would consult the Privy Council's advisers as to the likely success—on the basis that, he, (the Clerk) would give a "personal view" (emphasis in original) whether it was worth making a formal application. |
| Set II-viii | 29 June 1997 | A letter from the Clerk to the Privy Council to the Institute's solicitors. The letter is over six months later. The consultation with advisers is now over and he proposes a meeting. He says, "A point of particular relevance is the |

proportion of the corporate membership who are graduates. You will remember that we went into this aspect in some depth when we met last autumn."

| | | |
| --- | --- | --- |
| Set II-ix | 29 July 1997 | A letter from the Institute's solicitor to the Clerk to the Privy Council. The letter refers to a meeting that had taken place the previous week at the Privy Council Office "to discuss the issues bearing on a prospective Petition by the Institute for a Charter of Incorporation." |

Based upon the likelihood of the rise in the number of graduates among the corporate members, the Clerk to the Privy Council writes "to say that, without being able to pronounce authoritatively on the eventual reaction of the Privy Council, the prospects of a successful application are sufficiently encouraging for the Institute to submit a Petition."

The Institute is to submit a draft Charter and Byelaws, and a draft petition.

| | | |
| --- | --- | --- |
| Set II-x | 5 November 1997 | A letter from the Clerk to the Privy Council to the Institute's solicitors, acknowledging receipt of the draft Charter and Byelaws which would be shown to the Privy Council's advisers. |
| Set II-xi | 17 February 1998 | A letter from the Clerk to the Privy Council (the previous Clerk) to the Institute's solicitors regarding the outcome of the circulate of the draft Charter and Byelaws. Some advisers are still consulting, but the letter focuses on: |

The longevity of the Institute—the original draft Charter gave "the impression that the Institute came into being from scratch in 1994".

There was a need to focus upon charitable—what was drafted "implying the promotion of a profession". "People" is rather wide—proposed "people in the workplace.

Draft article 4.6—the letter says, "Would the library be open to the public? This bears on the question of whether the Institute's activities are wholly charitable."

There was a question over trading activity. "My understanding is that chartered bodies tend to confine trading activity to wholly-owned subsidiaries."

Byelaw 13 had suggested that a "Member shall cease to be a Member ipso facto when he becomes bankrupt. Such a provision

(Continued)

| Doc no | Date | Sender/Recipient, or writer |
|--------|------|------------------------------|
| | | would normally be appropriate only when a person was offering professional services to the public, whereas the Institute presumably include a large number of people working as employees." |
| | | An issue with the disciplinary code: "Can you say how your clients would propose to regulate disciplinary matters? It would normally be appropriate at least to include some basic safeguards as to procedure within the Bye-laws." |
| | | The Clerk to the Privy Council indicates that this letter contains some "issues of substance" that require clarification. |
| | 5 June 1998 | Missing from the bundle—a letter mentioned in document Set II-xiii, 7 September 1998, Deputy Clerk of the Privy Council to the Institute's solicitors. The letter raises some points for the Institute to answer concerning membership requirements; the Privy Council Office is concerned that the Byelaws address membership requirements. The substance is picked up again on 7 September 1998, Set II-xiii. |
| Set II-xii | 26 August 1998 | A letter from the Institute's solicitors to the previous Clerk to the Privy Council, enclosing the revised drafts of the petition and Charter. This letter refers to the letter of 5 June 1998 but does not address the issues specifically raised. The Byelaws here have been annotated with revisions. |
| | | The petition gives a history of the Institute, and particularly its history from 1994. |
| | | Point 2—"The objects of the Institute are to promote and develop the science and practice of the management and development of people (including the promotion of research and publication of the useful results of such research) for the public benefit." |
| | | Point 10—"The Institute offers access to membership for experienced practitioners through professional assessment and accreditation of prior certificated learning. This is achieved without compromising the Institute's high standards through rigorous quality assurance and systematic competence assessment." |

| Doc no | Date | Sender/Recipient, or writer |
|--------|------|------------------------------|
| | | Point 21 (against which there is in handwriting a question mark and exclamation mark)—The work of the Institute will be greatly promoted and facilitated by the grant of a Royal Charter of Incorporation by virtue of: |
| | | 21.1 the legal status afforded by such a charter |
| | | 21.2 the greater influence which the Institute would be able to exert, particularly in the promotion and improvement of the public benefit of the science and practice of the management and development of people |
| | | 21.3 the increased standing of the Institute which would make easier its liaison and co-operation with other organisations |
| | | 21.4 the prestige which a Royal Charter would bestow on the Institute, enabling it the better to seek the attainment of these objects; and |
| | | 21.5 the status of the Institute will be enhanced internationally |
| Set II-xiii | 7 September 1998 | A letter from the Deputy Clerk to the Privy Council to the Institute's solicitors, in response to the Institute's letter of 26 August. This letter acknowledges receipt of the documents which the Privy Council Office had invited the Institute to send. These documents are included with Set II-xii 26 August 1996. However, the Deputy Clerk specifically asks for a response to particular points asked in the letter of 5 June 1998, before the documents are "re-circulated" to the advisers. The Deputy Clerk is interested in the "specific provision for the application of specified minimum requirements". The letter states: "A professional body which aspires to chartered status should require applicants for corporate membership to hold a first degree or equivalent qualification in the discipline in question. Many chartered bodies, meanwhile, have a minimum experience requirement." |
| | 24 September 1998 | Missing—the Institute's returned documentation. |

(Continued)

(Continued)

| Doc no | Date | Sender/Recipient, or writer |
|--------|------|------------------------------|
| Set II-xiv | 7 December 1998 | A letter from the Clerk to the Privy Council to the Institute's solicitor who has followed up the Institute's petition by telephone. The Clerk reports that the Privy Council Office is still waiting for the adviser's comments on "revised drafts of the Petition and Charter" which the Institute's solicitor had sent on 26 August 1998, and which had been returned for amendment and sent back to the Privy Council Office on 24 September 1998. The letter concludes: "I am reasonably confident of bringing this stage of the process to a conclusion shortly and expect to have a small number of points of substance to discuss with you before the drafts are finalised." |
| | 3 February 1999 | Missing—a letter from the Institute's solicitor to the Deputy Clerk to the Privy Council; although the letter is missing from the bundle, it would appear to be a letter following up progress since the more encouraging letter of 7 December 1998, Set II-xiv. |
| Set II-xv | 9 February 1999 | A letter from the Clerk to the Privy Council to the Institute's solicitors Letter in response to letter 3/2/1999. "I am very sorry about this delay but I am anxious to ensure that the few remaining points of substances are tackled rigorously at this stage, so as to avoid difficulties in the wake of the submission of a formal petition by your clients." The Clerk assures the Institute's solicitors that he is "chasing matters on a regular basis". |
| Set II-xvi | 11 November 1999 | A letter from the Deputy Clerk of the Council to the Institute's solicitors with a copy to another person whose role is unclear, but she is dealing with the matter at the Privy Council. The letter responds to the solicitor's letter of 15 September 1999 (missing). "In particular, the Commission finds difficulty with the object "to promote . . . the practice of [personnel management]". The Commission considers such an object to be inconsistent with the Institute's charitable |

| Doc no | Date | Sender/Recipient, or writer |
|--------|------|------------------------------|
| | | status. They ask that the word "practice" be omitted from the objects and suggest that these be changed to "the promotion of the art and science of the management and development of people . . . for public benefit". Were the objects to retain the word "practice", the Commission would be reluctant to see the Institute being granted a Royal Charter whilst retaining its "charitable status." |

At this point, the correspondence appears to cease.

## 2002–2003: Set III

| Doc no | Date | Sender/Recipient, or writer |
|--------|------|------------------------------|
| Set III-i | 21 November 2002 | A letter from the Director-General to the Clerk to Privy Council which encloses proposed changes to the Charter and Byelaws. The letter refers to the discussion "a few weeks ago" "about our plans to apply for full members to use the chartered title on an individual basis". |
| | | The Director-General outlines the support the Institute has among its governing body and the membership "those attending our recent Annual General Meeting, where they were greeted with enthusiasm." |
| | | "The proposal is that all those coming into full membership would be eligible to use the chartered title. Transitional arrangements would provide that all existing full members would also be eligible to use the individual chartered title. |
| | | This would be subject to full members meeting the CIPD's regulations in respect of our professional standards (qualifications), experience, and continuing professional development. |
| | | The current requirements for entry to full membership are that individuals must have |
| | | • Met our professional standards, which are at postgraduate 'M' level (the Byelaws provide that they must be at least at the level of a first degree); |
| | | • Met our experience requirements, currently, these are three years experience at management level or equivalent; (apostrophe missing in the original) |

| Doc no | Date | Sender/Recipient, or writer |
|--------|------|-----------------------------|
| | | • Met our continuing professional development requirements as a condition of their application for full membership and subsequently as determined by the Institute." |
| | | The Director-General is seeking to determine whether this proposal has any legs, before the Institute puts this out to postal vote and ideally, he would like a response before the end of 2002. |
| Set III-ii | 4 Feb 2003 | A letter from an Official at the Privy Council Office to the Institute Secretary, which suggests that there had been telephone conversations. The letter outlines the Privy Council's advisers' comments: |
| | | "Although advisers do not have any objection in principle to the extension of the Chartered title to individual members of the Institute, they have pointed out that chartered status for an individual brings with it a high expectation of quality service, integrity and professional competence." This is the service ethos of the traditional professional model. |
| | | The correspondence continues: "It is, therefore, important that the arrangements are rigorous and fair. If chartered status is to be seen as a quality mark or a licence to practice then it is the competence of the individual, rigorously tested, which matters and this may be achieved by diverse routes. |
| | | The amended byelaws would seem to exclude from admission to chartered status those practitioners without a first degree in a "relevant discipline" although they are equally competent to graduate practitioners. As the details of admission seem to be a matter for regulations and requirements which advisers have not seen there may be other barriers which could act again the interests of certain groups. Advisers would need to be reassured that the arrangements made for chartered status include robust safeguards for equal opportunities. |
| | | It has been suggested, therefore, that the Institute ensures its arrangements are "equality proofed" to ensure no unintentional elements are introduced which would have the effect of discriminating against women, ethnic minorities, other disadvantaged groups on the grounds of age (in the light of forthcoming legislation). Advisers would also like entry to chartered status, while remaining rigorous, to be available to a wider group of practitioners |

| Doc no | Date | Sender/Recipient, or writer |
|--------|------|----------------------------|
| | | (e.g. competence-based qualifications recognised by QCA and SQA as equivalent to a higher education qualification should not be excluded as a basis for admission." |
| Set III-iii | 7 January 2003 (although this date must be a mistake) | A letter from the Institute Secretary to the official at the Privy Council Office, with a copy to the Institute's Member and Education Director. The letter is acknowledging receipt of the previous letter Set III-ii. It reads, "The concerns raised in your 4 February 2003 letter can be satisfied easily. The philosophy which underlines the comments made is mirrored in the approach we have taken, which is to make the profession as open access as possible. There is no requirement to hold a first degree in a 'relevant discipline' in order to become a full member and therefore a chartered member. This is not a requirement now and there is no intention to change this with the introduction of the chartered title. . . . We seek to make the profession as open access as possible and it is possible to qualify (i.e. meet the professional standards) through a member of routes which text both knowledge and competence. This allows individuals to choose a route which suits them and has been particularly effective in achieving a very high percentage of women in the profession. Over 80% of the people currently registered on our professional development scheme (PDS) are women". The idea that the Institute Secretary had to say something about the registration of women in the Institute says more about the gendered nature of the occupation. . . . "In addition we offer accreditation of prior learning (APCL) and have an advanced standing scheme which recognises a range of qualifications as substitutes for sections of the professional standards. As part of our open access arrangements we offer associate and licentiate membership to those who have completed the professional standards in part. This is thus inclusive of those who do not wish to study for the full qualification and provides a steppingstone for entry into full membership. Perhaps a misunderstanding has arisen because the existing Byelaws refer to graduate membership and state that the professional standards should |

(*Continued*)

(Continued)

| Doc no | Date | Sender/Recipient, or writer |
| --- | --- | --- |
| | | be at least at the level of a first degree (one would probably now refer to an NVQ level)?" |
| Set III-iv | 13 March 2003 | A letter from the Clerk to the Privy Council to the Institute Secretary at CIPD. The letter suggests that the correspondents are on first name terms. The Privy Council's advisers "are content with the proposals in the Director-General's letter of 21st November". |
| | | A letter of 7 January had assured the Privy Council. The final suggestion that they would make is that "university degree", also be followed by "or other qualification recognised by the Qualifications and Curriculum Authority or the Scottish Qualifications Authority as equivalent to a degree". |
| | | This was confirmation that there was no reason not to pursue the application for individual chartered status—"in the expectation of a fair wind". |
| Set III-v | 18 March 2003 | A letter from the Institute Secretary to the Clerk to the Privy Council with copies to the Director-General and the Director, Membership and Education, which expresses gratitude for the "encouraging news". |
| | | "We fully endorse the need to ensure the widest access to the profession and will continue to ensure that there are a range of qualification and competence based/assessed routes to membership". |
| | | The amendment that the Privy Council's advisers had suggested would cause "practical difficulties", requiring redrafting of other documents. The reason is the phraseology "at least at the level of a university degree" suits the international context—"We are increasingly operating within a wider international sphere, and of course within Europe the existing phraseology relates well to the terms of the Bologna declaration". Furthermore, the wording was required by the Privy Council when the Charter was granted in 2000. Institute Secretary adds, "Since this is relatively recent in members' minds to seek to amend it now might seem odd to them." |
| | | "Our current professional standards are at M level (i.e. above the level of a first degree) but may be met by following a range of qualification and other routes, including many within the remit of the QCA and SQA." |

| Doc no | Date | Sender/Recipient, or writer |
|---|---|---|
| Set III-vi | 5 June 2003 | A letter from the Institute Secretary to the Clerk to the Privy Council, to "formally request the Privy council to agree to a new byelaw to allow the Institute to grant individual full members the right to use the chartered title on an individual basis". The letter also details that at an EGM on 4 June 2003 "98.9% of those voting were in favour—significantly more than the 75% required by the byelaws, and an overwhelming indication of support". |

Institute Secretary points out that the requirements "more than meet the council's requirements".

Institute Secretary outlines the range of routes to full membership "which test both knowledge and competence. In practice many individuals combine these routes to meet out professional standards in full, selecting the combination which suits their individual circumstances best:

- By following a programme of study, full time or part time at a college or university. This may lead to an award of the qualification alone or may also lead to the award of a degree by the educational provider. The professional standards are at "M" level i.e. NVQ level 5
- Through a competence based route either:
- Through NVQs where this fully meets the depth and breadth of our professional standards (we are an awarding body)
- Through professional assessment based on a portfolio of evidence
- Through flexible learning

In addition we offer accreditation of prior learning (APCL) and have an advanced standing scheme which recognises a range of qualifications as substitutes for sections of the professional standards.

As part of our open access arrangements we offer associate and licentiate membership to those who have completed the professional standards in part. This is thus inclusive of those who do not wish to study for the full qualification and provides a stepping-stone for entry into full membership".

Institute Secretary proposes the post-nominal letters. In parenthesis, Institute Secretary adds "there is no generic word for entry into full membership".

Institute wants to be able to implement the change by October 2003.

(Continued)

(Continued)

| Doc no | Date | Sender/Recipient, or writer |
|--------|------|------------------------------|
| | | The objections raised by the Charity commission appears to have been dealt with. |
| Set III-vii | 8 July 2003 | An amendment to the Byelaw of the Institute granting the Institute the power to confer chartered status on individual members. |

# Appendix II Characteristics of Traditional Professionalism (Following Millerson 1964 and Hickson and Thomas 1969)

| Hickson and Thomas (1969)—constitutive and operational features of a profession, (following Millerson's 1964 literature review and analysis) | Hickson and Thomas (1969: 46)—characteristics signifying greater professionalisation | Analytical categories |
| --- | --- | --- |
| Community sanction/monopoly—only admitted qualifying members able to practice | Legal protection of specific work areas Self-regulation | |
| Organised—eight or more specialist committees for different purposes over and above the governing body | Organisation | |
| Annual subscriptions/membership review | Organisation | |
| Occupational title changed to signify development | Organisation | Collective Organisation |
| Recognised status—a Royal Charter of Incorporation | Royal Charter | |
| Independence | Self- regulation | |
| Professional/client relationship—a scale of recommended charges or fees | Self-regulation | |
| Competence tested: minimum age to the first corporate grade of membership, stages of examination (some exemptions possible); candidates proposed by admitted members | Competence tested | |
| Members prepared to contribute to development—Regular publication of a journal; Continuing Professional Development (CPD) | Continuing Professional Development | Knowledge |
| Skill, applied knowledge | Education and training | |
| Training and education—between 3 and 5 years; minimum education level | Education and training | |

(*Continued*)

(Continued)

| Hickson and Thomas (1969)—constitutive and operational features of a profession, (following Millerson's 1964 literature review and analysis) | Hickson and Thomas (1969: 46)—characteristics signifying greater professionalisation | Analytical categories |
|---|---|---|
| Non-manual | Education and training/ Organisation | |
| Code of Conduct/ethics—written code, disciplinary procedures | Adheres to a code of conduct | |
| Public service—therefore no advertising | Adheres to a code of conduct | |
| Fiduciary client relationship—express adherence to confidentiality | Adheres to a code of conduct | |
| Altruistic service | Adheres to a code of conduct | Values |
| Applied to the affairs of others | Adheres to a code of conduct/ Organisation | |
| Best impartial advice—members not permitted to undercut one another | Adheres to a code of conduct/self-regulation | |
| Loyalty to colleagues—no intra-profession criticism | Adheres to a code of conduct/self-regulation | |

# Index

Printed in the United States
by Baker & Taylor Publisher Services